THE
VEGETABLE GARDEN
PROBLEM
SOLVER
HANDBOOK

Patti —
Happy gardening in
your down-sized lot!
Susan Mulvihill

Brimming with creative inspiration, how-to projects, and useful information to enrich your everyday life, quarto.com is a favorite destination for those pursuing their interests and passions.

First Published in 2023 by Cool Springs Press, an imprint of The Quarto Group,
100 Cummings Center, Suite 265-D, Beverly, MA 01915, USA.
T (978) 282-9590 F (978) 283-2742 Quarto.com

Cool Springs Press titles are also available at discount for retail, wholesale, promotional, and bulk purchase. For details, contact the Special Sales Manager by email at specialsales@quarto.com or by mail at The Quarto Group, Attn: Special Sales Manager, 100 Cummings Center, Suite 265-D, Beverly, MA 01915, USA.

27 26 25 24 23   1 2 3 4 5

ISBN: 978-0-7603-7748-2

Digital edition published in 2023
eISBN: 978-0-7603-7749-9

Library of Congress Cataloging-in-Publication Data

Names: Mulvihill, Susan, author.
Title: The vegetable garden problem solver handbook : identify and manage diseases and other common problems on edible plants / Susan Mulvihill.
Other titles: Identify and manage diseases and other common problems on edible plants
Description: Beverly, MA : Cool Springs Press, 2023. | Includes index. |
    Summary: "The Vegetable Garden Problem Solver Handbook contains all-natural solutions for common problems plaguing your vegetable garden, including plant diseases, disorders, animal pests, and weather woes"--Provided by publisher.
Identifiers: LCCN 2022035186 (print) | LCCN 2022035187 (ebook) | ISBN 9780760377482 (trade paperback) | ISBN 9780760377499 (ebook)
Subjects: LCSH: Vegetable gardening. | Organic gardening. | Vegetables--Diseases and pests. | Handbooks and manuals.
Classification: LCC SB324.3 .M85 2023 (print) | LCC SB324.3 (ebook) | DDC 635--dc23/ eng/20220822
LC record available at https://lccn.loc.gov/2022035186
LC ebook record available at https://lccn.loc.gov/2022035187

Design, Page Layout, and Illustration: Mattie Wells
Photography: See credits on page 222.

Printed in China

SUSAN MULVIHILL

THE
VEGETABLE GARDEN
PROBLEM
SOLVER
HANDBOOK

Identify and manage diseases and other
common problems on edible plants

COOL
SPRINGS
PRESS

Growing your own food is so rewarding.

CONTENTS

2 VEGETABLE PLANT DISEASE GUIDE

3 CRITTERS IN THE GARDEN

INTRODUCTION

Organic vegetable gardening has been a passion of mine for most of my life. As much joy as it gives me, I'll be the first to admit that there are a few aspects that can be particularly challenging: insects, plant diseases, animal pests, and the frustrating things that happen because of the weather. As a longtime columnist, author, and Master Gardener, I am frequently asked a lot of questions about all these topics. While I don't mind answering those questions, I found myself repeatedly wondering why there aren't any simple-to-use guides that would help gardeners identify what they're dealing with and provide some solutions.

All the bug questions led me to write my previous book, *The Vegetable Garden Pest Handbook*. During that project, I analyzed all the ways a gardener could identify bugs—from plant damage to direct encounters with both good bugs and bad bugs—and presented the information in a way that I felt would be helpful. Not only that, I made sure all of the strategies for dealing with damaging pests involved organic methods.

After that book was published, I started thinking about plant diseases. They can be so difficult to diagnose and treat! But the more I thought about how I would want to present plant disease information, the more I realized there are other challenges and oddball gardening problems that have troubled me over the years: Why did the leaves on my seedlings turn white?

How do I protect my vegetable crops during heat waves? How come the little squash on my zucchini plant fell off? How do I keep deer and other critters out of my garden? I knew I wasn't the only gardener wondering about these things.

All these issues, and many more, have led to this new book, *The Vegetable Garden Problem Solver Handbook*. In it, I cover how to nurture your plants so they will produce well and be less likely to have problems, how to deal with the challenges Mother Nature throws our way, and the disorders that can affect our plants even when diseases aren't to blame. You'll learn everything you need to know about plant diseases—preventing, identifying, and controlling them—and be introduced to some appealing birds and animals that often do unappealing things to our vegetable gardens.

Just as with *The Vegetable Garden Pest Handbook*, my underlying goal for this book is to help you be a successful vegetable gardener. I want you to enjoy growing your own food and to provide you with a straightforward guide that you can consult when problems arise. Happy gardening!

Healthy vegetable plants yield abundant harvests.

1

NURTURE YOUR GARDEN & TROUBLESHOOT PROBLEMS

GET YOUR PLANTS OFF TO THE BEST START POSSIBLE

Vegetable gardening has long been a popular pursuit—and necessity—all around the world. In recent years, millions of new gardeners have joined the fold out of a desire to master the important skill of growing edible crops and increase their food security.

No matter what your motivation is, the act of growing your own food provides a great deal of satisfaction. You get to marvel at how plants grow, observe birds and bugs in your garden, and get some exercise. The best part is being able to feed yourself and your family plenty of flavorful, nutritious food. It's pretty hard to top the joy you feel as you bring in a harvest basket filled with veggies.

Growing vegetables is not difficult, provided you meet the plants' basic needs. But, to be honest, things don't always go according to plan. Sometimes problems occur that make us scratch our heads and quickly dampen the enthusiasm we felt at the start of the season.

To be a successful gardener, it's important to be alert to anything that impacts the normal growth of our plants. Put another way, knowing when to panic and leap into action is a valuable skill we all should strive for.

In this chapter, you'll learn how to meet your plants' needs so they have the best chance of growing well and being productive. Then I'll delve into the unexpected problems we might come across, such as poor seed germination, a lack of produce when flowers aren't pollinated, challenging weather conditions, what herbicides do to our plants, and how to deal with bug issues. There's also a section on physiological disorders—such as blossom-end rot, bitterness, and fruit-cracking–that are often weather-related.

In chapter 2, I'll shine the spotlight on vegetable plant diseases. You'll find a huge diagnostic chart that points to individual disease profiles. Each disease profile contains a description of the disease, which vegetable crops are most commonly impacted by it, lists of organic strategies and products you can employ to help your plants, and photos showing what plants look like when those diseases take hold. You'll also learn about the many organic strategies that will lessen the impact of a disease when it infects our plants and reduce the chance of future disease issues.

As if plant diseases weren't bad enough, many gardeners are all too familiar with the damage caused by certain animals and birds that love our gardens just as much as we do. In chapter 3, you'll have the opportunity to diagnose which type of critter is the source of the problem, learn more about them, and discover creative ways to put a stop to their activities.

As I wrote this book, I had one goal in mind: I want to help you be successful at growing your own delicious produce while enjoying the process it takes to make that happen. Let's start by considering the important steps we gardeners can take to get our plants off to the best start possible and keep them healthy.

When you nurture your plants and watch for potential problems, the end result is a bountiful harvest.

DON'T OVEREXTEND YOURSELF

It's easy to get carried away with gardening plans, especially if you're a new gardener. I can completely relate to the desire to grow as many veggies as possible. When we go to a garden center, we're greeted with seed displays that are hard to resist. We see photos of gorgeous edible gardens in magazines and vow to duplicate that in our own yards.

The problem is, if we create a large garden and plant a wide variety of crops without considering the time and labor needed to maintain and harvest that garden, it is possible to feel completely overwhelmed. Between the watering and weeding, it can be hard to maintain that initial enthusiasm. Falling behind in harvesting and losing some of your best produce can make you think that maybe vegetable gardening isn't such a great pursuit after all. I would hate for you to feel that way.

If this is a concern or sounds familiar, here are some ideas to avoid becoming overwhelmed by your garden:

> Ask yourself what you want from your garden. Are you planning a summer of garden-to-table meals or a combination of fresh and stored produce? Twelve to sixteen corn plants will contribute enough ears for several summer dinners, but if you are planning to freeze corn to enjoy later, you might want to double that quantity. Two tomato plants are perfect for fresh salads and sandwiches, but you will want several more if you are planning to make and store spaghetti sauce. Likewise, the number of plants you put in is dictated by the number of people you're feeding.

> If you will be watering your garden by hand, start with a small plot until you get an idea of the time commitment that task will require.

> Many vegetables require a small amount of time to get started in the garden and are fairly low maintenance until harvest time. Examples include onions, potatoes, garlic, and artichokes.

> Some vegetable crops need a bit of extra effort. Tomatoes need support. Root crops such as carrots, turnips, or beets have to be thinned so the roots will have enough room to fully develop.

> A few vegetables need to be harvested on their schedule, not yours. Salad greens should be picked frequently so they will continue producing more leaves. Peas are sweet and ready to be picked for a short window of time. When the corn is ripe, it will be sugary-sweet for about a week to ten days before the kernels start getting starchy.

As you are planning your garden, look for a balance of low-, medium-, and high-maintenance vegetables that will fit best into your gardening lifestyle.

One last thought: in gardening, sometimes things get missed. The peas that should have been harvested last week are now tough and starchy, the lettuce you grew under a cover bolted to seed and is bitter, and where did that giant zucchini come from?! Don't stress about it. The vegetables that are no longer fit for the table will make excellent additions to your compost pile and nurture next year's garden.

NURTURE YOUR GARDEN & TROUBLESHOOT PROBLEMS

LOCATION IS KEY

Nearly all vegetable crops require a minimum of six to eight hours of sunlight daily to thrive. Whether you are a new vegetable gardener or a highly experienced one, it's important to carefully evaluate the spot you've chosen for your garden. Are there trees or buildings that will rob your plants of that precious sunlight? Are there other factors that might make it difficult for the vegetables to grow?

As someone who has grown veggies for many decades, I have observed our garden setting and how it has changed over the years. If I don't trim back a hedge on the west side of our raised bed garden every other year, it will prevent the afternoon sun from hitting the row of beds located nearby. A few years ago, tree roots infiltrated our beds in a new area of the garden, which dramatically impacted the vegetable crops' ability to grow. When I noticed the plants were struggling, I had to address the issue if I wanted to continue raising vegetables in that area.

Study your garden site at different times of the day and consider making some changes—perhaps a bit of tree trimming or adjusting the garden boundaries—to provide your crops with more sunlight.

Grow your vegetable garden in the sunniest spot you can find in your landscape.

PLANT AT THE RIGHT TIME

There are cool-season crops (e.g., lettuce, radishes, and spinach) and warm-season crops (e.g., tomatoes, peppers, and squash). As you might guess, cool-season crops should be planted earlier in the season and are more tolerant of chilly temperatures. Warm-season crops prefer both warmer soil and weather, so you should wait until the danger of frost has passed before planting them from seed or transplanting seedlings you started indoors. The outdoor soil temperature should be at least 65°F (18°C). Consider purchasing a soil thermometer so you can keep an eye on conditions.

If you plant any of the above crops at the wrong time, they will either struggle or stop growing and die. That's not something any gardener wants to experience, right? To avoid this, be aware of your region's growing conditions. Know your average last frost date in the spring and when the first fall frosts typically arrive. Your seed packets will indicate when to start the plants indoors or sow them directly in the garden.

Peppers are an example of a warm-season crop that will languish or even die if planted too early in the season when the soil and air temperatures are still cold.

SPACE YOUR PLANTS APPROPRIATELY

While you're reading your seed packets or plant tags, take note of how far apart you should space the seeds or seedlings. I understand the desire to squeeze as many plants as possible into a bed, but if they're competing with each other for space, moisture, and nutrients, the plants will struggle. They might not have enough room to produce their crop and their close proximity can facilitate the spread of disease. As you'll see in chapter 2, proper spacing is a simple strategy for reducing disease problems because there will be good airflow around each plant.

On the opposite page are some standard guidelines for the spacing between plants and rows:

Space your vegetable plants so they have enough room to grow and good air circulation between them.

CROP NAME	SPACING BETWEEN PLANTS	SPACING BETWEEN ROWS
Artichoke	36" (91 cm)	36" (91 cm)
Arugula	3" (8 cm)	12–18" (30–46 cm)
Asparagus	12" (30 cm)	36" (91 cm)
Bean, bush	4" (10 cm)	12" (30 cm)
Bean, pole	3–4" (8–10 cm)	24–36" (61–91 cm)
Beet	4" (10 cm)	12" (30 cm)
Broccoli	12–18" (30–46 cm)	18" (46 cm)
Brussels sprouts	24" (61 cm)	18" (46 cm)
Cabbage	12–18" (30–46 cm)	24" (61 cm)
Carrot	3" (8 cm)	12" (30 cm)
Cauliflower	12–18" (30–46 cm)	18" (46 cm)
Celery	8" (20 cm)	12" (30 cm)
Corn	12" (30 cm)	24–30" (61–76 cm)
Cucumber	12" (30 cm)	24–36" (61–91 cm)
Eggplant	12–18" (30–46 cm)	24–36" (61–91 cm)
Kale	12–24" (30–61 cm)	18–36" (46–91 cm)
Kohlrabi	4–8" (10–20 cm)	12–18" (30–46 cm)
Leek	4" (10 cm)	12–18" (30–46 cm)
Lettuce	12" (30 cm)	18" (46 cm)
Melon	12–24" (30–61 cm)	36–48" (91–122 cm)
Okra	12–18" (30–46 cm)	36" (91 cm)
Onion	4–6" (10–15 cm)	12–24" (30–61 cm)
Parsnip	3–4" (8–10 cm)	12–18" (30–46 cm)
Pea	3" (8 cm)	18–24" (46–61 cm)
Pepper	12–18" (30–46 cm)	24–30" (61–76 cm)
Potato	24" (61 cm)	24–36" (61–91 cm)
Pumpkin	24–36" (61–91 cm)	36–48" (91–122 cm)
Radish	1–2" (3–5 cm)	8–12" (20–30 cm)
Rutabaga	8" (20 cm)	12–18" (30–46 cm)
Spinach	4–8" (10–20 cm)	12" (30 cm)
Squash, summer	18" (46 cm)	36" (91 cm)
Squash, winter	18" (46 cm)	36" (91 cm)
Swiss chard	10" (25 cm)	18" (46 cm)
Tomatillo	24" (61 cm)	24–36" (61–91 cm)
Tomato	36" (91 cm)	36" (91 cm)
Turnip	4" (10 cm)	12" (30 cm)

SUPPORT YOUR PLANTS TO KEEP THEM HEALTHY

Plant supports are one way to provide growing space while decreasing the chance of disease. Tomato plants are a perfect example of this because they are very susceptible to disease issues. By giving each plant a structure to grow up on—a large tomato cage or wire grid, for example—the plants aren't in contact with the soil and they benefit from increased air circulation around their foliage and developing fruits.

I love adding vertical elements to my vegetable garden. In addition to creating a "wow" factor, these supports keep my plants healthy and make harvesting a breeze. When it comes to the types of crops that need support, most folks think of eggplants, peas, peppers, pole beans, and tomatoes. I think supporting vining crops such as cucumbers, melons, pumpkins, and winter squash is a good idea, too.

Let's talk about tomato cages. Many years ago, garden centers began selling small, spindly cages. If you've ever used them, you've experienced how flimsy they are. As soon as a plant reached about 2 feet (61 cm) in height, the cage toppled over, usually damaging the plant and young fruits in the process. It was really frustrating. While those little cages might work for eggplants and peppers, they are not even an option for tomato plants. In recent years, manufacturers have begun offering taller and sturdier tomato cages. The most important thing

you need to know is that the support you use needs to accommodate the height and weight of a mature plant.

For years, I used tomato cages made with cylinders of recycled 47-inch (119 cm)-tall field fence. They were really sturdy and I always anchored each one with a heavy-duty metal stake as added insurance. If you want to use a tomato cage of some sort, no matter what size it is, always stake it in place.

About twenty years ago, I started using a different support method for tomatoes and have never gone

Be creative when looking for plant supports. I made this pea support from apple branches.

back to cages. To set it up, I pound heavy-duty metal fenceposts into the ground at about 8-foot (2.4 m) intervals. Then I secure 4-feet by 8-feet (1.2 by 2.4 m) sheets of concrete-reinforcing wire to them, with the 4-foot (1.2 m) width standing upright. Throughout the growing season, I tie the plants to the supports with jute twine. I grow a mix of determinate and indeterminate tomatoes, and this method has worked beautifully for both types. If you grow really tall indeterminates and have a long growing season, consider using taller wire.

I grow pole beans every year. They need supports that are a minimum of 6 feet (2 m) tall. My beans grow up and over a series of four powder-coated steel trellises. They are 44 inches (112 cm) wide, so they span the pathway between two raised beds and they are 7 feet (2.1 m) tall. By the time I anchor them in the soil, that shortens them to about 6½ (2 m) feet in height, which is ideal. In addition to keeping the vines off the ground, the beans are easy to harvest, and—best of all—I get to stand in the shade underneath the trellis while harvesting them during hot summer days.

Pea vines need support, too, or they would be really challenging to pick. Varieties range from 2 to 6 feet (0.6 to 2 m) in height. My favorite variety, 'Green Arrow', is about 40 inches (1 m) tall. I support them with the pruned branches from my apple trees. It's a great way to recycle the branches, and I have fun arranging them in interesting patterns.

What about vertical supports for vining crops such as winter squash and pumpkins? This is a good idea because it saves space (you don't have them sprawling all over your garden), significantly cuts down on the plant's contact with the soil, thus reducing chances of disease, and keeps their fruits away from ground-dwelling pests.

In my garden, I grow them up and over an arbor made from two livestock panels, which are sometimes referred to as cattle panels. The panels are 50 inches (127 cm) tall by 16 feet (5 m) long. Just as with the bean trellis, this arbor spans the pathway between two raised beds, which makes tending the plants a breeze. I recommend growing smaller-fruited varieties because heavier ones will require slings to support their weight as they get larger.

I grow my tomatoes on wire grids attached to metal fenceposts. This method keeps the plants off the ground and makes it easier for me to care for them.

PROVIDE THE RIGHT AMOUNT OF WATER

Plants need moisture to develop properly and be productive. But how much is enough? Because soil types, weather conditions, and watering systems vary widely, that's a challenging question to answer.

The easiest—and most reliable—way to test the moisture in your soil is by poking in your finger up to the second knuckle. How does the soil feel? Is it bone dry, lightly moist, or sopping wet? If the soil is really dry, the plants are probably struggling. If it's lightly moist, that is ideal. You certainly don't want the sopping wet scenario because no plant is going to thrive if its roots are standing in water all the time. As a matter of fact, that will kill a plant more quickly than you might realize.

I'm embarrassed to share the following story with you, but it illustrates my point. A few years ago, we were experiencing an extremely wet spring, which is very unusual for our region. I had transplanted some melon seedlings into the garden once the danger of frost had passed. When I checked on them two days later, they were wilting. It's easy to equate wilting with a plant not getting enough water, so I gave them a bit more. The next day, I checked on them and they were still wilting, so I watered them even more while puzzling over the situation.

You guessed it: I managed to kill those seedlings. When I dug them up, their poor little roots were brown. If I had taken a moment to check the amount of moisture in the soil, I would have realized the excessive rain saturated the soil to the point where it was just too much for little seedlings. The moral of the story is to check your soil moisture regularly and to take the weather conditions into account. If it's rainy, temporarily suspend watering the garden. When summertime temperatures start heating up, you'll need to increase your watering time.

The two most efficient ways to water are with drip irrigation systems or soaker hoses. Because they are placed directly on the soil, they deliver water to the base of the plants, right where roots can take it up. Overhead watering is less ideal because wet foliage can facilitate the spread of disease. If it is your only option, however, be sure to water in the early morning so the leaves can dry off fairly quickly. There is additional information about watering in chapter 2 on page 165 as it relates to disease issues.

I accidentally killed this little melon seedling by overwatering it. The white substance is wet diatomaceous earth to keep slugs away; it didn't contribute to the plant's demise.

Drip irrigation (shown here) and soaker hoses are the most efficient ways to water your vegetable plants.

NURTURE YOUR GARDEN & TROUBLESHOOT PROBLEMS

FEED YOUR SOIL

As gardeners, we tend to admire our plants without considering the huge role the soil plays in their growth. While we're marveling over the potential for a great crop of tomatoes, a complex ecosystem is working hard to make that happen.

Did you know that one teaspoon of healthy soil contains more microorganisms than there are humans on this planet? If you really stop and think about that, it's mind-boggling. Those microorganisms consist of bacteria, fungi, protozoans, nematodes, algae, and more; all benefit our plants in one way or another. For example, many microorganisms make water and nutrients available to our plants while others parasitize or attack pathogens that would threaten our vegetable crops with damaging diseases.

What can we do to support our soil? We should feed the soil by adding an inch or two (3 to 5 cm) of organic compost to the surface of our planting beds twice a year—in early spring and in the fall. You don't have to dig it in because the nutrients will filter down into the soil without our help.

Avoid disturbing your soil by rototilling it or turning it over with a shovel. While that used to be a common practice not long ago, it is now discouraged. That activity damages the structure of the soil, where microorganisms live and carry out their vital roles. The best practice is to gently loosen the top inch where you need to make planting furrows or dig small holes only where your seedlings will be transplanted.

Don't use synthetic (inorganic) fertilizers because they contain far more nutrients than our plants can utilize and the excess kills soil microorganisms. Always choose organic fertilizers and soil amendments.

Whenever you have a vacant bed or area in your garden, plant cover crops, which are also known as "green manures." These crops are planted for many purposes: to supply the soil with nutrients, fix nitrogen in the soil, reduce or prevent erosion, attract beneficial insects, and/or prevent soil pathogens from splashing up onto nearby plants. Examples of cover crops include field peas, buckwheat, vetch, clover, and rye grass. These crops are planted in the spring or fall, then cut down, and allowed to break down naturally in place.

Plant cover crops any time you have an empty planting bed. This buckwheat attracts pollinators and beneficial insects while it's growing and will add nutrients to the soil when it's cut down.

All these practices will enrich the life in your soil, which in turn will benefit your plants, and that means more food on your table.

I get a lot of questions from gardeners who have built new raised beds but are wondering where to get soil to fill them. When we created our raised bed garden, we planned to cover the pathways with landscape fabric and a few inches of bark mulch. It seemed a shame to cover good topsoil like that, so we used shovels to scrape the top 3 inches (8 cm) from the paths and added it to each bed. That was enough to fill each one about two-thirds of the way. We then mixed in compost, shredded leaves, and grass clippings from our untreated lawn.

I realize this method isn't an option for everyone. If you need to bring in soil from an outside source, be very careful where you get it. Most landscape suppliers sell topsoil, garden soil, or mixes of soil and compost. Visit potential sources, see what their products look like, and find out where the materials came from. Let them know you want to grow vegetables in the soil. Avoid getting overly sandy soil because water will run right through it.

Once you make your purchase and fill your beds, add in some organic amendments. I've often found that soil mixes tend to be a bit sterile, which will affect your plants' performance the first year or two. To prevent this, include material such as compost, shredded newspaper, grass clippings (provided you don't use herbicides), leaves, composted chicken manure, kitchen scraps, earthworms, and worm castings. Any or all of these items will jump-start your new garden!

COMPOST

Compost is the best organic amendment for your soil. It can be purchased from garden centers, or you can easily create your own. No matter which source you opt for, apply about an inch (3 cm) of compost over your garden soil in the spring and, if possible, again in the fall. As I mentioned earlier, you don't need to mix it into the soil.

Chances are that you've heard about making compost but felt overwhelmed because it sounds complicated. Let me reassure you that it's not difficult and you don't need to sweat the details. Just follow the basic concepts and you will be successful. Here is an overview of the composting process:

Compost is created by combining green materials (e.g., kitchen scraps or grass clippings from a lawn that hasn't been treated with herbicides) and brown materials (e.g., dried leaves and dead plant material), which are then allowed to decompose.

Green materials contain nitrogen while brown materials contain carbon. Both these materials should be added to a pile at a rate of two parts brown to one part green. Remember to keep this simple and go with general proportions. The smaller the pieces, the more quickly they will decompose, so consider chopping up or shredding the larger materials.

Two other essential components of a compost pile are air and moisture. The insects and microorganisms that decompose the materials in a pile need oxygen, and the moisture aids in decomposition as well as the ability of the soil organisms to move about.

When looking for a location for your compost pile, choose an area in or near your garden that has good airflow and access to a water source. You can build a set of three composting bins, purchase a composter, or loosely build a compost pile. Many of the critter profiles within chapter 3 mention the issue of compost attracting rodents or scavengers. If you know this will be a problem, use a closed composting system to keep them out.

Store-bought composters include tumblers that can easily be turned by cranking a handle, continuous composters to which you can repeatedly add materials, and rolling composters. Each of these is designed to make turning the compost pile easier. Because they are closed systems, it's important to monitor your pile to make sure it contains enough moisture and the microorganisms are getting enough oxygen.

The following tables list suggested green and brown materials to add to your compost pile:

GREENS (NITROGEN)

Coffee grounds and filters

Droppings from poultry or rabbits

Grass clippings from an untreated lawn

Kitchen scraps (vegetables, fruits)

Live plant material

Seaweed (rinse off salt first)

Tea bags

BROWNS (CARBON)

Animal bedding such as straw and sawdust

Branches (small diameter is best)

Cardboard (corrugated is best)

Dead plant material

Egg cartons (made from cardboard)

Eggshells (crush first)

Hair

Leaves, fallen

Newspaper (shred first)

Paper (shred first to speed decomposition)

Paper towels or napkins

Sawdust (do not add sawdust from treated lumber)

Straw or hay

Wood ash (use minimally as it makes soil more alkaline)

Avoid putting the following materials into a compost pile:

Bones*

Cooking oils*

Dairy products (milk, cheese)*

Diseased plants

Manure from cattle and horses**

Meat or fish*

Weeds that are difficult to control (e.g., bindweed, quackgrass, or thistle)

Never use animal waste from carnivorous animals—including dogs and cats—because it might contain dangerous pathogens.

Bones, cooking oils, dairy products, meat, and fish will attract rodents and scavengers.

**Cattle and horse manure may contain persistent herbicides.*

To create a compost pile, stack layers of green and brown materials. A manageable pile size is about 3 feet by 3 feet (1 m by 1 m). Moisten the pile until it contains the amount of moisture you'd feel in a wrung-out sponge.

Garden centers sell compost activators or accelerators, which are marketed as a means for speeding up this process. If you follow the information in this section while building and maintaining your compost pile, these products are unnecessary as you'll have plenty of microorganism activity. If you are interested in trying one, I would recommend selecting an activator that contains organic materials.

Consider purchasing a compost thermometer at your local garden center to monitor the temperature of the pile. It is exciting to watch the needle on the thermometer climb. Those higher temperatures mean the microbial activity in the pile is at its peak. The pile will go through many temperature peaks and valleys during the decomposition process.

Decide how you intend to manage the pile. If a hands-off approach works best for your lifestyle and gardening routine, that is perfectly acceptable. This is referred to as "cold composting," where you let nature take its course with minimal effort on your part. It can take anywhere from one to two years before the compost is ready to use in your garden.

For a quicker turn-around time, consider "hot composting." This involves turning the pile with a shovel or pitchfork once a week, which helps aerate the pile and makes more of the materials available to the host of insects and microorganisms that break them down. During the turning process, bring the materials from the outer parts of the pile to the inside. You'll also need to remoisten the pile whenever it gets dry to help those decomposers. With hot composting, you should have finished compost in a few months.

How do you know it's finished compost? The materials in the pile will no longer be recognizable. The compost

A compost thermometer will indicate what's happening within your compost pile.

These parsnips and carrots grew well because I added bonemeal to the soil prior to planting this bed.

should be crumbly and have a pleasant, earthy smell. If you can wait a month before using it, so much the better.

And speaking of smells, if your pile ever has an unpleasant odor, that usually means you've added too many green materials and/or too much water to the pile, which drastically cuts down on the amount of oxygen inside it. As mentioned earlier, the microorganisms that are decomposing the materials must have plenty of oxygen. You can resolve this by turning the pile and cutting back on the water.

MANURES

While barnyard manures are high in nitrogen and often free for the taking, there are a few caveats regarding the use of them in your vegetable garden:

1. Remember that a little goes a long way. If you apply manure to your soil, it should be in small quantities and preferably aged manure. Fresh manure will burn plant growth.

2. Do not use any animal waste that came from carnivorous animals. This includes waste from big cats at animal parks or zoos and dog or cat waste. It likely contains pathogens that are harmful to humans.

3. Avoid using manures from grazing animals such as horses and cows, especially those that have been fed Timothy hay. The hay might contain a persistent herbicide that doesn't break down as it passes through an animal's digestive system. Once you apply their manure to your garden, plants will have distorted growth and/or die. It takes several years for the herbicide to dissipate from the soil, so it's really not worth the risk. I personally would prefer to err on the side of caution.

4. The safest manures to use in a vegetable garden come from rabbits and chickens.

You will learn about how herbicides affect plants on page 37.

FEED YOUR PLANTS, BUT DON'T GO OVERBOARD!

While it's true that vegetable crops can benefit from added nutrition, it's important to understand which type of fertilizer is appropriate for the plants you are growing.

Garden centers sell many different types and formulations of fertilizers. The packages have three numbers listed on them, which indicate the amounts of nitrogen (N), phosphorus (P), and potassium (K) they contain, and they are listed in that order. For example, if the first number on the package is the highest, that indicates the fertilizer is high in nitrogen. If you've heard the term *balanced fertilizer*, that means there are equal proportions of the three nutrients. For example, 4-4-4 and 5-5-5 are balanced fertilizers.

I prefer to use organic fertilizers over synthetic fertilizers because they contain small amounts of diverse nutrients that plants can utilize.

Before making a selection, think about the crop you want to feed. If you are growing leafy greens such as lettuce, spinach, Swiss chard, or kale, they will benefit from a fertilizer that delivers a lot of nitrogen. Blood meal (12-0-0) is an example. Other organic sources of nitrogen include fish emulsion, soybean meal, cottonseed meal, and animal manure, preferably from chickens or rabbits.

Let's say you're growing tomatoes, melons, or squash. Because those plants need to bloom and set fruit, they will benefit from a fertilizer that is highest in phosphorus, the middle number on the package. Fish bonemeal (3-18-0), alfalfa meal, and rock phosphate are examples of amendments that are high in phosphorus. If you use a high-nitrogen fertilizer on them, they will have lush foliage at the expense of blooming and producing fruits. Many gardeners contact me to ask why their tomato plant isn't blooming or producing tomatoes. The first thing I ask is which type of fertilizer they've been using and, invariably, their answer is a nitrogen fertilizer. It's easy to make that mistake, but my goal is to help you understand what the essential nutrients do for plants.

Root crops such as carrots, onions, potatoes, and parsnips also benefit from high-phosphorus fertilizers because they facilitate root growth. What does potassium do for all vegetable plants? It is equally important because this nutrient aids in plant growth, facilitates the movement of water throughout the plant tissue, and helps plants fight disease. Kelp meal (1-0-2) is an organic fertilizer that supplies potassium. Wood ash also provides potassium, but go easy on it since it also will increase your soil's pH.

In addition to providing nitrogen, phosphorus, and potassium, some organic fertilizers provide the soil with beneficial microorganisms, trace elements, and minerals. For example, fertilizers that contain beneficial bacteria may help plants fight off fungal diseases.

Now that you have an understanding of these essential nutrients, I want to emphasize the importance of taking a "less is more" approach. Sometimes we love our plants too much and overfertilize them.

Here is how I approach this in my own garden: I start most of my vegetable plants indoors from seed. To germinate (sprout) and start growing, a seedling relies on the nutrients contained within the seed. By the

NUTRIENT	CROPS THAT BENEFIT
Nitrogen	Young seedlings, plus arugula, broccoli, Brussels sprouts, cabbage, cauliflower, celery, corn, kale, kohlrabi, lettuce, mustard, spinach, Swiss chard
Phosphorus	Artichokes, beans, beets, carrots, garlic, melons, onions, parsnips, peas, peppers, potatoes, pumpkins, radishes, rutabagas, shallots, squash (summer and winter), tomatoes, turnips, watermelons

time they begin producing their first "true" leaves (ones that resemble the mature leaves for that plant), the food stores have run out. Those young leaves will start producing energy through photosynthesis, but I like to help them out by feeding them with a highly diluted nitrogen fertilizer such as fish emulsion. If the label suggests mixing a tablespoon (14 g) of fertilizer with a gallon (4 L) of water, I use a half-tablespoon (7 g) of fertilizer to a gallon (4 L) of water. That's because the plants are small and don't need full-strength fertilizer at this point. I repeat the fertilizer application about two weeks later and again if I need to up-pot them into a larger container.

Every spring and fall, I add a couple of inches (about 5 cm) of organic compost to my garden beds because it contains readily available nutrients for the plants.

Prior to transplanting vegetable seedlings that will bloom and set fruit, I mix some bonemeal into the garden bed's soil, at the rate listed on the label directions. Bonemeal is an organic soil amendment that is high in phosphorus, so I know it will help those seedlings produce a good crop. At transplanting time, I give the seedlings one last dose of nitrogen fertilizer that has been mixed at full strength.

Most plants don't need additional fertilizing after they've been planted in the garden. There are a few crops that benefit from additional feedings of nitrogen throughout the growing season. That information is usually available on the seed packet or growing instructions from seed catalogs or nurseries.

KEEP AN EYE ON YOUR GARDEN

Monitoring your garden on a regular basis is one more way to nurture your plants. I walk through my garden at least once a day, partly because it's a lovely way to spend a few minutes outside but primarily to be on the lookout for any changes, good or bad.

More often than not, I make happy discoveries: the first ripe tomato, for example. Occasionally, I find insect damage or signs of a disease on a plant that warrants further investigation. By keeping a close eye on the plants, I can react quickly to problems that arise and, with a little luck, resolve them so the situation doesn't get worse. Taking a proactive approach is worth every minute I spend walking through the garden.

I also recommend jotting down some notes in a journal to detail any problems that arose and how you dealt with them. Many issues we encounter in our gardens are seasonal. When you keep a journal, you will see patterns and be prepared in future years. Don't forget to record the more pleasant things that occur in your garden. I find it helpful to note when a crop starts producing, an experiment that went particularly well, and new techniques I've learned from a workshop or podcast.

GO ORGANIC

I believe it is important to avoid the use of harmful chemicals, not just in the garden but in our daily lives as well. I'm primarily referring to synthetic chemical pesticides (insecticides), fertilizers, herbicides, and man-made products for controlling plant diseases

All these products throw off the natural balance that exists in the environment around us. For example, many pesticides kill both damaging pests and the

beneficial insects that would have controlled them for us. Synthetic fertilizers frequently contain higher quantities of nutrients than our plants can utilize, which causes other problems. Herbicides kill soil microorganisms and leave behind residues that remain in the environment for a long time. When it comes to disease control, I will list organic strategies and products that are available to help you deal with them.

TROUBLESHOOTING PROBLEMS
GERMINATION ISSUES

Growing plants from seed is an enjoyable and productive gardening activity. In addition to being a useful skill that saves us money, seed-starting allows us to grow varieties that otherwise might be difficult to find at garden centers and nurseries. This is especially true if we're looking for varieties that mature in a shorter period of time, or are resistant to certain diseases.

When the seeds you so carefully planted don't germinate well, it is really frustrating—especially if you garden in a short-season climate and you're on a tight timetable. Understanding why they didn't sprout can be a bit mystifying, so here are some thoughts:

How old are the seeds? Look at the date on the packet. The viability, or shelf life, of vegetable seeds varies quite a bit by crop. How the seeds are stored is equally important. Keep them in a cool (55°F to 60°F [13°C to 16°C]), dark location and protect them from moisture. Storing your seeds in the refrigerator or freezer is another option, but if your power goes out, the seeds can be damaged by a sudden increase in humidity. If you store the seeds with packets of an anti-desiccant such as silica gel, that will reduce the risk.

With that in mind, take a look at the table for some general guidelines on the number of years you should expect good germination rates.

Does this mean you shouldn't use older seeds? No. Many seeds remain viable for longer than you might think, and besides, we gardeners hate to waste anything, right? When in doubt, conduct a simple germination test.

Moisten a paper towel and place ten seeds near the middle. Carefully fold the paper towel around them and insert the towel—along with a label to identify the seeds—into a clear, plastic bag. Set the bag in a warm (70°F to 80°F [21°C to 27°C]) location. Check on the seeds every few days over the course of two weeks. At the end of that time, unfold the paper towel, count how many seeds have germinated, and multiply that number by ten. If all ten sprouted, that is a 100 percent

Seed Viability Table

VEGETABLE CROP	YEARS VIABLE
Artichoke	5
Arugula	3
Asparagus	3
Bean	3
Beet	4
Broccoli	3
Brussels sprouts	4
Cabbage	4
Carrot	3
Cauliflower	4
Celery	3
Collards	5
Corn	2
Cucumber	5
Eggplant	4
Kale	4
Kohlrabi	3
Leek	2
Lettuce	6
Melon	5
Mustard	4
Okra	2
Onion	1
Parsnip	1
Pea	3
Pepper	2
Pumpkin	4
Radish	5
Rutabaga	4
Spinach	3
Squash, summer/winter	4
Swiss chard	4
Tomato	4
Turnip	4

germination rate. If five sprouted, that is 50 percent. That's the beauty of testing ten seeds: It's easy to determine the percentage rate.

If the results of your test were 60 percent or lower, you have two options: Order new seeds or plant the old seeds more thickly, knowing you might need to thin them later so the seedlings won't be crowded.

Other factors can impact seed germination rates, too. Always read the back of your seed packets for any special instructions. Some seeds—tomatoes and peppers, for example—benefit from a warmer planting medium. A seedling heat mat can help with this. Certain seeds, such as lettuce, need light to germinate while others must be kept in the dark. Seed packets will

inform you of this, especially when they list the planting depth for the seeds. Some seeds need a little extra help breaking through their outer coating, such as New Zealand spinach and parsnip seeds. This is usually accomplished by soaking them in water for several hours prior to planting.

I know this sounds like a lot to keep in mind, but if you read your seed packets, you'll do great. There is one more issue that might arise, however. If your seeds don't germinate well or the young seedlings die very quickly, damping-off disease might be the culprit. You'll find everything you need to know in that disease profile (page 122).

My germination test of these four-year-old pole bean seeds resulted in a 100 percent germination rate because all ten seeds sprouted.

POLLINATION ISSUES

Most of the flowering vegetable crops we grow require pollination by bees and other types of insects. For the most part, this works beautifully, and the end result is a bountiful harvest. It's not uncommon for problems to arise, however. Here are some pollination-related issues that gardeners most frequently encounter and ways to solve them:

CORN

If your corn patch wasn't very productive last year or the cobs were missing a lot of kernels, chances are the plants were arranged in single or double rows rather than being planted in multirow blocks. At pollination time, corn plants send up tassels with pollen-containing anthers attached to them. The silks, which are part of the female flowers, are wind-pollinated. When conditions are right, the pollen grains are released from the anthers and drop onto the silks below. The best pollination rates occur within block plantings rather than individual rows, because the close proximity within a block provides the pollen with many more "targets." The next time you grow corn, plant them in rows of four or more for optimal pollination rates.

NIGHTSHADE FAMILY

Tomato, pepper, and eggplant flowers are self-pollinating, but if the plants aren't producing fruits, there are some simple methods to help them out. To move the pollen within the blossoms, consider shaking or flicking them. Some gardeners use a battery-operated toothbrush to vibrate the flower stalks, which mimics bee pollination activities.

Plant corn in blocks to get the best possible pollination rates.

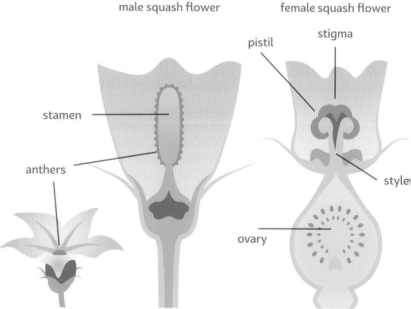

male squash flower

female squash flower

stigma

pistil

stamen

anthers

style

ovary

Male reproductive organs of a squash flower.

Female reproductive organs of a squash flower.

Female squash flowers have a bulbous base, which is a tiny squash.

The male flowers do not produce any squash; their sole purpose is for pollination.

Hand-pollination of a female squash flower.

CUCURBITS

It's not unusual for members of the cucurbit family (cucumbers, melons, pumpkins, and squash) to experience pollination-related problems. In these cases, the plants are growing well and blooming, but they aren't producing any fruit. Let's look at the most common reasons for this:

1. There might be a lack of pollinators in your garden. Look around it. Do you see insects? If not, it could be due to pesticide use in your neighborhood that killed bees and other pollinating insects. This is a very good reason to choose organic products that are safe to use around these essential creatures. Attract pollinators by planting some annual flowers in your vegetable garden. A quick solution is to hand-pollinate your squash flowers, which is a fun skill to learn. Follow the steps in the sidebar at right.

2. Sometimes cucurbit plants go through a period where they only produce the flowers of one sex. That is definitely a showstopper! Early in the season, the plants typically produce only male flowers, but the good news is they're still important because they will start attracting pollinators to the area. Soon, the female flowers will appear on the plants. Once bees pollinate those flowers, the squash will develop and mature. If a female flower hasn't been pollinated, the tiny squash will abort by shriveling up and falling off.

3. Sometimes, plants don't develop female flowers at all. This often takes place when the weather is excessively hot or cool but can also result from the repeated application of nitrogen to the soil. With a little luck, the weather will go back to normal, you will heed my earlier plea to avoid overfertilizing your plants, and the female flowers will appear.

HOW TO HAND-POLLINATE SQUASH BLOSSOMS

The following steps apply to hand-pollinating all types of cucurbit family crops (cucumbers, melons, pumpkins, summer or winter squash):

1. Early morning is the best time to hand-pollinate your female squash blossoms because that is when the most pollen will be available on the male flowers.

2. Pluck a male flower from a plant and remove its petals.

3. Rub the anther of the male flower onto the stigma of the female flower. This will pollinate the squash and it should develop normally.

4. You will find additional information on pollination issues in the Physiological Disorders section (page 43).

WEATHER-RELATED ISSUES

Sometimes the weather thwarts our best efforts. Early or surprise frosts, heat waves, or high winds can negatively impact the seedlings we so lovingly planted at the start of the season. While we can't change what Mother Nature throws our way, we can use many strategies that help our gardens survive and even flourish.

FROST

Even though water freezes at 32°F (0°C), did you know crops can sustain frost damage at temperatures above that? Early and late in the season, gardeners need to watch the weather forecasts closely and be prepared to protect sensitive plants at a moment's notice.

How do frosts impact plants? The cells within leaves and other plant tissue contain water. As temperatures drop toward freezing, ice crystals form and burst the cell walls. A lot of vegetable crops can survive light frosts, but heavier frosts cause severe damage to the plants. If you venture out to your garden early on a frosty morning, your plants might look fine, but once the sun comes up, the extent of the damage will be much more apparent.

When you look at the table on the opposite page, notice how some crops—specifically warm-season crops—are very sensitive to frosts, while cool-season crops will often escape undamaged until repeated and severe frosts occur. I find it interesting that the flavor of many cool-season crops actually improves once they've been frosted. For example, carrots will become much sweeter.

Frost protection

You can protect your plants from frost both early and late in the season by covering them. **Floating row cover** is one of my favorite tools for this purpose. This fabric allows sunlight and moisture to pass through it and, depending on the weight you use, also provides a few degrees of frost protection. Row covers come in varying weights, which correspond to the amount of protection they provide. It should be noted that the

Late frosts or unusually early snowstorms can present gardeners with extra challenges.

These winter squash vines look pretty pathetic after a hard frost.

CROPS THAT ARE SENSITIVE TO FROSTS	CROPS THAT ARE MORE TOLERANT OF FROSTS
Beans, corn, cucumbers, eggplants, melons, peppers, potatoes, pumpkins, summer and winter squash, tomatillos, tomatoes	Artichokes, arugula, beets,* broccoli, cabbage, carrots,* cauliflower, celery, garlic, kale, kohlrabi,* leeks,* lettuce, mustard, onions, parsnips,* peas, radishes, rutabagas,* shallots, spinach, Swiss chard, turnips*

*The flavor of these crops improves after being frosted.

heavier weights do not allow much light transmission so they shouldn't be used on a long-term basis or they should be removed during the daytime. Refer to the table below for specifics.

Clear plastic sheeting is an alternative to floating row cover and it also should be suspended on hoops over the crop. This setup is referred to as a "low tunnel." Because plastic doesn't "breathe" like fabric, open the ends of the plastic during the daytime so that plants won't get overheated or burned. In addition to regular plastic sheeting, you can purchase special plastic containing either slits or small pre-punched holes to alleviate that problem. Of course, if you're caught off guard by an unexpected frost warning, use blankets, sheets, or tarps to cover your most sensitive plants.

Floating row cover offers frost protection to susceptible plants. For best results, lay it on hoops over the bed you want to protect.

FLOATING ROW COVER GRADES

ROW COVER WEIGHT	FROST PROTECTION	LIGHT TRANSMISSION LEVEL
Lightweight* (.45 oz./sq. yd.)	None	90%
Medium (.55 oz./sq. yd.)	Down to 28°F (-2°C).	85%
Heavy (1.5 oz./sq. yd.)	Down to 24°F to 28°F (-4°C to -2°C).	30–50%

*Use only as an insect barrier rather than for frost protection.

What gardener wouldn't love to have a row of elaborate cold frames like these? They are located in The Lost Gardens of Heligan, in St. Austell, England.

Cold frames are another useful tool for protecting plants. They are usually rectangular in shape and constructed from materials that allow light to pass through them, such as old windows or twin-wall polycarbonate. The walls can be constructed with wood, straw bales, or concrete blocks, which are then covered with an old window or other clear material. Many gardeners sink the lower part of the structure into the ground for added insulation from the cold. You can make your own or purchase commercially built cold frames from garden centers and online sources.

The front side of the structure is often lower, both to permit more light to hit the plants inside and to allow easier access to them. Cold frames should face south to take maximum advantage of sunlight at a time when the sun is lower in the sky.

In addition to being used for frost protection both early and late in the season, cold frames have other uses. You can start seeds inside them or harden-off seedlings that you started indoors before transplanting them into the garden. Depending upon the severity of your winters, you might be able to grow vegetable crops in a cold frame during the colder months of the year, when traditional gardening isn't an option. For the best success, choose cold-tolerant varieties.

No matter how you use a cold frame, it's important to check on the plants regularly to make sure the soil remains lightly moist and vent it on bright, sunny days so it doesn't get too hot inside.

Cloches also protect plants from the cold. Stemming from the French word for "bell," these bell-shaped glass covers were used for this purpose dating back to the seventeenth century. While they make a beautiful addition to a garden, it's important to understand that on a bright, warm day, the light and heat transmitted through the glass will burn the foliage of plants growing underneath it. These days, plastic or wax-paper cloches are available at garden centers and online. You can even transform an empty plastic, gallon (4 L)-sized milk jug into a cloche. Cut off the bottom of the jug and hang on to the screw-on lid. While keeping an eye on the weather, take off the lid when temperatures are warm and replace it in the evening or on chilly days. You might need to attach a stake to lightweight cloches so you can anchor them to the soil and prevent them from blowing away on a windy day.

I use our **small hoop house**—which is a plastic-covered greenhouse—to extend the garden season into the fall and winter. How is this possible when our winters are so cold? After all, it isn't heated. The secret is to choose

These very old glass bells, known as *cloches*, were used in the early 1900s to protect plants from the cold and are part of a collection at Chateau de Chenonceau in France's Loire Valley.

I use this small, unheated hoop house to grow cold-tolerant crops during the fall and winter months.

cold-tolerant vegetables such as kale, miner's lettuce (*Claytonia*), corn salad (mâche), and certain varieties of lettuce and spinach. If you're wondering why I go to this "trouble," allow me to explain.

I always preserve a good portion of each summer's harvest to enjoy through the winter months. My basement is stocked with home-canned fruits, tomato sauce, salsa, and jellies. There are boxes of winter squash, pumpkins, garlic, shallots, and onions. In the garage, I've got bins of apples, potatoes, beets, carrots, and parsnips. As wonderful as all this produce is, the one thing I really miss during the off-season is fresh salad greens.

Several years ago, my husband designed and built our little hoop house. It is 10 feet wide by 9 feet (3 by 2.7 m) long, and it fits over two raised beds. It is lightweight and portable so we can move it to different areas of our garden.

I use the hoop house year-round. I grow cold-tolerant crops during the fall and winter and warm-season crops such as peppers or melons during the spring and summer.

In late summer, I start the seeds of my cold-season crops indoors so they will be ready to transplant out into the hoop house as soon as its summertime crops have been harvested. In between plantings, I replenish the soil with compost or we move the hoop house to new beds that have already been prepared.

In the fall, we have to turn off the sprinkler system, which means I need to hand-carry water to the hoop house beds once or twice weekly. As soon as the temperatures drop, the moisture stays in the soil longer and the condensation that builds up on the inside of the plastic will rain down, watering the plants for me.

There is one other change that comes with the temperature drop: I suspend floating row cover on hoops over each of the beds. This adds a little extra cold protection for the plants.

Growing a winter garden is both a luxury and a treat!

HAIL

There's nothing quite like venturing out to your garden after a hailstorm and feeling heartbroken when you see the damage it has caused. Depending upon the severity of the storm, you will likely see small to large holes punched into plant leaves, ripped or shredded leaves, or plants that have collapsed from the onslaught of those ice pellets. I've found that large-

The leaves of this squash plant contain holes and tears from a summer hailstorm, but the plant continued to grow and produce normally.

Shade cloth is useful for protecting plants during heat waves.

My corn-staking method keeps the plants safe during windstorms.

leaved crops such as squash and pumpkins tend to sustain the most damage.

If you have enough warning, cover your crops with row covers, blankets, and tarps. Fortunately, most plants will recover from the damage; they just won't look as pretty as they did before.

HEAT WAVES

A few summers ago, our Spokane, Washington, garden was presented with three major challenges: an exceptional drought, a weeks-long heat wave that included peak temperatures of 114°F (46°C), and thick smoke from regional wildfires. To be honest, I nearly gave up when I observed how this began affecting my plants.

Many regions have been experiencing unusually high summertime temperatures, which makes it challenging to grow a healthy, productive garden. During our heat wave, I employed a few strategies to help the plants:

1. I suspended 50 percent shade cloth over our tomato and broccoli beds to lessen the intensity of the sunlight.

2. I did a lot of supplemental watering, primarily in the early morning and early evening hours. I focused on watering the soil rather than the plants' leaves to lessen the chance of certain types of disease.

3. A thick layer of mulch on the surface of every bed helped the soil retain moisture.

4. I researched heat-tolerant vegetable varieties to plant in my garden. The crops impacted the most were corn, tomatoes, and pole beans so I am experimenting with other varieties. The cucurbit family crops (cucumbers, melons, pumpkins, and summer and winter squash) were the least impacted.

Hot temperatures can cause other problems for vegetables. You'll find many examples of this in the Physiological Disorders section (page 43).

HIGH WINDS

Whether you grow vegetables in a rural area, in a city lot, or in pots on a balcony, wind can be an issue. For the most part, plants are resilient and manage just fine in breezy conditions. That isn't the case in windstorms where the gusts range from 40 to 60 miles (64 to 97 km) per hour or more. If your weather forecast calls for strong winds, you will want to take action to protect your plants. I live in an area that can get pretty windy at times. Here's what I do to prevent damage and some other suggestions.

I love growing corn and am always amazed at how quickly the cornstalks grow. Invariably, when the plants are at their tallest, they are also at their most vulnerable to wind. I can tell you from personal experience that there is nothing more depressing than going out to your garden the morning after a windstorm and seeing your entire corn patch lying flat on the ground. It's a heartbreaking sight.

Corn plants have short, stubby roots, which makes it difficult for them to hold on to the soil during strong winds. If you're growing corn in the ground, consider "hilling up" the plants. This method involves mounding extra soil around the base of each plant. Since I grow my corn in raised beds, that method isn't an option. So, I came up with an alternative that I think works even better.

Every year, I set up a staking system that runs around the perimeter of each raised bed. When the corn plants are about 3 feet (1 m) high, I place a sturdy stake at each corner of the bed and add a stake at the midway point of each long side of the bed. Next, I tie jute twine at a height of 2½ feet (0.8 m) to the stakes, all the way around the bed. Once the plants have grown about 4

feet (1.2 m) tall, I run another line of twine, just below the cornstalks' height, around the perimeter of the bed. I repeat this process one more time when the plants are close to their mature height. When we get a windstorm, the cornstalks might waver a little, but the jute prevents the extreme movements that would snap the stalk right above the root system. This method has been very successful and it takes less time to implement than it does to describe it.

Strong winds can damage tomato, pepper, and eggplant stalks and branches, along with other plants. Place hoops over a susceptible planting, lay floating row cover on top, and anchor down the lower edges with bricks or scrap boards. This will create a nice shelter for the crops.

To prevent climbing plants from getting ripped out of the ground in a storm, always anchor their supports or cages with a stake. It also helps to tie branches that are heavy with fruit to the support. Relocate all container plants that can be moved before bad storms arrive.

My husband and I live in a windy location, where the wind primarily comes from the west. Many years ago, we planted hedges along the west side of the main part of our vegetable garden. They have done a good job of protecting most of our crops, but they also have caused problems over time. As the hedges grew, roots started infiltrating our westernmost raised beds. In addition, the hedges also shade the same beds late in the afternoon. If you decide to go this route for wind protection, be aware of these two issues. If you're able to allow extra space between your planting beds and the hedge to avoid—or at least lessen—the root and shade problems, it will be worth it.

HERBICIDE DAMAGE

It's frustrating enough when the weather or a disease adversely impacts your plants, but there is an even more discouraging issue that we never anticipate: herbicide damage. This can occur when a neighbor sprays weeds near your garden or from adding tainted manure or compost to your soil.

In either case, your plants won't look normal. They might wilt or their leaves and stems are twisted or otherwise deformed.

If the damage was caused by nearby spraying and you know where it originated, this is an opportunity for you to diplomatically explain what happened to your plants as a result. A little healthy communication goes a long way as folks often don't realize how herbicides impact non-weedy plants. It will also be helpful to learn which herbicide they used and check the label for additional information on what to do.

When you notice plant damage in beds that contain manure, it was likely caused by the presence of persistent herbicides. How does it end up in manure? The herbicides are often sprayed in hay fields to control broadleaf weeds. When horses or other livestock eat the hay, the herbicide doesn't break down as it goes through their digestive systems.

In the past, gardeners occasionally encountered problems from using compost produced from yard waste that had been exposed to the herbicide. Fortunately, residential use of persistent herbicides has been widely banned.

No matter where you got the tainted manure—a garden center, a landscape supply company, or a farmer at no cost—this is really bad news for your garden. Most of these herbicides take several years to dissipate. In many cases, gardeners have had to remove the soil from their garden and replenish it with fresh soil.

There is a simple way to avoid dealing with the heartbreak of this problem: Conduct a bioassay test of the manure before adding it to your garden. Legumes (beans and peas) are very sensitive to herbicides so they will help you detect their presence. Fill one planting flat or pot with one part soil and one part manure and then plant ten bean or pea seeds in it. Fill another flat or pot with soil from a garden bed where you've successfully grown vegetables and plant it with another ten seeds; this is your control group, which should germinate and grow normally. If the seeds germinate well (70 percent or better) in the manure mix and the plants are growing normally, rather than twisting, the manure likely doesn't contain persistent herbicides. If you had minimal or no germination, or the seedlings are distorted, do not use that manure—no matter how good of a deal it was!

These deformed tomato leaves exhibit damage caused by a persistent herbicide.

BUG ISSUES

Bugs can certainly be a problem throughout the growing season, but it's important to remember that the damaging ones are actually in the minority. Of the approximately 1 million insect species that have been identified on our planet, roughly 99 percent of them are either beneficial or benign. Pollinators and predators are examples of beneficial bugs. Many benign insects aid in the decomposition of organic matter instead of damaging our crops. This means that only 1 percent of the species are the ones gardeners contend with in various regions of the world.

When you come across an insect in your garden, start by positively identifying it before deciding if you need to take action. I've encountered some scary-looking bugs that fall into either the beneficial or benign category. When that happens, I'm glad I took the time to figure out what it was because I discovered they were an important part of the environment.

Out in our gardens, so many insects are quietly doing good things for us without our knowledge. I encourage you to embrace the beneficial bugs you encounter.

In addition to using my cell phone to study the physical characteristics of a new-to-me bug, I also have a magnifying glass that enables me to take a good look at them. Usually, a reference book or quick internet search is all that is necessary to get a positive identification of a bug.

If it turns out you've got a troublesome bug, and it has more buddies in the garden, observe what they're doing to your plants. This is where the principles of Integrated Pest Management (IPM) come into play. If the bugs are causing damage, decide upon a course of action. The goal is to choose the most environmentally friendly method of dealing with the pest. If they are confined to one leaf on a plant, squish the bugs and discard the leaf.

A proactive approach for bugs you've dealt with in the past is to exclude them from a planting. Lightweight floating row cover is my preferred tool. Sunlight and moisture easily pass through it, but it also acts as a barrier to keep insects off the plants they love. Here's how to use it: As soon as you plant the seeds or seedlings of a susceptible crop, place hoops over the planting and suspend the row cover on top of them. Weigh down the cover around the edges so it won't blow off. This works great for aphids. If you've covered a plant that will bloom later and needs to be pollinated, remove the cover when you start seeing flower buds. Those plants will have gotten off to a great start.

For persistent or especially damaging bugs, rest assured there are a lot of options for dealing with them. I would encourage you to use organic methods and/or products at all times. Please avoid chemical insecticides that are touted as a quick fix. The fact is, along with killing the insects that are harming your vegetables, they also kill beneficial insects that may have taken care of the problem for you.

After you implement a control method, document how well it worked. If things went well, you will know what to do next time. If it didn't go well, you'll want to use another method. With IPM, if the organic approach didn't work and the problem is ongoing, the final step is to use chemicals. I prefer to stay with organic methods, so I do not go that route. Chemicals do more harm within our environment than good.

Let's take a look at some of the most commonly encountered damaging bugs, which plants they're most attracted to, the damage they cause, and the organic methods for controlling them.

Spotted asparagus beetles and many other insects can be problematic in the garden. Both damaging and beneficial bugs are covered in great detail in my book, *The Vegetable Garden Pest Handbook*.

THE TOP TEN GARDEN BUGS AND HOW TO DEAL WITH THEM

THUMBNAIL	NAME/SIZE	FAVORITE PLANTS	SIGNS OF DAMAGE	ORGANIC CONTROLS
	Aphid Family name: Aphididae ⅛" (0.3 cm) long	Cabbage family crops (arugula, broccoli, Brussels sprouts, cabbage, cauliflower, collards, kale, kohlrabi, mustard, radishes, rutabaga, turnips)	Puckered, curled leaves; honeydew; presence of ants; stunted new growth; tiny insects mainly on leaf undersides	Cover seeds or seedlings with floating row cover as soon as you plant them. Crush aphids. Blast them off plants with a strong jet of water from the hose. Apply horticultural oil, insecticidal soap, Neem, or plant extracts.
	Cabbage worm (larva of imported cabbage white butterfly) *Pieris rapae* 1½" (4 cm) long	Cabbage family crops (arugula, broccoli, Brussels sprouts, cabbage, cauliflower, collards, kale, kohlrabi, mustard, radishes, rutabaga, turnips)	Irregular holes in the leaves; excrement on and below the plant; green caterpillars on leaf midribs	Cover planting with floating row cover for entire season. Hand-pick the larvae, and crush eggs. Apply *Bacillus thuringiensis* variety *kurstaki* as soon as you see damage.
	Colorado potato beetle *Leptinotarsa decemlineata* ½" (1 cm) long	Primarily potatoes but also eggplants, peppers, tomatillos, tomatoes	Chewed foliage; dark excrement; yellow or orange eggs on leaf undersides	Crush eggs, and hand-pick beetles and larvae. Cover planting with floating row cover; leave it over potatoes for entire season; remove it from other crops as soon as they begin blooming. Apply kaolin clay, Neem, plant extracts, or spinosad.
	Cutworm Family name: Noctuidae 2" (5 cm) long	Asparagus, beans, cabbage family crops (arugula, broccoli, Brussels sprouts, cabbage, cauliflower, collards, kale, kohlrabi, mustard, radishes, rutabaga, turnips), corn, cucurbit family crops (cucumbers, melons, pumpkins, squash), lettuce, peas, peppers, potatoes, tomatoes	Seedlings or plant stems cut off near the soil surface; tips of asparagus spears deformed from chewing damage; cavities chewed into potato tubers	Go out at night with a flashlight to look for cutworms and hand-pick. Make barriers to protect seedling stems (1" [2 cm] above soil, 1½" [4 cm] below). Sprinkle diatomaceous earth around the base of each seedling. Apply *Bacillus thuringiensis* variety *kurstaki*, beneficial nematodes, Neem, or plant extracts.

THUMBNAIL	NAME/SIZE	FAVORITE PLANTS	SIGNS OF DAMAGE	ORGANIC CONTROLS
	Flea beetle Family name: Chrysomelidae ¹⁄₁₆" to ¼" (0.2 to 0.6 cm) long	Beet family crops (beets, spinach, Swiss chard), cabbage family crops (arugula, broccoli, Brussels sprouts, cabbage, cauliflower, collards, kale, kohlrabi, mustard, radishes, rutabaga, turnips), nightshade family crops (eggplants, peppers, potatoes, tomatillos, tomatoes)	Numerous holes in the leaves that are less than ⅛" (0.3 cm) diameter; wilted, stunted seedlings	Cover planting bed with reflective plastic mulch before planting seedlings through X's in it (the reflective surface makes it hard for flea beetles to locate the plants). Control weeds in garden. Clean up garden debris at end of season. Apply diatomaceous earth, kaolin clay, Neem, plant extracts, or spinosad.
	Hornworm *Manduca quinquemaculata* (tomato), *Manduca sexta* (tobacco, pictured) 4" (10 cm) long	Primarily tomatoes but also eggplants, peppers, potatoes, tomatillos	Chewed foliage and fruits; defoliated plants; dark excrement on the leaves and soil below the feeding damage	Hand-pick caterpillars. Apply *Bacillus thuringiensis* variety *kurstaki*, insecticidal soap, Neem, or spinosad.
	Japanese beetle *Popillia japonica* ½" (1 cm) long	Basil, beans, collards, corn, eggplants, leafy greens, peppers, tomatoes	Skeletonized leaves; chewed corn silks; dead sections of lawn (caused by the grubs)	Hand-pick the beetles early in the season. Do not use Japanese beetle traps because the lures attract more beetles to the area. To control beetles, apply kaolin clay, Neem, or *Bacillus thuringiensis* variety *galleriae*; to control grubs, apply beneficial nematodes, milky spore (*Paenibacillus popilliae*), or *Bacillus thuringiensis* variety *galleriae*.

THUMBNAIL	NAME/SIZE	FAVORITE PLANTS	SIGNS OF DAMAGE	ORGANIC CONTROLS
	Slug and snail *Deroceras reticulatum* (gray garden slug), *Cornu aspersum* (brown garden snail) Slugs: 2" (5 cm) long (pictured), Snails: 1¼" (3 cm) long	Artichokes, basil, beans, beet family crops (beets, spinach, Swiss chard), cabbage family crops (arugula, broccoli, Brussels sprouts, cabbage, cauliflower, collards, kale, kohlrabi, mustard, radishes, rutabaga, turnips), lettuce, peppers, tomatoes	Irregularly shaped holes in leaves; slime trails	Hand-pick them. Trap them under boards during the day (they are nocturnal). Use beer traps or barriers made with copper tape. Apply diatomaceous earth or plant extracts. Apply organic slug and snail bait.
	Squash bug *Anasa tristis* ⅝" (1.5 cm) long	Primarily pumpkins and winter squash, but also cucumbers, melons, and summer squash	Tiny specks on leaves; leaves turn yellow, then brown, and start wilting; plant dies; reddish-brown eggs on stems or leaf undersides; nymphs and adults scurry away when you approach	Use row cover at planting time; leave in place until plants begin blooming. Don't use mulch under plants because it provides hiding places. Hand-pick adults and nymphs; crush eggs.
	Stink bug Family: Pentatomidae Brown marmorated stink bug (*Halyomorpha halys*), pictured ⅝" (1.5 cm) long	Artichokes, beans, corn, peas, peppers, squash, tomatoes	Holes in artichoke heads and dark, damaged scales; dark excrement; mottled skin of fruits; dimpled or distorted fruits or plants; sunken skin; sunken bean seeds and pods	Use stink bug traps that contain pheromones to attract both sexes. Hand-pick adults and nymphs; crush eggs. Use floating row cover over susceptible crops, and remove when they start blooming. Apply insecticidal soap, kaolin clay, or pyrethrins.

I have so much more information about bugs that I want to share with you, but there just isn't enough room to do the topic justice within this book. You will find extensive information on dealing with damaging insect pests in my previous book, *The Vegetable Garden Pest Handbook*. It is filled with the details and photos you need to correctly identify what's bothering your veggies and how to control them by employing effective, organic methods. There are useful descriptions of the organic products available to you and do-it-yourself projects for making traps, barriers, row cover hoops, and even an insect hotel to draw in the beneficials. I encourage you to pick up a copy of this indispensable resource.

PHYSIOLOGICAL DISORDERS

Sometimes our vegetable plants, or the crops they produce, don't develop normally. When pests or diseases aren't the cause, these problems are known as physiological disorders because they are caused by environmental conditions or a cultural issue. Abiotic disorder is another name for problems caused by non-living organisms. Chances are, many of the following disorders are ones you have seen in your own garden but didn't know the cause:

BITTERNESS

DESCRIPTION

Have you ever picked a cucumber, expecting a delicious flavor, only to discover it is extremely bitter? Or harvested lettuce for a summer salad but the lettuce tasted awful? These issues are caused by environmental stresses. Let's look at cucumbers first, which are members of the cucurbit family.

Cucurbits contain natural chemicals called cucurbitacins. Environmental conditions such as extended periods of high temperatures or even cooler than normal temperatures cause cucurbitacin levels to rise, resulting in bitter fruits. Irregular watering is another trigger for this. For example, if a gardener only waters the plants periodically, it stresses them. Low soil pH is another potential cause of bitterness.

What causes bitter lettuce or other salad greens? Because lettuce is a cool-season crop, you can expect its flavor to degrade as summertime temperatures heat up. Just like with cucumbers, irregular watering can lead to bitterness of the leaves. Leafy greens will develop a flower head in order to produce seeds before they die; refer to Bolting on page 48 for additional information.

Cucumbers will be bitter if they don't receive enough moisture or are picked when they are past their prime.

CROPS MOST IMPACTED BY THIS CONDITION:

Primarily cucumbers but other members of the cucurbit family (melons, pumpkins, squash), lettuce, and other leafy greens

STRATEGIES

> Water your plants regularly.
> Pick cucumbers while they are young and most flavorful.
> In cucumbers and other cucurbits, the majority of the bitterness is located at the stem end of the fruits. If you remove that area and peel the skin, the fruits should be more palatable.
> Consider growing hybrid cucumbers because bitterness occurs less frequently in them.
> Place mulch around lettuce and other salad greens to help the soil retain moisture.
> Use shade cloth to extend cool-season crops' growing season into the summer.

NURTURE YOUR GARDEN & TROUBLESHOOT PROBLEMS

BLOSSOM DROP

DESCRIPTION

It's always exciting when your fruit-producing crops begin flowering, but if those flowers shrivel up and fall off, that is cause for concern. Blossom drop results from a lack of pollination caused by environmental conditions. Ideal daytime temperatures for pollination range between 70°F and 85°F (21°C and 29°C); if it is too cold or too hot, the unpollinated flowers will drop off. In addition, excessively low or high relative humidity affects the mobility of pollen; levels between 40 and 70 percent are optimal.

Other causes include windy conditions that dry out the flowers, planting warm-season crops too early or where they don't receive enough sunlight, irregular watering, or too much nitrogen fertilizer, which makes plants use their energy for leaf development rather than flowers. Even pest or disease problems will cause blossom drop because stressed plants produce fewer flowers. The good news is that blossom drop is usually a temporary disorder that will resolve as weather conditions improve.

Gardeners commonly encounter this problem with their tomato, eggplant, and pepper plants. As members of the nightshade family, they have "perfect flowers," meaning each one contains both the male and female components necessary for pollination. The flowers are pollinated by the wind or by bees and other pollinators.

CROPS MOST IMPACTED BY THIS CONDITION:

Beans, nightshade family crops (eggplants, peppers, tomatoes)

STRATEGIES

> Plant warm-season crops after the danger of frost has passed. If you planted them too early, cover them with floating row cover for some protection (refer to page 30).

> Make sure they are planted in a location that receives at least 6 to 8 hours of sunlight daily.

> Water your plants regularly to keep the soil lightly moist.

> Cover plants with lightweight (30 percent) shade cloth when temperatures are unusually hot.

> If your garden is in a very windy location, protect plants with a barrier to prevent flowers from drying.

> Avoid repeated use of high-nitrogen fertilizers.

> Choose varieties that perform well in your region. If your summers are extremely hot, select varieties that mature in a shorter period of time.

> You can also shake the flower stalks (or buzz them with a battery-operated electric toothbrush) to move the pollen to the stigma.

If none of the above causes of blossom drop relate to your situation, consider applying a blossom set spray containing the plant growth hormone kinetin.

Tomato plants are often affected by blossom drop early in the growing season.

BLOSSOM-END ROT

DESCRIPTION

Blossom-end rot is most easily recognized by the presence of a sunken, brown bottom tip on the developing fruits of tomatoes and zucchinis, but it also can occur on other crops. The underlying problem is a calcium deficiency within the developing fruits. The primary causes are hot, dry conditions and irregular watering. For fruits to develop normally, plant roots need to be able to transport calcium from the soil into the plants and up to the fruits. To do that, the roots require moisture. Overuse of high-nitrogen fertilizers also causes blossom-end rot because they promote leafy growth, which robs calcium from the fruits. You might think that applying calcium to your soil is the answer, but if the soil around the plants isn't watered regularly, there is no way for the calcium to get into the plants through the roots. Foliar applications of calcium won't help either because it isn't able to move from the leaves to the fruits. While blossom-end rot can affect nearly every variety of tomato, it impacts elongated plum tomatoes the most. Cherry tomatoes are typically not affected by it at all.

CROPS MOST IMPACTED BY THIS CONDITION:

Cucurbit family crops (melons, pumpkins, summer and winter squash), nightshade family crops (eggplants, peppers, tomatoes)

STRATEGIES

> Water your plants consistently and increase the watering time during exceptionally hot, dry conditions.

> Place mulch around the base of susceptible crops to help the soil retain moisture. Ideal materials include shredded leaves or grass clippings from a lawn that hasn't been treated with herbicides.

> Avoid overfeeding your plants with high-nitrogen fertilizers. Refer to the Fertilizing Issues section on fertilizers on page 24 for more information.

> Don't cultivate near the roots of susceptible crops because damaged roots will not transport as much calcium into the plants as heathy roots.

> Use shade cloth during excessive heat to shelter susceptible plants from the intensity of the sun.

> Most soils contain sufficient calcium for growing vegetables. If your plants suffer from blossom-end rot every year and you are consistent about watering, consider testing your soil before adding calcium.

Blossom-end rot causes the tips of developing tomatoes to turn brown.

Blossom-end rot on a young zucchini squash.

BOLTING

DESCRIPTION

Bolting refers to plants blooming and setting seeds for the next generation, before their growing season is over. Cool-season crops are more susceptible to this, and it most frequently occurs when the day length and temperatures increase. Yet, it also can happen when plants are suddenly exposed to cool temperatures. Bolting affects the taste of these crops because they usually become bitter and sometimes tough. Once plants bolt, they will stop producing new leaves. Besides heat stress, bolting also can occur when plants struggle due to a lack of space, insufficient sunlight, or insect or disease problems.

CROPS MOST IMPACTED BY THIS CONDITION:

Bok choy, broccoli, Brussels sprouts, cabbage, carrots, cauliflower, cilantro, lettuce and other types of salad greens, onions grown from sets or plant starts, radishes, spinach, Swiss chard

These carrot plants bolted in reaction to a heat wave. I left them in place because I knew their flowers would attract more pollinators to the garden.

STRATEGIES

> When seed shopping, look for varieties that are labeled as "slow to bolt" or "bolt resistant."
> Plant cool-season crops as soon as conditions are right to allow them enough time to grow and produce before the hot weather arrives. If you missed that opportunity, consider planting that crop in late summer and harvest it in the fall.
> Water your plants consistently.
> Avoid disturbing the plants' roots as this can trigger bolting. Many of these crops fare much better when their seeds are sown directly in the garden.
> Place mulch around the base of crops that tend to bolt. This helps the soil retain moisture.
> If you catch the problem early enough, you might be able to pinch off the flowers and keep the plants going for a bit longer, but the plants will be on borrowed time.
> Those gardening in regions with hot summers should consider protecting susceptible crops with lightweight (30 percent) shade cloth.
> Avoid planting biennial crops such as onions, carrots, and parsley earlier than is recommended. These crops grow in the first season and then bloom and set seed the following year—provided you haven't harvested them before that. The cold temperatures in late winter and very early spring can trigger the bolting response.
> If you're not anxious to replant the bed, help the pollinators by letting the bolted plants bloom.

BUTTONING

DESCRIPTION

Buttoning refers to the premature development of small heads on broccoli and cauliflower plants. Sudden exposure to colder temperatures is the most common reason for this. Other causes revolve around stressors such as infrequent watering, a lack of nitrogen in the soil, transplant shock, weed competition while the plants are young, damaged roots, and pest attacks. High concentrations of salt in your soil also will stress the plants and promote buttoning. This can be caused by poorly draining soil, erratic watering practices, the use of water softeners, or locating your planting bed next to a walkway where de-icer is used during the winter months.

CROPS MOST IMPACTED BY THIS CONDITION:

Broccoli, cauliflower

Buttoning is the development of small heads on broccoli (shown here) or cauliflower plants.

STRATEGIES

> Wait until the soil temperature is at least 50°F (10°C) before transplanting your seedlings.

> Time your indoor seed sowing so the transplants will have no more than four to six mature leaves when it's time to move them out to the garden. Larger transplants are more susceptible to buttoning, likely due to the stress of being pot-bound.

> Avoid transplant shock by planting broccoli or cauliflower on an overcast day and watering them right away.

> Water regularly throughout the season. The soil should be lightly moist.

> Feed these crops with nitrogen fertilizer on a regular basis; apply it as recommended on the package.

> Place mulch around the base of broccoli or cauliflower plants to help the soil retain moisture. Ideal materials include shredded leaves or grass clippings from a lawn that hasn't been treated with herbicides.

> To prevent stress from insect pests, cover the seedlings with floating row cover at planting time. Broccoli and cauliflower do not require pollination, so you can leave the cover on all season. The floating row cover will act as a physical barrier to keep aphids and cabbage worms away from the plants.

> Weed the bed regularly, especially while the plants are young.

FRUIT-CRACKING

DESCRIPTION

Most gardeners have seen this problem on their tomatoes, but fruit-cracking can occur on several types of vegetable crops. The most common cause is rainfall or excessive watering following prolonged dry spells. The problem is that the skin of the fruit is often unable to expand with the rapidly growing inner tissue. Maturing tomatoes experience different types of cracking: radial (from the stem to the tip), concentric (in a circle at the shoulder of the fruit), or irregular cracks. Unfortunately, the exposed tissue is more prone to rotting and deterioration. It's not uncommon for a beautiful head of cabbage to suddenly split wide open after a summertime rainstorm or even from the heat—usually right before you intended to pick it! Fortunately, the head is still salvageable if you harvest it right away. Root crops such as carrots and parsnips are also susceptible to cracking as a reaction to changing moisture in the soil. No matter which crops you're growing, cracking happens more frequently in fruits that are reaching maturity.

This tomato cracked following a late summer rainstorm.

CROPS MOST IMPACTED BY THIS CONDITION:

Cabbage, carrots, cucumbers, nightshade family crops (eggplants, peppers, tomatoes), parsnips, watermelons

STRATEGIES

> Water your garden consistently, but don't overwater.

> Place mulch on the surface of your beds to help the soil retain moisture. Ideal materials include shredded leaves or grass clippings from a lawn that hasn't been treated with herbicides.

> During especially hot summers, suspend a lightweight (30 percent) shade cloth over susceptible crops.

> Allow leaves to cover developing fruits, to provide some protection.

> Consider harvesting some of your vegetables a bit early—especially if a rainstorm is in the forecast—and allow them to ripen indoors. This works especially well with tomatoes that are just starting to show a bit of color.

> Look for crack-resistant varieties of vegetables.

MISSHAPEN FRUITS

DESCRIPTION

It's discouraging when, despite your best efforts, you end up with some deformed crops. Environmental stresses are the main reason, but certain insects or diseases also can cause this problem. Most gardeners are familiar with forked or split carrots, knobby or cracked potatoes, and strangely shaped cucumbers, but other crops are affected as well. If carrots or other root crops aren't properly spaced, the roots won't develop normally. These vegetables prefer light, sandy soil that that does not contain a lot of nitrogen, which promotes leaves over root development. Most root crops grow better when direct-sown in the garden rather than being started indoors and transplanted later. Transplanting damages the roots' growth tips, potentially resulting in deformed roots later. Knobby potato tubers develop during prolonged heat spells or from high levels of nitrogen in the soil. Extended periods of drought interrupt the tubers' development as well. Cracks or fissures in potatoes occur while they are developing and particularly when the moisture in the soil changes dramatically (e.g., little water early in the season followed by excessive amounts). Insufficient pollination is the primary reason for deformed cucumbers as well as irregular watering, too much nitrogen fertilizer, or high heat and humidity.

This deformed carrot root was likely the result of irregular watering.

CROPS MOST IMPACTED BY THIS CONDITION:

Beets, carrots, cucurbit family crops (mainly cucumbers, summer and winter squash), kohlrabi, parsnips, potatoes

STRATEGIES

For root crops:

> Prior to planting, loosen the soil as deep as you expect the roots to grow. Add sand and/or compost to heavy clay soils. Avoid rocky soils, which will impede root development; consider growing these crops in raised beds or containers instead.

> Don't walk on the soil surrounding the planting because this will compact the roots.

> Direct-sow root crops.

> Always thin seedlings to provide enough room for the roots to develop.

> Avoid using high-nitrogen fertilizers. Root crops benefit from the addition of phosphorus; bonemeal is an organic soil amendment that works well.

Other crops:

> Apply a balanced fertilizer to the soil rather than high-nitrogen supplements.

> Water consistently.

> Apply mulch to the soil surface to help it retain moisture and cool down a bit, if temperatures are hot.

> Weed beds regularly to eliminate competition for moisture and nutrients.

> To prevent pollination issues, avoid the use of pesticides in your garden and plant flowers to attract pollinators.

PHYSIOLOGICAL LEAF ROLL

DESCRIPTION

It's a bit unsettling when the leaves on certain vegetable crops start curling. Most of the time, this is due to environmental stresses, but it also can be caused by viral diseases or herbicide exposure. Physiological leaf roll is most commonly seen on tomato plants but does occur on a few other crops. Tomato leaves become thick and leathery, and the outer edges of the leaves curl upward forming a roll or tube. On watermelons and potatoes, the leaves have upward cupping while stressed beans and peppers exhibit downwardly cupped leaves. Researchers believe leaf distortion is a plant's strategy for minimizing both moisture loss and exposure to intense sunlight. Physiological leaf roll generally occurs in late spring and early summer, but it also can happen during extended heat waves. The lower leaves of tomato plants are usually affected first. The great news is that the disorder does not affect the productivity or flavor of the fruits. If weather conditions return to normal quickly, the leaves will usually return to normal. Other causes include cool weather early in the growing season, transplant shock, insufficient watering, too much nitrogen in the soil, root damage from cultivation, and excessive pruning.

How do you tell if the rolled leaves are the result of viral diseases or herbicide damage, rather than physiological leaf roll? It is important to carefully examine the leaves first. Virus-afflicted leaves are yellow or have a mottled appearance, and they impact the plant's ability to grow. With herbicides, the leaves and stems will be twisted and otherwise distorted.

CROPS MOST IMPACTED BY THIS CONDITION:

Primarily on tomatoes but also seen on beans, peppers, potatoes, watermelons

STRATEGIES

> Plant warm-season crops such as beans, peppers, tomatoes, and watermelons two weeks after the danger of frost has passed. Protect young seedlings with floating row cover during unseasonably cool weather early in the growing season.

> Harden-off your seedlings before transplanting them into the garden. Refer to opposite page for details.

> Water consistently.

> Don't cultivate around the roots because root damage stresses the plants.

> Avoid overfertilizing any of these crops with nitrogen.

> Protect plants with shade cloth during extended periods of heat and drought.

Physiological leaf roll on a 'Costoluto Genovese' tomato plant.

SUNBURN (ALSO KNOWN AS LEAF SCORCH)

DESCRIPTION

While you might think only people get sunburns, it happens to plants as well and can be much more devastating. At the very least, the plants will struggle, but if the damage is severe enough, they will die. With sunburn, which is also referred to as leaf scorch, the leaf tissue turns white or brown and usually wilts. This happened to three of the leaves on my zucchini plant one year and they looked terrible. I initially thought the plant had a disease, but as soon as our hot summertime temperatures subsided, it recovered and produced enough zucchini for our neighborhood.

It's not unusual for sunburn to impact young seedlings. Sunburn most commonly occurs when gardeners fail to acclimate seedlings to direct sunlight and outdoor temperatures before moving them permanently out to the garden. There is a huge difference between the amount of light an indoor grow light puts out and the intensity of the sun outdoors. Because the leaves of young seedlings are very tender, it's important to put them through the hardening-off process to acclimate them to the great outdoors.

When a seedling has been sunburned, the leaves turn white and wilt.

CROPS MOST IMPACTED BY THIS CONDITION:

Young seedlings, most vegetable crops

STRATEGIES

> Harden-off your seedlings over the course of a week:
>> On the first day, move your seedlings outside to an area with filtered sunlight for one hour and then move them back inside. On day two, move them out for two hours and bring them back indoors. Each subsequent day, add an hour to their outdoor time while moving them into brighter sunlight. This might sound tedious, but it is well worth your time. By the end of those seven days, it will be safe to transplant your seedlings into the garden.
> If you didn't harden-off your seedlings before transplanting them and they're exhibiting mild cases of sunburn, place a shade cloth above the bed for a few days to give them some relief. Do not remove the damaged leaves because they still should be able to conduct photosynthesis, which will help the plants recover.
> Water plants regularly to reduce stress on them.
> If you have advance warning about a heat wave, consider using shade cloth to protect susceptible plants.

SUNSCALD

DESCRIPTION

If you've ever seen papery white patches on the developing fruits of any crops listed at right, that is sunscald. It occurs when the fruits are suddenly exposed to intense sunlight during periods of hot weather. Under normal circumstances, leaves provide shade for the fruits. If a plant has lost a large percentage of its leaves due to damage from pests or diseases, or from excessive pruning, the fruits will be very susceptible to sunscald. This will be exacerbated if the plants aren't being watered regularly because it increases their stress. When tomato plants first show signs of disease, a good way to slow the spread is by removing any affected leaves. Unfortunately, this can lead to sunscald of the fruits since they will suddenly lose some of the leaf canopy that had been protecting them. If this situation arises in your garden, you'll need to get creative to provide extra shade for the tomatoes. It is safe to eat sunscald-affected fruits, provided they don't contain black mold on the surface. While sunscald and sunburn (also known as leaf scorch) might sound like the same problem, sunscald impacts the fruits whereas sunburn/leaf scorch affects the foliage. Learn more about the latter on page 53.

The light patch on this tomato is from sunscald.

CROPS MOST IMPACTED BY THIS CONDITION:

Cucurbit family crops (cucumbers, melons, summer and winter squash, watermelons), nightshade family crops (eggplants, peppers, tomatoes)

STRATEGIES

> Avoid removing large portions of the leaf canopy that are shading fruits, especially during the peak of summer. While it might be tempting to remove some leaves from squash plants to make harvesting easier and less painful (due to those prickly leaf stems), this will expose developing fruits to too much sunlight.

> Place mulch on the surface of the soil in tomato beds to lessen the chance of soilborne diseases coming into contact with the plant foliage.

> If you must remove diseased leaves, shade the fruits on the plant with shade cloth or another barrier that will decrease the intensity of the sunlight they are exposed to.

> Water your plants consistently and provide them with good nutrition throughout the growing season to keep them unstressed.

TOMATO CATFACING

DESCRIPTION

It is relatively easy to identify catfacing on tomato fruits: They are deformed on the blossom end, having scars, creases, small holes, brown corky tissue, and occasionally exposed locules, which are the cavities inside the fruit. There hasn't been a great deal of research on what causes catfacing. The main theory is that the exposure of young seedlings to cool temperatures (below 54°F [12°C]) damages their flower buds, which will affect the later development of the fruits. Another potential cause is the excessive pruning of indeterminate tomato plants because this reduces the amounts of auxins (growth hormones); as a result, it impacts early flower bud development. Overuse of nitrogen fertilizers, inconsistent watering, or flower bud damage from thrips also has the potential to cause catfacing. Another theory is that exposure to certain types of herbicides can lead to catfacing; but in this instance, only the flowers and fruits are damaged rather than the plants' leaves. Large, round cultivars and some heirloom tomato varieties seem to be more prone to catfacing.

'Costoluto Genovese' heirloom tomatoes are delicious but prone to catfacing.

CROPS MOST IMPACTED BY THIS CONDITION:

Tomatoes

STRATEGIES

> Watch the weather forecasts closely to time the planting of your tomato seedlings. Consider waiting two weeks after the danger of frost has passed. If there is a sudden cooldown in the forecast later, protect your seedlings at night with floating row covers, blankets, or tarps.

> Avoid intensive pruning, particularly of indeterminate varieties, while they are actively growing and developing fruits.

> Water plants regularly.

> If catfacing frequently occurs on a specific tomato variety in your garden, look for another one that is less prone to this problem.

NURTURE YOUR GARDEN & TROUBLESHOOT PROBLEMS

Beans are susceptible to a number of diseases, but when the plants are healthy, they are so prolific.

VEGETABLE PLANT DISEASE GUIDE

I'm going to be honest with you: Plant diseases are one of the most challenging aspects of growing a garden. At times, it's hard to pinpoint whether a plant is ailing from extreme weather conditions or a cultural issue where we haven't met its needs, or if it's struggling with a disease.

For this chapter, I've written profiles of the most commonly encountered vegetable plant diseases. There are three main types: bacterial, fungal, and viral. I have arranged all the disease profiles in alphabetical order so you can quickly locate a specific profile without having to know the type ahead of time. In the index on this page, I have grouped them by their type. As you can see, the vast majority of vegetable diseases are fungal, but bacterial and viral diseases are just as worrisome.

It would be easy for us to think that all fungi and bacteria are bad for our plants. After all, this chapter is filled with many examples of the ones that wreak havoc with our plants and affect our ability to get a decent harvest. It's important for us to remember some bacteria and fungi positively impact our plants and the environment around us.

For example, most gardeners are familiar with the beneficial bacteria known as *Bacillus thuringiensis*—or *Bt*, for short. Several strains help us control damaging pests. *Bt kurstaki* (*Btk*) kills the caterpillar stage of insects such as armyworms, cabbage worms, and cutworms. *Bt galleriae* (*Btg*) controls both Japanese beetles and their larvae. *Saccharopolyspora spinosa* is a fermented soil bacterium that is the active ingredient in a commonly used organic product called spinosad. It controls a wide range of damaging pests.

Fungi benefit plants in some significant ways as well. For example, mycorrhizal fungi have a symbiotic relationship with plant roots. The fungi absorb nutrients from the soil and make them available to plants. In return, decomposing plant materials provide fungi with the nutrients they need to survive. Mycorrhizal fungi also protect plants against certain types of soilborne fungal diseases, such as *Fusarium* and *Phytophthora*. Scientists have been studying the benefits of fungal networks within the soil that connect plants to each other and, more recently, are investigating how they are able to store vast amounts of carbon in the soil. Yes, this chapter is about vegetable plant diseases, but I did want to put things into perspective.

There are a lot of similarities between identifying a disease on a plant and in a human being. When a person is ill, their doctor asks them about their symptoms, examines them, and perhaps orders a few tests. Let's say they have contracted strep throat. Their **symptoms** might be a fever and sore throat, which are how our bodies react to this bacterial disease. When a swab test shows the presence of the bacteria, *Streptococcus pyogenes*, that is a positive **sign** of the disease.

With plant diseases, we need to be very observant of what is going on, with the plant itself and the environment surrounding it. **Symptoms** might include yellow leaves, wilting, or stunted growth. All of these are examples of a plant's reactions to the presence of a disease. If you notice leaves with a white coating or that a plant has fluids oozing from its pores, those are actual **signs** of a disease.

For a disease to infect a plant, three components must be present: a host plant, a pathogen, and the right environmental conditions. This is what is known as the *disease triangle*. The disease won't occur if any of these components are missing.

For example, if a pathogen exists in your garden and conditions are ideal, but you're not growing any of its host plants, the disease won't develop. Put another way, if a pathogen needs cool, moist conditions to spread disease but your weather is hot and dry, the disease won't infect your plants.

If all three items are present and environmental conditions are particularly favorable to spread the pathogens, the disease will impact your plants much more severely.

As gardeners, we have control over many things that can prevent or reduce the spread of disease. You will find plenty of suggestions for how to accomplish this within the disease profiles and explanations of how they work in the Organic Strategies Explained section, beginning on page 158.

Diseases are caused by living pathogens that can spread easily from one plant to the next. Some are specific to a crop or plant family, while others infect a wide variety of vegetables. Let's look at the properties of bacteria, fungi, and viruses so you will have a better understanding of how each of these functions and affects plant growth.

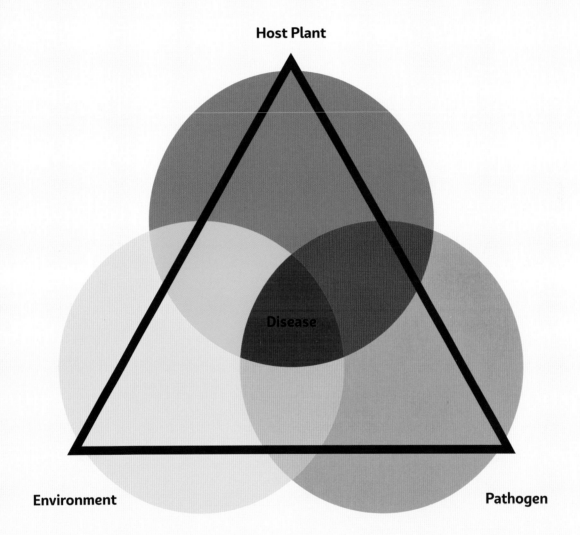

This diagram illustrates the "disease triangle": A disease will not occur
unless there is a host, a pathogen, and favorable conditions.

BACTERIA

Bacteria are microscopic prokaryotic organisms. This means they don't have a nucleus or internal membranes. They asexually reproduce by splitting their single cell into two individual cells. Their bodies can be rod-shaped, round, spiral-shaped, or threadlike; most move about via a whiplike tail called a flagellum.

They enter hosts through wounds or tiny, natural openings (stomata) on plant leaves and stems. Some of the most common symptoms bacteria cause include wilting, leaf spots, rotting, and deformities such as scabs and cankers. Bacteria kill plant cells with toxins, break down cell walls, or interfere with the transportation of moisture and nutrients within a plant's vascular system.

To gain a better understanding of bacterial diseases, let's look at how bacterial wilt disease (*Erwinia tracheiphila*) might affect a cucumber vine in your garden. The plant had been growing reasonably well until cucumber beetles started feeding on it. You soon notice yellow spots developing on the leaves and spots on the young cucumbers. What's even more worrisome is that the leaves suddenly start wilting during the day. You water the plant, thinking it must have dried out; when you check on it again in the evening, the leaves have recovered. This happens again the next day, but soon the vine dies. When you cut through the stem to investigate, you notice two things: The tissue in the stem has dark streaks in it and the stem is also oozing a clear, sticky liquid.

What happened? The cucumber beetles fed elsewhere on infected plants and brought the disease to your plant. Their feeding activities caused wounds, through which the bacteria entered the plant. Once inside, the bacteria multiplied at an astounding rate and quickly blocked the plant's vascular system. That is what caused the wilting and eventual death of the plant.

Bacteria spread via rain, wind, insect vectors, and contaminated tools. To control them, look for resistant varieties, disinfect your tools, avoid causing plant wounds, use crop rotation methods, and consider using biological controls. You will find information about products later in this chapter.

SIGNS AND SYMPTOMS OF BACTERIAL DISEASES

- Brown leaf spots, sometimes surrounded by yellow halos
- Spots on fruits
- V-shaped wedges of yellow leaf tissue
- Oozing leaf spots, sometimes accompanied by a foul odor
- Dead areas on leaves
- Corky lesions
- Water-soaked tissues
- Sudden wilting of leaves and stems
- Sudden plant death

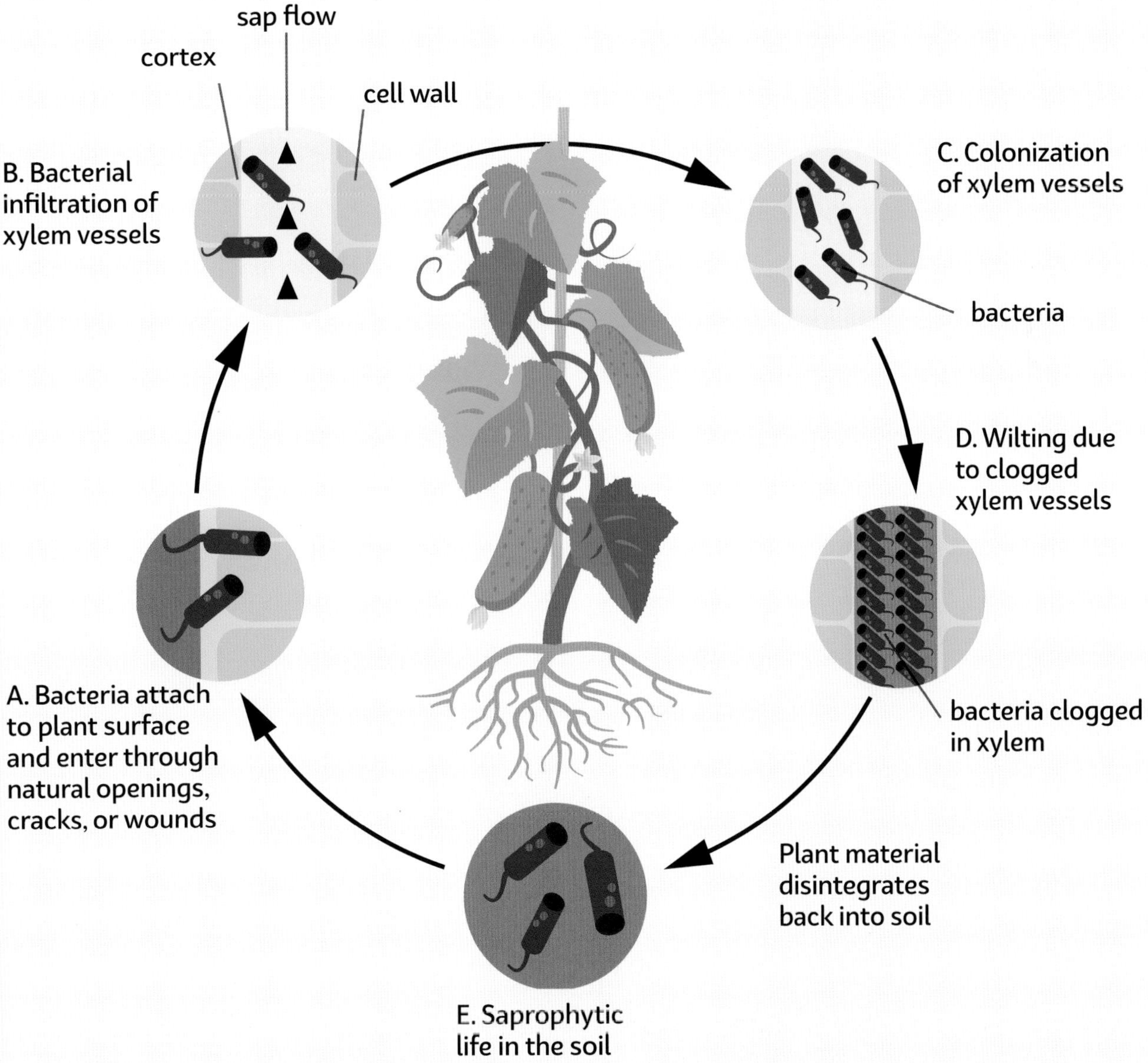

cortex

sap flow

cell wall

B. Bacterial
infiltration of
xylem vessels

C. Colonization
of xylem vessels

bacteria

D. Wilting due
to clogged
xylem vessels

bacteria clogged
in xylem

A. Bacteria attach
to plant surface
and enter through
natural openings,
cracks, or wounds

Plant material
disintegrates
back into soil

E. Saprophytic
life in the soil

This illustration shows the life cycle of bacterial wilt disease.

FUNGI

Fungi and fungi-like microorganisms are responsible for the majority of vegetable plant diseases. From a historical standpoint, the most devastating fungus has been *Phytophthora infestans*, which causes potato late blight. Back in the 1800s, the people of Ireland were completely dependent upon their potato crops. When this disease struck, it destroyed the foliage and tubers of their plants for successive years. This led to the Irish potato famine, which began in 1845. Over one million people starved to death as a result. This is a sobering example of the potential for certain diseases to severely impact the crops humans rely upon for food.

Fungi are eukaryotic organisms, which have a cell nucleus. They absorb nutrients through filament-like hyphae. Some are unique to a specific host while others have many different hosts. Just like bacteria and viruses, fungi can enter a host via wounds or natural openings (stomata), but they have another tool in their armory: appressoria. These specialized hyphae enable them to enter and infect plant hosts.

Fungi and fungi-like microorganisms are either saprophytic, which survive on decaying or dead tissue, or are parasitic, where they are able to survive on both live and dead tissue.

Since late blight (*Phytophthera infestans*) on potatoes continues to be a concern to this day, let's look at it as a typical example of fungal infections. Let's say you planted several tubers in the spring, but, unbeknownst to you, some were infected with late blight. Your potato bed is looking great, with lots of green foliage on the plants. The weather has been a mix of rainy and windy days. Soon, changes start taking place. The first things you notice are pale green water-soaked spots on the lowest leaves of the plants. Lesions are at the edges of the leaves, which soon turn black. Some of the lesions have yellow halos and you also notice a pale mold on them. In just a few days, spores that developed in the lesions of that infected plant have drifted onto other plants in the bed, and now all the plants have some brown spots with yellow halos. After doing some exploratory digging around the base of the plant, you discover depressions on the tubers and discoloration of their skin. When you cut into one of the tubers, a red rot is visible. That is a pretty disheartening scenario, isn't it?

Late blight is primarily caused by infected tubers and spreads rapidly when conditions are especially wet. Once the spores develop, they move to other plants via rain and wind. Infection of the plant occurs when spores land on wet foliage. When spores land on wet soil and make contact with developing tubers, they infect them as well.

To control these microorganisms, look for resistant varieties, especially if you've experienced fungal diseases in the past or they are prevalent in your region. Water your plants consistently, but avoid overwatering them. Remove infected plant tissues and dispose of them, rather than composting them. Practice crop rotation. Avoid injuring your plants while caring for them and consider using organic products that control fungi.

SIGNS AND SYMPTOMS OF FUNGAL DISEASES

- Gray or white fuzzy growth or powder
- Brown, yellow, or rust spots on leaves
- Center of spots occasionally drops out of leaves
- V-shaped leaf lesions
- Wilting leaves
- Stunted plants
- Water-soaked lesions
- Brown spots on fruits
- Rotting fruits
- Rotting seeds
- Dead seedlings
- White to black sclerotia (resting fungal structures)

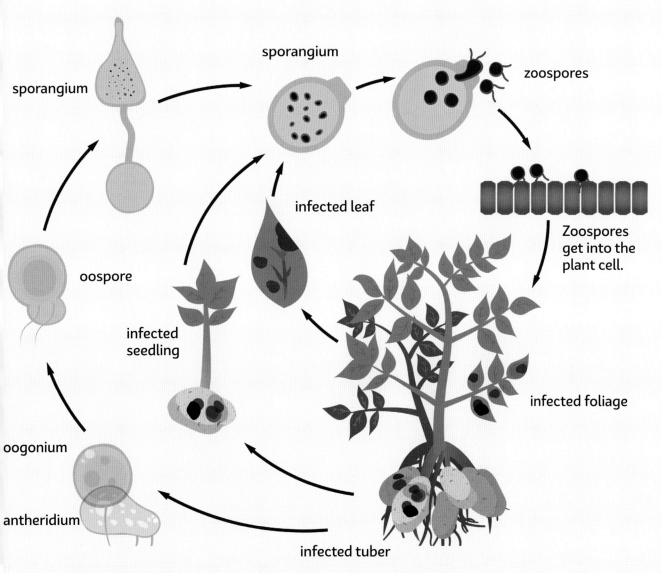

sporangium

sporangium

zoospores

infected leaf

Zoospores get into the plant cell.

oospore

infected seedling

infected foliage

oogonium

antheridium

infected tuber

This illustration shows the life cycle of the potato late blight fungus (*Phytophthora infestans*).

VIRUSES

Viruses live inside cells and are so tiny that they can only be seen with an electron microscope. They have a protein coating that surrounds their central core, which contains either RNA or DNA. Viruses require a wound to enter a host cell. This might be the result of the natural development of roots or other plant tissue, gardening activities such as pruning or propagation techniques, or other organisms previously infecting the cell; this includes insect vectors that carry pathogens. Viruses are also transmitted in seeds.

Viruses must have a living host or they will die. Once they enter a cell, they shed their protein coating and multiply. They move through the vascular system of the host plant, which disrupts its normal processes and causes the plant to die.

When a plant is infected with a virus, it's a pretty alarming sight. In this final scenario, let's look at what happens to a tomato plant when tomato spotted wilt virus (TSWV) strikes. You have nice, healthy tomato plants. In your daily visits to the garden, you don't even notice that tiny insects called thrips have arrived and are feeding on them. In a few short days, the plants' leaves are covered with small, dead spots and some leaves are cupping downwardly. What's more, the stems have dark streaks on them, and when you lift some leaves to look at the fruits, you discover the tomatoes are blotchy with raised patches and concentric rings.

What happened was insect vectors—in this case, thrips—picked up the virus by feeding on an infected plant and then spread it to your healthy plants through feeding wounds. The virus rapidly multiplied within the plant tissue, moving from the leaves to the stems and impacting each plant's ability to transport moisture and nutrients.

Controlling viruses in your garden is challenging. For one thing, they cause a diverse number of symptoms in the plants they infect so it can be hard to pinpoint exactly what's going on. If viruses have been a problem in previous garden seasons, or certain viruses are prevalent in your region, look for resistant varieties when purchasing seeds or seedlings. Remove any plants that show symptoms of a virus and dispose of them, rather than adding them to your compost pile. Use crop rotation methods to avoid repeatedly planting virus-prone crops in the same location. There aren't any organic products that will control viruses, but if there are known insect vectors in your garden, use organic products and strategies to reduce or eliminate them.

SIGNS AND SYMPTOMS OF VIRAL DISEASES

- Distorted leaves with puckering, twisting, or rolling
- Purple leaf veins
- Mottled leaves
- Bronze leaves
- Abnormally-developing fruits
- Lack of fruits or undersized fruits
- Sunken lesions on fruits often surrounded by rings

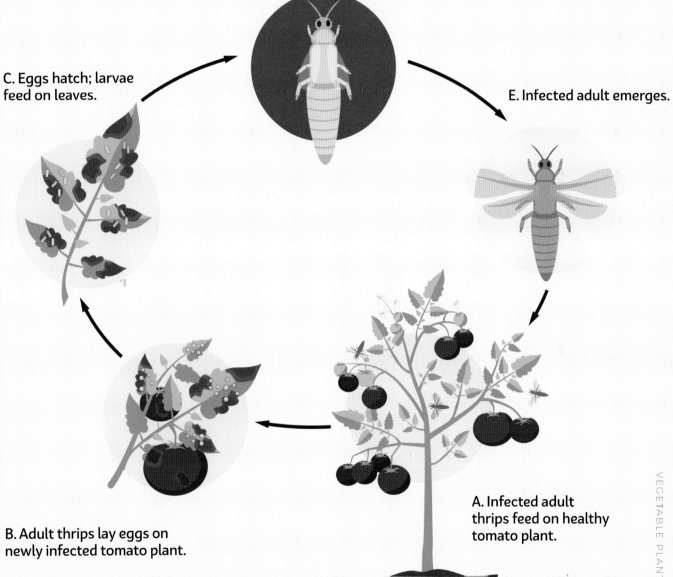

D. Infected larvae pupate underground.

C. Eggs hatch; larvae feed on leaves.

E. Infected adult emerges.

A. Infected adult thrips feed on healthy tomato plant.

B. Adult thrips lay eggs on newly infected tomato plant.

This illustration shows the life cycle of tomato spotted wilt virus (TSWV).

DISEASE TROUBLESHOOTING

When determining what is adversely impacting your plants, there are several important things to look for:

> What is different about the plant(s)?
> - The leaves might have changed color or are wilting.
> - If leaf spots are present, examine where are they are located (on the upper surface, the undersides, or both; or perhaps just between the leaf veins). The color of the spots is also helpful information.
> - If the plants are wilting, check the base of the plant stalk and the roots. If you see dead tissue, take note of that. In addition, look for any signs of animal activity. Pocket gophers reside in tunnels beneath the soil surface and frequently chew on the roots of plants, causing them to wilt and die. You can learn more about dealing with them on page 190.
> - Distorted growth such as twisting or puckered leaves is a very important detail that will assist with your diagnosis.

> When did you first notice this problem, and, if it spread, how quickly did that happen?
> Did anything change in your garden before the problem became evident? This might include new amendments to the soil, the application of fertilizers, severe weather disturbances, or new insect activity.

INTEGRATED PEST MANAGEMENT (IPM)

You might think that Integrated Pest Management, or IPM, only applies to managing damaging insect pests in your garden, but it is just as relevant for any disease issues you might encounter.

The fundamental principle of IPM is to choose the most environmentally friendly method for dealing with these types of challenges. This involves approaching problems in a systematic way:

1. Monitor your garden on a regular basis.

2. If you observe a problem with the plants, examine them closely, take note of what you're seeing, and attempt to identify it. A small magnifying glass is helpful for this and remember that garden centers and educational institutions with horticultural programs can assist in the diagnosis.

3. If a disease problem appears to be worsening, look at your control options or strategies. You'll find plenty of them within the disease profiles.

4. As I mentioned in chapter 1, there is one step of Integrated Pest Management that I don't agree with: If you aren't able to resolve the disease problem organically, you should apply chemical controls as a last resort. To be honest, I believe synthetic chemicals cause far more problems than they solve. If I'm not able to resolve the issue through organic means, my solution will likely be to avoid growing a certain crop or family of crops if they are particularly susceptible to a disease.

5. The final—and most important step—is to document what you saw on your plants, the control method you used, and how well it worked. Take note of what you might do differently if the problem arises in the future. By taking a systematic approach to monitoring, identifying, and dealing with plant diseases, you should be able to grow a healthy, productive garden.

As you learn about the diseases, it's important to know if a certain disease targets more than one crop belonging to a specific plant family. There are three reasons for this:

1. It is crucial that you keep an eye on those other crops if that disease is present in your garden.

2. If you're growing a crop that isn't listed in the Vegetable Crops and Potential Diseases chart (beginning on page 70), you can check the plant family table to the right to discover the other crops that belong to the same family. Then you can look for one of them in the Vegetable Crops and Potential Diseases chart (beginning on page 70) and see which diseases might affect it.

3. You also can use the plant family table as a tool for crop rotation. When you read through the disease profiles in this chapter, you'll notice that crop rotation keeps surfacing as a strategy for preventing, or at least reducing, the occurrence of plant diseases. Look for an explanation of how this works in the Organic Strategies Explained section, beginning on page 158.

Monitoring your garden regularly is the first step to keeping your plants healthy and spotting problems as soon as they arise.

VEGETABLE PLANT FAMILIES AND THEIR MEMBERS

PLANT FAMILY NAME	VEGETABLES WITHIN THIS FAMILY
Asparagus (*Asparagaceae*)	Asparagus
Beet (*Amaranthaceae*)	Beet, spinach, Swiss chard
Cabbage or mustard (*Brassicaceae*)	Arugula, broccoli, Brussels sprouts, cabbage, cauliflower, collard greens, kale, kohlrabi, mustard, radish, rutabaga, turnip
Carrot (*Apiaceae*)	Carrot, celery, chervil, cilantro, dill, fennel, parsley, parsnip
Cucurbit (*Cucurbitaceae*)	Cucumber, melon, pumpkin, squash (summer and winter)
Grass (*Poaceae*)	Corn
Legume (*Fabaceae*)	Bean, pea
Mallow (*Malvaceae*)	Okra
Nightshade (*Solanaceae*)	Eggplant, pepper, potato, tomatillo, tomato
Onion (*Amaryllidaceae*)	Chives, garlic, leek, onion, shallot
Aster or sunflower (*Asteraceae*)	Artichoke, endive, lettuce, sunflower, tarragon

It's time to delve into the most common vegetable plant diseases you might encounter. In my previous book, *The Vegetable Garden Pest Handbook*, I asked readers not to freak out when they saw all of the types of bugs that can (potentially) wreak havoc with our crops. As I explained, just because there are a lot of bugs in the world, that doesn't mean all of them will visit your garden!

Now I'm going to ask the same favor of you in this book. While there are a lot of vegetable plant diseases, you probably won't encounter many of them. Take a deep breath, absorb the information I'm about to present to you, and just think of all the new things you're going to learn here.

This chapter contains one of the most useful diagnostic tools for identifying the diseases you might encounter: the Vegetable Crops and Potential Diseases chart (page 70). In it, you'll find the most commonly grown vegetables and descriptions of how each disease manifests itself on those crops. When you read through the descriptions, notice how they point you to the name of the disease that matches what you're seeing on the plant. That's where you'll find the page number of the disease profile that you're interested in.

TERMS TO KNOW

My goal for this book has been to present all the information in a straightforward manner that makes sense to gardeners with all levels of experience. I didn't want it to be overly technical, but it's important to understand the concepts and how things work. Before you read through the disease profiles, here are the definitions of some terms you might not be familiar with:

Canker: Dead areas on the stems of plants; they can be caused by fungi and bacteria.

Chlorosis/chlorotic: The yellowing of leaves that should normally be green, caused by a lack of chlorophyll.

Hyphae: Microscopic filaments that form the body of a fungus and absorb nutrients.

Lesion: A diseased area of a plant leaf or stem; it is often sunken in appearance.

Mosaic: An abnormal coloration of leaves, usually with a combination of dark green and light green or yellow markings.

Mycelium, mycelia: Branching filaments that are the vegetative part of a fungus. For example, a white, fuzzy growth.

Nematode: A microscopic, soil-dwelling roundworm. There are both harmful and beneficial species of nematodes.

Pathogen: An organism that causes disease.

Petiole: A stalk that connects a leaf to the stem of a plant.

Phloem: Tissue that is part of the vascular system of a plant; it moves water and energy generated by photosynthesis to different areas of the plant.

Pustule: A raised spot on a leaf or other plant tissue that is a common sign of rust diseases.

Sclerotium, sclerotia: The singular and plural forms of resting structures of a fungus.

Shothole: When the centers of leaf spots drop off, they leave holes that are similar in appearance to that of an object that has been shot with a shotgun.

Sign: Physical evidence of a pathogen on a plant. This includes cankers that ooze bacteria, rust pustules, and fungal filaments on plants that have been infected with powdery mildew.

Sporagium, sporangia: The singular and plural forms of capsules where spores are produced.

Spore: A fungal reproductive cell that spreads pathogens.

Stomata: Natural openings in plant tissues, such as pores.

Symptom: A visible manifestation of a plant's reaction to a disease, such as wilting leaves.

Teliospores: The resting spores of some fungi, such as rust.

Vascular system of plants: A network of plant tissues that transport moisture and nutrients. This includes the xylem, which connects the roots to the aboveground plant parts, and the phloem, which moves water and energy generated by photosynthesis to areas of the plants. Normal vascular tissue does not contain any streaks, whereas diseased tissue can have dark streaks throughout it.

Vector: Organisms that transport pathogens from one plant to another. This includes insect vectors such as leafhoppers and cucumber beetles.

Vein-clearing: Leaf veins lose their normal green color, often due to viral diseases.

Water-soaked spots: Areas of leaves or stems that appear wet and have a dark, almost translucent appearance; they are often sunken.

Xylem: Tissue that is part of the vascular system of a plant; it connects the roots to the aboveground plant parts.

Chlorosis, or the yellowing of leaves, results from a lack of chlorophyll.

Find out which diseases target corn plants in the Vegetable Crops and Potential Diseases chart.

VEGETABLE CROPS AND POTENTIAL DISEASES

PLANT NAME	PLANT FAMILY	PROBLEMS/DAMAGE	POSSIBLE DISEASE
Artichoke	Sunflower (*Asteraceae*)	Seeds rot before they can germinate; young seedlings fall over and die shortly after emerging from the soil	Damping-off disease (page 122)
		Flower bracts turn brown on the exterior, gray inside	Gray mold (page 128)
		Yellow blotches on the leaves	Mildew, powdery (page 134)
		Sticky leaves; leaves covered with dark green or black dots or a film; stunted plants	Sooty mold (page 144)
		Wilting plants; yellow leaves; stunted plants and flower buds	Verticillium wilt (page 152)
Arugula	Brassica (*Brassicaceae*)	Round, brown leaf spots containing concentric rings	Alternaria leaf spot (page 100)
		Small water-soaked spots on leaves turn brown, sometimes have a purple border; leaves become dry and brittle	Bacterial leaf spot (page 106)
		Water-soaked tissue; rotting tissue usually accompanied by oozing liquids and a foul odor	Bacterial soft rot (page 108)
		Seedlings die; older plants develop yellow, V-shaped lesions with brown centers along edges of leaves; stems and petioles have black tissue	Black rot (page 114)
		Round, white spots with dark borders; leaves turn yellow	Cercospora leaf spot (page 118)
		Seeds rot before they can germinate; young seedlings fall over and die shortly after emerging from the soil; canker on main stem	Damping-off disease (page 122)
		Older leaves of plants turn yellow and wilt, often on one side at first; leaves wilt during the day and recover at night; plants die; brown vascular tissue	Fusarium wilt (page 126)
		Brown spots appear on both sides of leaves; white mold on undersides	Mildew, downy (page 132)
		White, powdery spots on the leaves	Mildew, powdery (page 134)
		Yellow spots on upper leaf surfaces, yellow pustules on undersides	Rust (page 140)

PLANT NAME	PLANT FAMILY	PROBLEMS/DAMAGE	POSSIBLE DISEASE
Arugula	Brassica (*Brassicaceae*)	Sticky leaves; leaves covered with dark green or black dots or a film; stunted plants	Sooty mold (page 144)
		Yellow, wilting leaves; stunted growth; plants die	Verticillium wilt (page 152)
		Lesions on stems; leaves on a single stem die; sudden wilting or death of plant; masses of white fuzzy growth	White mold (page 154)
Asparagus	Asparagus (*Asparagaceae*)	Brown lesions with red borders on needles and stems that progress upward; ferns turn yellow and die	Cercospora leaf spot (page 118)
		Yellowing ferns; brownish-red lesions on roots, stems, and crowns; plants wilt and die	Fusarium wilt (page 126)
		Gray or brown fuzzy areas on spears	Gray mold (page 128)
		Pale green spots on shoots and branches; rust-colored pustules on spears	Rust (page 140)
		Water-soaked lesions on stems; ferns turn yellow; rotting crowns and roots	Southern blight (page 146)
Bean	Legume (*Fabaceae*)	Small, brown lesions on lower leaves that steadily grow larger; older lesions drop out of leaves, creating a hole; leaves drop prematurely; pods have tiny brown/black spots	Alternaria leaf spot (page 100)
		Dark lesions on the cotyledons; reddish-brown lesions on stems and leaf undersides that become sunken; stems break above damage; pods have dark, sunken spots; stunted growth; seeds in pods have sunken brown lesions	Anthracnose (page 102)
		Dry, brown spots and lesions along leaf margins; sunken spots on pods; water spots on undersides of leaves; lesions oozing a crusty liquid; dead leaves on plant	Bacterial blight (page 104)
		Yellow, deformed leaves; stunted growth; abnormal pods	Beet curly top virus (page 112)
		Tan spots with purple margins; upper leaves fall off; young plants stunted and die	Cercospora leaf spot (page 118)
		Seeds rot before they can germinate; young seedlings fall over and die shortly after emerging from the soil	Damping-off disease (page 122)
		Dark, water-soaked lesions on pods; brown streaks on stems; fuzzy gray spores on stems and pods	Fusarium wilt (page 126)

PLANT NAME	PLANT FAMILY	PROBLEMS/DAMAGE	POSSIBLE DISEASE
Bean	Legume (*Fabaceae*)	Yellow spots on leaves; gray fuzzy growth on leaf undersides; lesions on pods; mold inside pods	Gray mold (page 128)
		Reddish-brown spores on leaves, stems, and pods	Mildew, downy (page 132)
		Small white spots develop on stems, leaves, and pods	Mildew, powdery (page 134)
		Yellow-and-green mottled pattern on leaves; stunted plants; little or no flowers and pods	Mosaic virus (page 136)
		Yellow spots on upper leaf surfaces, yellow pustules on undersides	Rust (page 140)
		Sticky leaves; leaves covered with dark green or black dots or a film; stunted plants	Sooty mold (page 144)
		A brown canker covered with white mold on the stem above the soil surface; leaves turn yellow; plants wilt and die due to rotten stem	Southern blight (page 146)
		Bronze leaves; lesions and streaks on stems; yellow or brown rings on leaves	Tomato spotted wilt virus (page 150)
		Lesions on stems or pods; leaves on a single stem die; sudden wilting or death of plant; masses of white fuzzy growth	White mold (page 154)
Beet	Beet (*Amaranthaceae*)	Water-soaked tissue; rotting tissue usually accompanied by oozing liquids and a foul odor	Bacterial soft rot (page 108)
		Puckered, twisted leaves; deformed roots	Beet curly top virus (page 112)
		Small round spots with light centers and purple margins on leaves and petioles; leaves wilt and die	Cercospora leaf spot (page 118)
		Seeds don't germinate or young seedlings quickly turn black, wilt, and die	Damping-off disease (page 122)
		Gray, fuzzy mold on fleshy root, usually when in storage	Gray mold (page 128)
		Pale green spots on upper surface of leaves; puckered leaves; gray fuzz on both leaf surfaces; wilted leaves	Mildew, downy (page 132)
		White, powdery spots on the leaves	Mildew, powdery (page 134)

PLANT NAME	PLANT FAMILY	PROBLEMS/DAMAGE	POSSIBLE DISEASE
Beet	Beet (*Amaranthaceae*)	Raised, corky lesions on the fleshy roots	Potato scab (page 138)
		Yellow spots on upper leaf surfaces, yellow pustules on undersides	Rust (page 140)
		Sticky leaves; leaves covered with dark green or black dots or a film; stunted plants	Sooty mold (page 144)
		Yellow, wilting leaves and stems; lesions on roots	Southern blight (page 146)
		Mottled leaves	Tobacco Mosaic virus (page 148)
		Yellow leaves; stunted plants; vascular tissue turns brown	Verticillium wilt (page 152)
Broccoli	Brassica (*Brassicaceae*)	Tiny, dark specks on lower leaves or stems, which grow and form a bull's eye with yellow margin; leaves fall off; dark mold spores on curd	Alternaria leaf spot (page 100)
		Tiny dark spots with yellow margins on outer leaves and stems	Bacterial leaf spot (page 106)
		Water-soaked areas of plant become soft and rot very quickly; strong odor present	Bacterial soft rot (page 108)
		Seedlings die; older yellow, V-shaped blotches on leaf margins that spread; wilting leaves; black or brown leaf veins	Black rot (page 114)
		Round, white spots with dark borders; leaves turn yellow	Cercospora leaf spot (page 118)
		Seeds rot before they can germinate; young seedlings fall over and die shortly after emerging from the soil; canker on main stem	Damping-off disease (page 122)
		Older leaves of plants turn yellow and wilt, often on one side at first; leaves wilt during the day and recover at night; plants die; brown vascular tissue	Fusarium wilt (page 126)
		Pale green spots on tops of leaves that turn yellow; gray fuzzy growth on leaf undersides; dark streaks inside stalks	Mildew, downy (page 132)
		White, powdery spots on the upper surfaces of leaves	Mildew, powdery (page 134)
		Yellow spots on upper leaf surfaces, yellow pustules on undersides	Rust (page 140)

PLANT NAME	PLANT FAMILY	PROBLEMS/DAMAGE	POSSIBLE DISEASE
Broccoli	Brassica (*Brassicaceae*)	Sticky leaves; leaves covered with dark green or black dots or a film; stunted plants	Sooty mold (page 144)
		Lower leaves are chlorotic between veins; wilting lower leaves that fall off; stunted growth; black stems and roots	Verticillium wilt (page 152)
		Lesions on stems; leaves on a single stem die; sudden wilting or death of plant; masses of white fuzzy growth	White mold (page 154)
Brussels sprouts	Brassica (*Brassicaceae*)	Tiny, dark specks on lower leaves or stems, which grow and form a bull's eye with yellow margin; leaves fall off	Alternaria leaf spot (page 100)
		Tiny, dark spots with yellow margins on outer leaves and stems; water-soaked leaf spots	Bacterial leaf spot (page 106)
		Water-soaked areas of plant become soft and rot very quickly; strong odor present	Bacterial soft rot (page 108)
		Seedlings die; older yellow, V-shaped blotches on leaf margins that spread; wilting leaves; black or brown leaf veins; dark vascular tissue	Black rot (page 114)
		Round, white spots with dark borders; leaves turn yellow	Cercospora leaf spot (page 118)
		Seeds rot before they can germinate; young seedlings fall over and die shortly after emerging from the soil; canker on main stem	Damping-off disease (page 122)
		Lower leaves are chlorotic between veins; wilting lower leaves that fall off; stunted growth; black stems and roots	Fusarium wilt (page 126)
		Pale green spots on tops of leaves that turn yellow; gray fuzzy growth on leaf undersides; dark streaks inside stalks	Mildew, downy (page 132)
		White, powdery spots on the upper surface of leaves	Mildew, powdery (page 134)
		Yellow spots on upper leaf surfaces, yellow pustules on undersides	Rust (page 140)
		Sticky leaves; leaves covered with dark green or black dots or a film; stunted plants	Sooty mold (page 144)
		Lower leaves are chlorotic between veins; wilting lower leaves that fall off; stunted growth; black stems and roots	Verticillium wilt (page 152)

PLANT NAME	PLANT FAMILY	PROBLEMS/DAMAGE	POSSIBLE DISEASE
Brussels sprouts	Brassica (*Brassicaceae*)	Lesions on stems; leaves on a single stem die; sudden wilting or death of plant; masses of white, fuzzy growth	White mold (page 154)
Cabbage	Brassica (*Brassicaceae*)	Small dark spots on leaves with concentric rings that crack in center; lesions on stems and petioles	Alternaria leaf spot (page 100)
		Water-soaked areas of plant become soft and rot very quickly; strong odor present	Bacterial soft rot (page 108)
		Seedlings die; older yellow, V-shaped blotches on leaf margins that spread; wilting leaves; black or brown leaf veins; dark vascular tissue	Black rot (page 114)
		Round, white spots with dark borders; leaves turn yellow	Cercospora leaf spot (page 118)
		Seeds rot before they can germinate; young seedlings fall over and die shortly after emerging from the soil; canker on main stem	Damping-off disease (page 122)
		Lower leaves are chlorotic between veins; wilting lower leaves that fall off; stunted growth; black stems and roots	Fusarium wilt (page 126)
		Fuzzy, gray fungus; brown, rotting plant tissue; dark lesions on plants; wilting leaves	Gray mold (page 128)
		Pale green spots on tops of leaves that turn yellow; gray fuzzy growth on leaf undersides; dark streaks inside stalks	Mildew, downy (page 132)
		White, powdery spots on the leaves	Mildew, powdery (page 134)
		Yellow spots on upper leaf surfaces, yellow pustules on undersides	Rust (page 140)
		Sticky leaves; leaves covered with dark green or black dots or a film; stunted plants	Sooty mold (page 144)
		Lower leaves are chlorotic between veins; wilting lower leaves that fall off; stunted growth; black stems and roots	Verticillium wilt (page 152)
		Lesions on stems; leaves on a single stem die; sudden wilting or death of plant; masses of white fuzzy growth	White mold (page 154)

PLANT NAME	PLANT FAMILY	PROBLEMS/DAMAGE	POSSIBLE DISEASE
Carrot	Carrot (*Apiaceae*)	Water-soaked tissue; rotting tissue usually accompanied by oozing liquids and a foul odor	Bacterial soft rot (page 108)
		Small brown, water-soaked spots on leaves and petioles with yellow halos; leaf undersides turn gray	Cercospora leaf spot (page 118)
		Seeds rot before they can germinate; young seedlings fall over and die shortly after emerging from the soil	Damping-off disease (page 122)
		Gray, fuzzy mold on fleshy root, usually when in storage	Gray mold (page 128)
		White, powdery spots on the leaves	Mildew, powdery (page 134)
		Raised, corky lesions on the fleshy roots	Potato scab (page 138)
		Yellow spots on upper leaf surfaces, yellow pustules on undersides	Rust (page 140)
		Taproot is decayed at soil surface; yellow, wilting leaves	Southern blight (page 146)
		Sudden wilting or death of plant; masses of white fuzzy growth	White mold (page 154)
Cauliflower	Brassica (*Brassicaceae*)	Round, brown leaf spots containing concentric rings; sooty spores on leaves and curds	Alternaria leaf spot (page 100)
		Tiny, black spots with yellow halos on outer leaves that coalesce into large, papery tissue	Bacterial leaf spot (page 106)
		Water-soaked tissue; rotting tissue usually accompanied by oozing liquids and a foul odor	Bacterial soft rot (page 108)
		Seedlings die; older yellow, V-shaped blotches on leaf margins that spread; wilting leaves; black or brown leaf veins; dark vascular tissue	Black rot (page 114)
		Round, white spots with dark borders; leaves turn yellow	Cercospora leaf spot (page 118)
		Seeds rot before they can germinate; young seedlings fall over and die shortly after emerging from the soil; canker on main stem	Damping-off disease (page 122)
		Older leaves of plants turn yellow and wilt, often on one side at first; leaves wilt during the day and recover at night; plants die; brown vascular tissue	Fusarium wilt (page 126)

PLANT NAME	PLANT FAMILY	PROBLEMS/DAMAGE	POSSIBLE DISEASE
Cauliflower	Brassica (*Brassicaceae*)	Pale green spots on tops of leaves that turn yellow; gray fuzzy growth on leaf undersides	Mildew, downy (page 132)
		White, powdery spots on the leaves	Mildew, powdery (page 134)
		Yellow spots on upper leaf surfaces, yellow pustules on undersides	Rust (page 140)
		Sticky leaves; leaves covered with dark green or black dots or a film; stunted plants	Sooty mold (page 144)
		Lower leaves are chlorotic between veins; wilting lower leaves that fall off; stunted growth; black stems and roots	Verticillium wilt (page 152)
		Lesions on stems; leaves on a single stem die; sudden wilting or death of plant; masses of white fuzzy growth	White mold (page 154)
Celery	Carrot (*Apiaceae*)	Water-soaked spots that turn yellow, then change to brown dead spots that have yellow halos	Bacterial leaf spot (page 106)
		Water-soaked tissue; rotting tissue usually accompanied by oozing liquids and a foul odor	Bacterial soft rot (page 108)
		Seeds rot before they can germinate; young seedlings fall over and die shortly after emerging from the soil	Damping-off disease (page 122)
		Fuzzy, gray fungus; brown, rotting plant tissue; dark lesions on plants; wilting leaves	Gray mold (page 128)
		Young petioles curl downward; veins lose their normal green color; mosaic pattern on leaves	Mosaic virus (page 136)
		Small, yellow spots on leaves and petioles that turn brown; leaves die	Septoria leaf spot (page 142)
		Yellow blotches, dead patches, and concentric rings on leaves	Tomato spotted wilt virus (page 150)
		Yellow, wilting leaves; plants die	Verticillium wilt (page 152)
		Lesions on stems; leaves on a single stem die; sudden wilting or death of plant; masses of white fuzzy growth	White mold (page 154)

PLANT NAME	PLANT FAMILY	PROBLEMS/DAMAGE	POSSIBLE DISEASE
Corn	Grass (*Poaceae*)	Oval, water-soaked spots on leaves with light centers and dark borders; leaves dying	Anthracnose (page 102)
		Water-soaked tissue; rotting tissue usually accompanied by oozing liquids and a foul odor	Bacterial soft rot (page 108)
		Gray or black powdery galls covered by a membrane on any aboveground portion of a plant; distorted kernels	Corn smut (page 120)
		Seeds rot before they can germinate; young seedlings fall over and die shortly after emerging from the soil	Damping-off disease (page 122)
		Rusty-brown pustules on upper and lower leaf surfaces; spores on corn ears and tassels	Rust (page 140)
		Sticky leaves; leaves covered with dark green or black dots or a film; stunted plants	Sooty mold (page 144)
Cucumber	Cucurbit (*Cucurbitaceae*)	Round, brown leaf spots containing concentric rings; leaves die	Alternaria leaf spot (page 100)
		Leaf spots with yellow halo; stems with elongated brown streaks; round, water-soaked lesions on fruits	Anthracnose (page 102)
		Water-soaked tissue; rotting tissue usually accompanied by oozing liquids and a foul odor	Bacterial soft rot (page 108)
		Sudden wilting of leaves and stems; leaves wilt during the day, recover at night; spots on fruits; yellow leaves with brown edges, which wilt and die; entire vine dies	Bacterial wilt (page 110)
		Yellow, deformed leaves; stunted growth; fruits misshapen, undersized, or don't develop at all	Beet curly top virus (page 112)
		Round leaf spots with brown centers and yellow halos	Cercospora leaf spot (page 118)
		Seeds rot before they can germinate; young seedlings fall over and die shortly after emerging from the soil	Damping-off disease (page 122)
		Older leaves of plants turn yellow and wilt, often on one side at first; leaves wilt during the day and recover at night; plants die; brown vascular tissue	Fusarium wilt (page 126)
		Fuzzy, gray fungus; brown, rotting plant tissue; dark lesions on plants; wilting leaves	Gray mold (page 128)

PLANT NAME	PLANT FAMILY	PROBLEMS/DAMAGE	POSSIBLE DISEASE
Cucumber	Cucurbit (*Cucurbitaceae*)	Pale green spots on tops of leaves that turn yellow; gray fuzzy growth on leaf undersides	Mildew, downy (page 132)
		White, powdery spots on the leaves	Mildew, powdery (page 134)
		Yellow mosaic pattern on leaves; deformed leaves that curl down; stunted plants; fruits distorted and undersized; vines wither	Mosaic virus (page 136)
		Small, brown, or white water-soaked leaf spots; older spots have small black fruiting bodies (spores); fruits have small, white, raised spots	Septoria leaf spot (page 142)
		Sticky leaves; leaves covered with dark green or black dots or a film; stunted plants	Sooty mold (page 144)
		Leaves with light and dark green mottling; distorted or small leaves; stunted plants; few if any fruits	Tobacco Mosaic virus (page 148)
		Yellow leaves; stunted plants	Tomato spotted wilt virus (page 150)
		Yellow, V-shaped leaf spots that spread; leaves wilt and die; plant dies	Verticillium wilt (page 152)
		Lesions on stems; leaves on a single stem die; sudden wilting or death of plant; masses of white fuzzy growth; fruits rot	White mold (page 154)
Eggplant	Nightshade (*Solanaceae*)	Round, sunken spots on fruits; spots on leaves and stems	Anthracnose (page 102)
		Water-soaked tissue; rotting tissue usually accompanied by oozing liquids and a foul odor	Bacterial soft rot (page 108)
		Sudden wilting; rotting roots; brown stem cankers; plants die	Bacterial wilt (page 110)
		Small, pale leaf spots that turn brown and tiny, dark circles of spores	Cercospora leaf spot (page 118)
		Seeds rot before they can germinate; young seedlings fall over and die shortly after emerging from the soil	Damping-off disease (page 122)
		Brown leaf spots with concentric rings and yellow halos, starting on oldest leaves first; dark, sunken spot with concentric circles on the stem end of fruits	Early blight (page 124)

PLANT NAME	PLANT FAMILY	PROBLEMS/DAMAGE	POSSIBLE DISEASE
Eggplant	Nightshade (*Solanaceae*)	Older leaves turn yellow and wilt, often on one side at first; leaves wilt during the day and recover at night; plants die; brown vascular tissue in stem, crown, or roots	Fusarium wilt (page 126)
		Fuzzy, gray fungus on fruits; round, gray spots on leaves	Gray mold (page 128)
		Water-soaked spots on younger leaves; white mold on the undersides of leaf lesions; brown spots coalesce and have yellow or light green halo; dark lesions on stems	Late blight (page 130)
		White, powdery spots on the leaves	Mildew, powdery (page 134)
		Small, brown spots with yellow halos on leaves and stems; leaves turn yellow and fall off plant	Septoria leaf spot (page 142)
		Sticky leaves; leaves covered with dark green or black dots or a film; stunted plants	Sooty mold (page 144)
		Dark lesion on stem at soil surface; stems or entire plants suddenly wilt, fall over, and die; white mold on stem and nearby soil; small brown sclerotia; fruit rots if touching soil	Southern blight (page 146)
		Leaves with light and dark green mottling; distorted or small leaves; stunted plants; few if any fruits	Tobacco Mosaic virus (page 148)
		Bronzing of leaves; tip dieback; leaves cup downward; fruits have pale spots with concentric rings	Tomato spotted wilt virus (page 150)
		Stunted plants; V-shaped lesions on leaves that are wider at the leaf margins; yellow leaves roll inward; stems and leaves wilt; vascular system has dark coloration	Verticillium wilt (page 152)
Garlic	Onion (*Amaryllidaceae*)	Stunted plants; leaves turn yellow and wilt; roots and neck rot; white, fuzzy growth on roots, bulb, and neck; tiny black spots on bulbs	Allium white rot (page 98)
		Gray mold between garlic cloves; gray spores on necks, tiny black sclerotia on necks; bulbs rot	Gray mold (page 128)
		Mottled and striped leaves; stunted plants; undersized bulbs	Mosaic virus (page 136)

PLANT NAME	PLANT FAMILY	PROBLEMS/DAMAGE	POSSIBLE DISEASE
Kale	Brassica (*Brassicaceae*)	Round, brown leaf spots containing concentric rings; leaves die	Alternaria leaf spot (page 100)
		Tiny, black spots with yellow halos on outer leaves that coalesce into large, papery tissue	Bacterial leaf spot (page 106)
		Water-soaked tissue; rotting tissue usually accompanied by oozing liquids and a foul odor	Bacterial soft rot (page 108)
		Seedlings die; older yellow, V-shaped blotches on leaf margins that spread; wilting leaves; black or brown leaf veins; dark vascular tissue	Black rot (page 114)
		Round, white spots with dark borders; leaves turn yellow	Cercospora leaf spot (page 118)
		Seeds rot before they can germinate; young seedlings fall over and die shortly after emerging from the soil; canker on main stem	Damping-off disease (page 122)
		Older leaves of plants turn yellow and wilt, often on one side at first; leaves wilt during the day and recover at night; plants die; brown vascular tissue	Fusarium wilt (page 126)
		Pale green spots on tops of leaves that turn yellow; gray fuzzy growth on leaf undersides	Mildew, downy (page 132)
		White, powdery spots on the leaves	Mildew, powdery (page 134)
		Yellow spots on upper leaf surfaces, yellow pustules on undersides	Rust (page 140)
		Sticky leaves; leaves covered with dark green or black dots or a film; stunted plants	Sooty mold (page 144)
		Yellow, wilting leaves; plants die	Verticillium wilt (page 152)
		Lesions on stems; leaves on a single stem die; sudden wilting or death of plant; masses of white fuzzy growth	White mold (page 154)
Kohlrabi	Brassica (*Brassicaceae*)	Round, brown leaf spots containing concentric rings; leaves die	Alternaria leaf spot (page 100)
		Water-soaked tissue; rotting tissue usually accompanied by oozing liquids and a foul odor	Bacterial soft rot (page 108)
		Seedlings die; older yellow, V-shaped blotches on leaf margins that spread; wilting leaves; black or brown leaf veins; dark vascular tissue	Black rot (page 114)

PLANT NAME	PLANT FAMILY	PROBLEMS/DAMAGE	POSSIBLE DISEASE
Kohlrabi	Brassica (*Brassicaceae*)	Round, white spots with dark borders; leaves turn yellow	Cercospora leaf spot (page 118)
		Seeds rot before they can germinate; young seedlings fall over and die shortly after emerging from the soil; canker on main stem	Damping-off disease (page 122)
		Older leaves of plants turn yellow and wilt, often on one side at first; leaves wilt during the day and recover at night; plants die; brown vascular tissue	Fusarium wilt (page 126)
		Pale green spots on tops of leaves that turn yellow; gray fuzzy growth on leaf undersides	Mildew, downy (page 132)
		White, powdery spots on the leaves	Mildew, powdery (page 134)
		Yellow spots on upper leaf surfaces, yellow pustules on undersides	Rust (page 140)
		Sticky leaves; leaves covered with dark green or black dots or a film; stunted plants	Sooty mold (page 144)
		Yellow, wilting leaves; plants die	Verticillium wilt (page 152)
		Lesions on stems; leaves on a single stem die; sudden wilting or death of plant; masses of white fuzzy growth	White mold (page 154)
Lettuce	Sunflower (*Asteraceae*)	Small, rounded, water-soaked spots on the outer leaves that turn brown; the centers often fall out, leaving holes	Anthracnose (page 102)
		Small, angular, water-soaked spots that spread between veins; brown areas that turn black	Bacterial leaf spot (page 106)
		Water-soaked tissue; rotting tissue usually accompanied by oozing liquids and a foul odor	Bacterial soft rot (page 108)
		Seeds rot before they can germinate; young seedlings fall over and die shortly after emerging from the soil	Damping-off disease (page 122)
		Older leaves of plants turn yellow and wilt, often on one side at first; leaves wilt during the day and recover at night; plants die; brown vascular tissue	Fusarium wilt (page 126)
		Brown, decaying crown; rotting outer leaves and stems	Gray mold (page 128)

PLANT NAME	PLANT FAMILY	PROBLEMS/DAMAGE	POSSIBLE DISEASE
Lettuce	Sunflower (*Asteraceae*)	White, powdery spots on the leaves	Mildew, powdery (page 134)
		Stunted, deformed leaves on young plants; yellow, distorted leaves on older plants, brown spots on outer leaves	Mosaic virus (page 136)
		Yellow spots on upper leaf surfaces, yellow pustules on undersides	Rust (page 140)
		Mottled or yellowed leaves	Tobacco Mosaic virus (page 148)
		Dark brown or dead spots on leaves; distorted leaves; stunted plants	Tomato spotted wilt virus (page 150)
Melon (including watermelon)	Cucurbit (*Cucurbitaceae*)	Round, brown leaf spots containing concentric rings; leaves die	Alternaria leaf spot (page 100)
		Brown leaf spots with center of some spots dropping out; leaves and vines die; young fruits turn black and die; mature fruits develop round, water-soaked lesions	Anthracnose (page 102)
		Water-soaked tissue; rotting tissue usually accompanied by oozing liquids and a foul odor	Bacterial soft rot (page 108)
		Sudden wilting of leaves and stems; leaves wilt during the day, recover at night; spots on fruits; yellow leaves with brown edges that wilt and die; entire vine dies	Bacterial wilt (page 110)
		Yellow, deformed leaves; stunted growth; fruits misshapen, undersized, or don't develop at all	Beet curly top virus (page 112)
		Round leaf spots with brown centers and yellow halos	Cercospora leaf spot (page 118)
		Seeds rot before they can germinate; young seedlings fall over and die shortly after emerging from the soil	Damping-off disease (page 122)
		Older leaves of plants turn yellow and wilt, often on one side at first; leaves wilt during the day and recover at night; plants die; brown vascular tissue	Fusarium wilt (page 126)
		Fuzzy, gray fungus; brown, rotting plant tissue; dark lesions on plants; wilting leaves	Gray mold (page 128)
		Pale green spots on tops of leaves that turn yellow; gray fuzzy growth on leaf undersides	Mildew, downy (page 132)

PLANT NAME	PLANT FAMILY	PROBLEMS/DAMAGE	POSSIBLE DISEASE
Melon (including watermelon)	Cucurbit (*Cucurbitaceae*)	White, powdery spots on the leaves	Mildew, powdery (page 134)
		Yellow mosaic pattern on leaves; deformed leaves that curl down; stunted plants; fruits distorted and undersized; vines wither	Mosaic virus (page 136)
		Small brown or white water-soaked leaf spots; older spots have small black fruiting bodies (spores); fruits have small, white, raised spots	Septoria leaf spot (page 142)
		Sticky leaves; leaves covered with dark green or black dots or a film; stunted plants	Sooty mold (page 144)
		Dark lesion on stem at soil surface; stems or entire plants suddenly wilt, fall over, and die; white mold on stem and nearby soil; small brown sclerotia; fruit rots if touching soil	Southern blight (page 146)
		Leaves with light and dark green mottling; distorted or small leaves; stunted plants; few or undersized fruits	Tobacco Mosaic virus (page 148)
		Yellow, V-shaped leaf spots that spread; leaves wilt and die; plant dies	Verticillium wilt (page 152)
		Lesions on stems; leaves on a single stem die; sudden wilting or death of plant; masses of white fuzzy growth; fruits rot	White mold (page 154)
Mustard	Brassica (*Brassicaceae*)	Round, brown leaf spots containing concentric rings; leaves die	Alternaria leaf spot (page 100)
		Water-soaked tissue; rotting tissue usually accompanied by oozing liquids and a foul odor	Bacterial soft rot (page 108)
		Seedlings die; older yellow, V-shaped blotches on leaf margins that spread; wilting leaves; black or brown leaf veins; dark vascular tissue	Black rot (page 114)
		Round, white spots with dark borders; leaves turn yellow	Cercospora leaf spot (page 118)
		Seeds rot before they can germinate; young seedlings fall over and die shortly after emerging from the soil; canker on main stem	Damping-off disease (page 122)
		Older leaves of plants turn yellow and wilt, often on one side at first; leaves wilt during the day and recover at night; plants die; brown vascular tissue	Fusarium wilt (page 126)

PLANT NAME	PLANT FAMILY	PROBLEMS/DAMAGE	POSSIBLE DISEASE
Mustard	Brassica (*Brassicaceae*)	Pale green spots on tops of leaves that turn yellow; gray fuzzy growth on leaf undersides	Mildew, downy (page 132)
		White, powdery spots on the leaves	Mildew, powdery (page 134)
		Yellow spots on upper leaf surfaces, yellow pustules on undersides	Rust (page 140)
		Sticky leaves; leaves covered with dark green or black dots or a film; stunted plants	Sooty mold (page 144)
		Yellow, wilting leaves; plants die	Verticillium wilt (page 152)
		Lesions on stems; leaves on a single stem die; sudden wilting or death of plant; masses of white fuzzy growth	White mold (page 154)
Okra	Mallow (*Malvaceae*)	Seeds rot before they can germinate; young seedlings fall over and die shortly after emerging from the soil	Damping-off disease (page 122)
		White, powdery spots on the leaves	Mildew, powdery (page 134)
		Yellow leaves wilt and die; plant dies	Verticillium wilt (page 152)
Onion	Onion (*Amaryllidaceae*)	Stunted plants; leaves turn yellow and wilt; roots and neck rot; white, fuzzy growth on roots, bulb, and neck; tiny black spots on bulbs	Allium white rot (page 98)
		Onion leaves turn yellow and brown; onion necks are soft; rotting scales inside onion bulbs	Bacterial soft rot (page 108)
		Neck rots; white, sunken spots on leaves	Gray mold (page 128)
		Brown or purple spots on leaves with fuzzy mold; bulbs stunted or rotting	Mildew, downy (page 132)
Pea	Legume (*Fabaceae*)	Sunken, brown marks on stems; red leaf veins that turn brown; reddish-brown spots on the pods	Anthracnose (page 102)
		Dry, brown spots and lesions along leaf margins; sunken spots on pods; water spots on undersides of leaves; lesions oozing a crusty liquid; dead leaves on plant	Bacterial blight (page 104)
		Seeds rot before they can germinate; young seedlings fall over and die shortly after emerging from the soil	Damping-off disease (page 122)

| --- | --- | --- | --- |
Pea	Legume (*Fabaceae*)	Lower leaves on pea plants turn yellow; plants produce stunted or few pods	Fusarium wilt (page 126)
		Fuzzy, gray fungus; brown, rotting plant tissue; dark lesions on plants; wilting leaves	Gray mold (page 128)
		Yellow spots on leaves; gray fuzzy growth on leaf undersides; lesions on pods; mold inside pods	Mildew, downy (page 132)
		White, powdery spots on the leaves	Mildew, powdery (page 134)
		Yellow-and-green mottled pattern on leaves; stunted plants; little or no flowers and pods	Mosaic virus (page 136)
		Sticky leaves; leaves covered with dark green or black dots or a film; stunted plants	Sooty mold (page 144)
		Lesions on stems and pods; leaves on a single stem die; sudden wilting or death of plant; masses of white fuzzy growth	White mold (page 154)
Pepper	Nightshade (*Solanaceae*)	Round, sunken spots on fruits; spots on leaves and stems	Anthracnose (page 102)
		Dead spots on leaves, stems, and fruits; water-soaked spots on leaf undersides; leaves turn yellow and fall off; fruits have raised scabs	Bacterial leaf spot (page 106)
		Water-soaked tissue; rotting tissue usually accompanied by oozing liquids and a foul odor	Bacterial soft rot (page 108)
		Sudden wilting; rotting roots; brown stem cankers; plants die	Bacterial wilt (page 110)
		Leaves roll upward and twist, are thick, and turn yellow; stunted plants; abnormal fruits	Beet curly top virus (page 112)
		Leaves roll upward, twist, become thick and turn yellow; veins turn purple; abnormal fruits or none at all; stunted growth; plants die	Buckeye rot (page 116)
		Small brown spots on fruits that enlarge into lesions with tan and brown concentric rings; fruits rot internally	Cercospora leaf spot (page 118)
		Seeds rot before they can germinate; young seedlings fall over and die shortly after emerging from the soil	Damping-off disease (page 122)

PLANT NAME	PLANT FAMILY	PROBLEMS/DAMAGE	POSSIBLE DISEASE
Pepper	Nightshade (*Solanaceae*)	Older leaves of plants turn yellow and wilt, often on one side at first; leaves wilt during the day and recover at night; plants die; brown vascular tissue in stem, crown, or roots	Fusarium wilt (page 126)
		Fuzzy, gray fungus; brown, rotting plant tissue; dark lesions on plants; wilting leaves	Gray mold (page 128)
		Water-soaked spots on younger leaves; white mold on the undersides of leaf lesions; brown spots coalesce and have yellow or light green halo; dark lesions on stems	Late blight (page 130)
		Yellow blotches on the leaves	Mildew, powdery (page 134)
		Narrow, small leaves; smaller and fewer fruits; mosaic pattern on leaves	Mosaic virus (page 136)
		Small, brown spots with yellow halos on leaves and stems; leaves turn yellow and fall off plant	Septoria leaf spot (page 142)
		Sticky leaves; leaves covered with dark green or black dots or a film; stunted plants	Sooty mold (page 144)
		Dark lesion on stem at soil surface; stems or entire plants suddenly wilt, fall over, and die; white mold on stem and nearby soil; small brown sclerotia; fruit rots if touching soil	Southern blight (page 146)
		Leaves with light and dark green mottling; distorted or small leaves; stunted plants; few if any fruits	Tobacco Mosaic virus (page 148)
		Sudden yellowing of leaves; necrotic long streaks on stems; fruits have dead streaks and spots; dead fruits	Tomato spotted wilt virus (page 150)
		Stunted growth; leaves that wilt and die; plant dies	Verticillium wilt (page 152)
		Lesions on stems; leaves on a single stem die; sudden wilting or death of plant; masses of white fuzzy growth; fruits rot	White mold (page 154)
Potato	Nightshade (*Solanaceae*)	Brown or gray discoloration of tubers; all plant parts covered with tiny black spots	Anthracnose (page 102)
		Tubers develop lesions that become soft and rot; lesions on stems sometimes contain a slimy liquid; rotting can occur during storage	Bacterial soft rot (page 108)

PLANT NAME	PLANT FAMILY	PROBLEMS/DAMAGE	POSSIBLE DISEASE
Potato	Nightshade (*Solanaceae*)	Sudden wilting; rotting roots; brown stem cankers; plants die	Bacterial wilt (page 110)
		Distorted leaves that cup upwards; tubers undersized or don't develop at all	Beet curly top virus (page 112)
		Brown leaf spots with concentric rings and yellow halos; tubers develop lesions that become sunken	Early blight (page 124)
		Leaves turn yellow, bronze, or red, and curl up and in; wilting leaves; tubers are sunken where they attach to stem	Fusarium wilt (page 126)
		Fuzzy, gray fungus; brown, rotting plant tissue; dark lesions on plants; wilting leaves	Gray mold (page 128)
		Brown blotches on leaves; tuber skin is brown or purple with sunken areas	Late blight (page 130)
		White, powdery spots on the leaves	Mildew, powdery (page 134)
		Raised, corky lesions on the skin of the tubers	Potato scab (page 138)
		Yellow spots on upper leaf surfaces, yellow pustules on undersides	Rust (page 140)
		Small, brown spots with yellow halos on leaves and stems; leaves turn yellow and fall off plant	Septoria leaf spot (page 142)
		Sticky leaves; leaves covered with dark green or black dots or a film; stunted plants	Sooty mold (page 144)
		Dark lesion on stem at soil surface; stems or entire plants suddenly wilt, fall over, and die; white mold on stem and nearby soil; small brown sclerotia	Southern blight (page 146)
		Leaves with light and dark green mottling; distorted or small leaves; stunted plants	Tobacco Mosaic virus (page 148)
		Yellow or brown spots; dead ringspots with pale halos; distorted leaves; tubers have ringspots and discoloration	Tomato spotted wilt virus (page 150)
		Leaves and vines turn yellow and die prematurely; plant dies	Verticillium wilt (page 152)
		Lesions on stems; leaves on a single stem die; sudden wilting or death of plant; masses of white fuzzy growth	White mold (page 154)

PLANT NAME	PLANT FAMILY	PROBLEMS/DAMAGE	POSSIBLE DISEASE
Pumpkin	Cucurbit (*Cucurbitaceae*)	Round, brown leaf spots containing concentric rings; leaves die	Alternaria leaf spot (page 100)
		Brown leaf spots with center of some spots dropping out; leaves and vines die; young fruits turn black and die; mature fruits develop round, water-soaked lesions	Anthracnose (page 102)
		Water-soaked tissue; rotting tissue usually accompanied by oozing liquids and a foul odor; can occur during storage	Bacterial soft rot (page 108)
		Sudden wilting of leaves and stems; leaves wilt during the day, recover at night; spots on fruits; yellow leaves with brown edges, which wilt and die; entire vine dies	Bacterial wilt (page 110)
		Yellow, deformed leaves; stunted growth; fruits misshapen, undersized, or don't develop at all	Beet curly top virus (page 112)
		Round leaf spots with brown centers and yellow halos	Cercospora leaf spot (page 118)
		Seeds rot before they can germinate; young seedlings fall over and die shortly after emerging from the soil	Damping-off disease (page 122)
		Older leaves of plants turn yellow and wilt, often on one side at first; leaves wilt during the day and recover at night; plants die; brown vascular tissue	Fusarium wilt (page 126)
		White, powdery spots on the leaves	Mildew, powdery (page 134)
		Yellow mosaic pattern on leaves; deformed leaves that curl down; stunted plants; fruits distorted and undersized; vines wither	Mosaic virus (page 136)
		Small brown or white water-soaked leaf spots; older spots have small black fruiting bodies (spores); fruits have small, white, raised spots	Septoria leaf spot (page 142)
		Sticky leaves; leaves covered with dark green or black dots or a film; stunted plants	Sooty mold (page 144)
		Dark lesion on stem at soil surface; stems or entire plants suddenly wilt, fall over, and die; white mold on stem and nearby soil; small brown sclerotia; fruit rots if touching soil	Southern blight (page 146)

PLANT NAME	PLANT FAMILY	PROBLEMS/DAMAGE	POSSIBLE DISEASE
Pumpkin	Cucurbit (*Cucurbitaceae*)	Leaves with light and dark green mottling; distorted or small leaves; stunted plants; few if any fruits	Tobacco Mosaic virus (page 148)
		Yellow, V-shaped leaf spots that spread; leaves wilt and die; plant dies	Verticillium wilt (page 152)
		Lesions on stems; leaves on a single stem die; sudden wilting or death of plant; masses of white fuzzy growth; fruits rot	White mold (page 154)
Radish	Brassica (*Brassicaceae*)	Round, brown leaf spots containing concentric rings; leaves die	Alternaria leaf spot (page 100)
		Water-soaked tissue; rotting tissue usually accompanied by oozing liquids and a foul odor	Bacterial soft rot (page 108)
		Seedlings die; older yellow, V-shaped blotches on leaf margins that spread; wilting leaves; black or brown leaf veins; dark vascular tissue	Black rot (page 114)
		Round, white spots with dark borders; leaves turn yellow	Cercospora leaf spot (page 118)
		Seeds rot before they can germinate; young seedlings fall over and die shortly after emerging from the soil; canker on main stem	Damping-off disease (page 122)
		Older leaves of plants turn yellow and wilt, often on one side at first; leaves wilt during the day and recover at night; plants die; brown vascular tissue	Fusarium wilt (page 126)
		Pale green spots on tops of leaves that turn yellow; gray fuzzy growth on leaf undersides	Mildew, downy (page 132)
		White, powdery spots on the leaves	Mildew, powdery (page 134)
		Raised, corky lesions on the roots	Potato scab (page 138)
		Yellow spots on upper leaf surfaces, yellow pustules on undersides	Rust (page 140)
		Sticky leaves; leaves covered with dark green or black dots or a film; stunted plants	Sooty mold (page 144)
		Yellow, V-shaped leaf spots that spread; leaves wilt and die; plant dies	Verticillium wilt (page 152)
		Lesions on stems; leaves on a single stem die; sudden wilting or death of plant; masses of white fuzzy growth	White mold (page 154)

PLANT NAME	PLANT FAMILY	PROBLEMS/DAMAGE	POSSIBLE DISEASE
Rutabaga	Brassica (*Brassicaceae*)	Round, brown leaf spots containing concentric rings; leaves die	Alternaria leaf spot (page 100)
		Water-soaked tissue; rotting tissue usually accompanied by oozing liquids and a foul odor	Bacterial soft rot (page 108)
		Seedlings die; older yellow, V-shaped blotches on leaf margins that spread; wilting leaves; black or brown leaf veins; dark vascular tissue	Black rot (page 114)
		Round, white spots with dark borders; leaves turn yellow	Cercospora leaf spot (page 118)
		Seeds rot before they can germinate; young seedlings fall over and die shortly after emerging from the soil; canker on main stem	Damping-off disease (page 122)
		Older leaves of plants turn yellow and wilt, often on one side at first; leaves wilt during the day and recover at night; plants die; brown vascular tissue	Fusarium wilt (page 126)
		Gray, fuzzy mold on fleshy root, usually when in storage	Gray mold (page 128)
		Pale green spots on tops of leaves that turn yellow; gray fuzzy growth on leaf undersides; stunted fleshy root	Mildew, downy (page 132)
		White, powdery spots on the leaves	Mildew, powdery (page 134)
		Raised, corky lesions on the fleshy roots	Potato scab (page 138)
		Yellow spots on upper leaf surfaces, yellow pustules on undersides	Rust (page 140)
		Sticky leaves; leaves covered with dark green or black dots or a film; stunted plants	Sooty mold (page 144)
		Yellow, V-shaped leaf spots that spread; leaves wilt and die; plant dies	Verticillium wilt (page 152)
		Lesions on stems; leaves on a single stem die; sudden wilting or death of plant; masses of white fuzzy growth	White mold (page 154)
Spinach	Beet (*Amaranthaceae*)	Small, round, water-soaked spots on leaves; spots turn brown or tan	Anthracnose (page 102)
		Water-soaked tissue; rotting tissue usually accompanied by oozing liquids and a foul odor	Bacterial soft rot (page 108)

PLANT NAME	PLANT FAMILY	PROBLEMS/DAMAGE	POSSIBLE DISEASE
Spinach	Beet (*Amaranthaceae*)	Yellow, deformed leaves; stunted growth	Beet curly top virus (page 112)
		Small, round tan to brown spots with red borders	Cercospora leaf spot (page 118)
		Seeds rot before they can germinate; young seedlings fall over and die shortly after emerging from the soil	Damping-off disease (page 122)
		Older leaves turn yellow and wilt, often on one side at first; leaves wilt during the day and recover at night; stunted plants; plants die; brown vascular tissue in stem, crown, or roots	Fusarium wilt (page 126)
		Pale green spots on upper surface of leaves; puckered leaves; gray fuzz on both leaf surfaces; wilted leaves	Mildew, downy (page 132)
		Yellow spots and mottling of leaves; puckered leaves	Mosaic virus (page 136)
		Yellow spots on upper surface of leaves; white pustules on the undersides	Rust (page 140)
		Yellow leaves with necrotic spots; stunted growth	Tomato spotted wilt virus (page 150)
		Yellow leaves; stunted plants; vascular tissue turns brown	Verticillium wilt (page 152)
Squash (summer and winter)	Cucurbit (*Cucurbitaceae*)	Round, brown leaf spots containing concentric rings; leaves die	Alternaria leaf spot (page 100)
		Brown leaf spots with center of some spots dropping out; leaves and vines die; young fruits turn black and die; mature fruits develop round, water-soaked lesions	Anthracnose (page 102)
		Water-soaked tissue; rotting tissue usually accompanied by oozing liquids and a foul odor; can occur during storage	Bacterial soft rot (page 108)
		Sudden wilting of leaves and stems; leaves wilt during the day, recover at night; spots on fruits; yellow leaves with brown edges, which wilt and die; entire vine dies	Bacterial wilt (page 110)
		Yellow, deformed leaves; stunted growth; fruits misshapen, undersized, or don't develop at all	Beet curly top virus (page 112)
		Round leaf spots with brown centers and yellow halos	Cercospora leaf spot (page 118)

PLANT NAME	PLANT FAMILY	PROBLEMS/DAMAGE	POSSIBLE DISEASE
Squash (summer and winter)	Cucurbit (*Cucurbitaceae*)	Seeds rot before they can germinate; young seedlings fall over and die shortly after emerging from the soil	Damping-off disease (page 122)
		Older leaves of plants turn yellow and wilt, often on one side at first; leaves wilt during the day and recover at night; plants die; brown vascular tissue	Fusarium wilt (page 126)
		Pale green spots on tops of leaves that turn yellow; gray fuzzy growth on leaf undersides	Mildew, downy (page 132)
		Yellow mosaic pattern on leaves; deformed leaves that curl down; stunted plants; fruits distorted and undersized; vines wither	Mosaic virus (page 136)
		Small brown or white water-soaked leaf spots; older spots have small black fruiting bodies (spores); fruits have small, white, raised spots	Septoria leaf spot (page 142)
		Sticky leaves; leaves covered with dark green or black dots or a film; stunted plants	Sooty mold (page 144)
		Leaves with light and dark green mottling; distorted or small leaves; stunted plants; few or undersized fruits	Tobacco Mosaic virus (page 148)
		Yellow, V-shaped leaf spots that spread; leaves wilt and die; plant dies	Verticillium wilt (page 152)
		Lesions on stems; leaves on a single stem die; sudden wilting or death of plant; masses of white fuzzy growth; fruits rot	White mold (page 154)
Swiss chard	Beet (*Amaranthaceae*)	Water-soaked tissue; rotting tissue usually accompanied by oozing liquids and a foul odor	Bacterial soft rot (page 108)
		Small, round tan to brown spots with red borders	Cercospora leaf spot (page 118)
		Seeds rot before they can germinate; young seedlings fall over and die shortly after emerging from the soil	Damping-off disease (page 122)
		Pale green spots on upper surface of leaves; puckered leaves; gray fuzz on both leaf surfaces; wilted leaves	Mildew, downy (page 132)
		Yellow spots on upper leaf surfaces, yellow pustules on undersides	Rust (page 140)

PLANT NAME	PLANT FAMILY	PROBLEMS/DAMAGE	POSSIBLE DISEASE
Tomato	Nightshade (*Solanaceae*)	Round, sunken spots on fruits; spots on leaves and stems	Anthracnose (page 102)
		Dead spots on leaves, stems, and fruits; water-soaked spots on leaf undersides; leaves turn yellow and fall off; fruits have raised scabs	Bacterial leaf spot (page 106)
		Water-soaked tissue; rotting tissue usually accompanied by oozing liquids and a foul odor	Bacterial soft rot (page 108)
		Sudden wilting; rotting roots; brown stem cankers; plants die	Bacterial wilt (page 110)
		Leaves roll upward and twist, are thick, and turn yellow; stunted plants; abnormal fruits	Beet curly top virus (page 112)
		Small brown spots on fruits that enlarge into lesions with tan and brown concentric rings; fruits rot internally	Buckeye rot (page 116)
		Leaves have lesions in between the leaf veins; leaves curl	Cercospora leaf spot (page 118)
		Seeds rot before they can germinate; young seedlings fall over and die shortly after emerging from the soil	Damping-off disease (page 122)
		Brown leaf spots with concentric rings and yellow halos, starting on oldest leaves first; dark, sunken spot with concentric circles on the stem end of fruits	Early blight (page 124)
		Older leaves turn yellow and wilt, often on one side at first; leaves wilt during the day and recover at night; plants die; brown vascular tissue in stem, crown, or roots	Fusarium wilt (page 126)
		White or yellow halos on immature and mature fruits; gray or brown mold on leaves and stems	Gray mold (page 128)
		Water-soaked spots on younger leaves; white mold on the undersides of leaf lesions; brown spots coalesce and have yellow or light green halo; dark lesions on stems; tomato fruits are mottled with gold to brown sunken spots, which turn dark and become leathery	Late blight (page 130)
		Yellow blotches on the leaves	Mildew, powdery (page 134)

PLANT NAME	PLANT FAMILY	PROBLEMS/DAMAGE	POSSIBLE DISEASE
Tomato	Nightshade (*Solanaceae*)	Narrow, small leaves; yellow leaves with mosaic pattern; stunted plants; little or no fruit	Mosaic virus (page 136)
		Small brown spots with yellow halos on leaves and stems; leaves turn yellow and fall off plant	Septoria leaf spot (page 142)
		Sticky leaves; leaves covered with dark green or black dots or a film; stunted plants	Sooty mold (page 144)
		Dark lesion on stem at soil surface; stems or entire plants suddenly wilt, fall over, and die; white mold on stem and nearby soil; small brown sclerotia; fruit rots if touching soil	Southern blight (page 146)
		Leaves with light and dark green mottling; distorted or small leaves; stunted plants; few or undersized fruits; tomato fruits may have sunken lesions	Tobacco Mosaic virus (page 148)
		Bronzing of leaves; tip dieback; dark streaks on leaves and petioles; leaves cup downward; stunted growth; immature fruits have light green rings and raised centers; mature fruits have orange and red rings	Tomato spotted wilt virus (page 150)
		Stunted plants; yellow leaves roll inward and die; plant dies	Verticillium wilt (page 152)
		Lesions on stems; leaves on a single stem die; sudden wilting or death of plant; masses of white fuzzy growth; fruits rot	White mold (page 154)
Turnip	Brassica (*Brassicaceae*)	Round, brown leaf spots containing concentric rings; leaves die	Alternaria leaf spot (page 100)
		Water-soaked tissue; rotting tissue usually accompanied by oozing liquids and a foul odor	Bacterial soft rot (page 108)
		Seedlings die; older yellow, V-shaped blotches on leaf margins that spread; wilting leaves; black or brown leaf veins; dark vascular tissue	Black rot (page 114)
		Round, white spots with dark borders; leaves turn yellow	Cercospora leaf spot (page 118)
		Seeds rot before they can germinate; young seedlings fall over and die shortly after emerging from the soil; canker on main stem	Damping-off disease (page 122)

PLANT NAME	PLANT FAMILY	PROBLEMS/DAMAGE	POSSIBLE DISEASE
Turnip	Brassica (*Brassicaceae*)	Older leaves of plants turn yellow and wilt, often on one side at first; leaves wilt during the day and recover at night; plants die; brown vascular tissue	Fusarium wilt (page 126)
		Gray, fuzzy mold on fleshy root, usually when in storage	Gray mold (page 128)
		Pale green spots on tops of leaves that turn yellow; gray fuzzy growth on leaf undersides; stunted root	Mildew, downy (page 132)
		White, powdery spots on the leaves	Mildew, powdery (page 134)
		Raised, corky lesions on the fleshy roots	Potato scab (page 138)
		Yellow spots on upper leaf surfaces, yellow pustules on undersides	Rust (page 140)
		Sticky leaves; leaves covered with dark green or black dots or a film; stunted plants	Sooty mold (page 144)
		Yellow, V-shaped leaf spots that spread; leaves wilt and die; plant dies	Verticillium wilt (page 152)
		Lesions on stems; leaves on a single stem die; sudden wilting or death of plant; masses of white fuzzy growth	White mold (page 154)

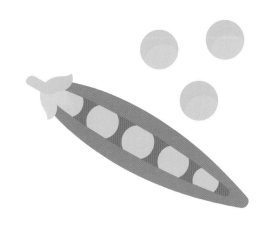

DISEASE PROFILES

Are you ready to learn about the most common vegetable plant diseases? In each profile, you'll see photos of what they can do to plants, learn helpful background information on the disease, find a list of which crops can be impacted by it, the signs and symptoms to look for on your plants, and a list of organic strategies and products available to you.

Immediately following the final disease profile, you'll discover even more resources. First up is a discussion about root-knot nematodes, which are microscopic roundworms that cause a lot of problems. While that might sound more like a pest-related issue, these nematodes damage the roots of plants, which makes them susceptible to disease pathogens. I've listed several helpful strategies for controlling root-knot nematodes in your garden.

After that, you'll find descriptions of the organic disease-controlling strategies that I suggested in each profile. These include important information on sterilizing and sanitizing your tools and equipment, ideal materials for mulching your planting beds, watering methods to prevent diseases, how to solarize your soil, and much more.

Finally, there are descriptions of organic disease control products that are available to you at garden centers and online. You'll learn how the products work and which diseases they target.

It's very common for winter squash and pumpkin leaves to be affected by powdery mildew, especially near the end of the growing season. You'll learn everything you need to know about this fungal disease on page 132.

ALLIUM WHITE ROT

Type: Fungal   **Caused by:** *Sclerotium cepivorum, Stromatinia cepivorum*

DESCRIPTION

If you enjoy growing onions, garlic, and other members of the allium family, you must read this disease profile. Why? If your plants become infected with allium white rot, you will have to wait many years before growing them again in your garden. This is an extremely destructive fungal disease because once it has been introduced into the soil, it can survive there for up to thirty years without the presence of host plants. It appears during the cool, wet part of the growing season and is easily spread by contaminated soil, bulbs, cloves, and roots.

If you notice any of the signs listed below, carefully inspect one of the plants to make sure the yellow leaves and rotting bulb haven't been caused by onion maggots. Even though they are a damaging pest, it would be much better to have them than allium white rot!

CROPS MOST COMMONLY IMPACTED:

Allium family (garlic, leeks, onions, shallots), with garlic and onions being the most susceptible. This disease also infects ornamental alliums.

White fungus on onion bulbs is a sign of allium white rot.

WHAT TO LOOK FOR

Stunted plants; oldest leaves turn yellow and wilt; the neck of the plant turns brown and rots; plants are easy to pull up because the roots have rotted; white, fuzzy growth (mycelia) on the roots, bulbs, and neck; black sclerotia (masses of fungal tissue the size of poppy seeds) on the bulbs.

ORGANIC STRATEGIES

Ask your local agricultural agency if allium white rot has been identified in your area. If it hasn't been detected, be careful about your allium sources:

> Purchase allium sets (small bulbs), cloves, or seedlings from a reliable source. They must be certified to be disease-free.

> Do not plant garlic cloves from your grocery store; they might carry the disease but not show any symptoms.

> Grow allium family crops from seeds.

If you have discovered allium white rot in your garden:

> Stop watering your plants immediately. This won't eradicate the disease, but it will slow its spread.

> Remove all infected plants and dispose of them; do not add them to your compost pile. Remove the surrounding soil as well.

> Sanitize your hands, clothes, shoes, and tools if you come into contact with diseased plants and contaminated soil. Refer to the Organic Strategies Explained section (page 164) to learn the best practices for this.

> Do not try to grow any members of the allium family—including ornamental alliums—if allium white rot has infected the planting area. Most reliable sources recommend waiting at least eight years before attempting to plant alliums again in your garden.

Here are some strategies for trying to live with allium white rot:

> If you have a planting location well away from the contaminated area of your vegetable garden, you could try planting alliums there.

> Plant allium family crops in containers filled with sterile potting soil.

> At this time, researchers are testing biological controls for allium white rot, but they are not effective as a cure for the disease. In addition, they haven't gotten consistent results from organic products. There were no resistant varieties of alliums available at the time of publication.

Allium white rot caused these onion leaves to wilt and die.

ALTERNARIA LEAF SPOT

Type: Fungal   **Caused by:** Several species of *Alternaria*

DESCRIPTION

Alternaria leaf spot, which is also referred to as Alternaria leaf blight, is a common fungal disease that affects members of the cabbage and cucurbit families of crops. Melons are particularly susceptible. It can be brought into the garden on contaminated seeds and seedlings, or blown in from neighboring gardens. The fungus overwinters on infected plant debris and weed hosts for up to two years. When conditions are warm and moist, spores are spread by wind or splashed up from the ground onto plants by rain or overhead watering. Moisture also helps the spores attach to a new host, and crowded plantings facilitate plant-to-plant spread. Subsequent spores germinate from leaf spots when the leaves are wet. The fungus can be moved around the garden via contaminated tools or clothing. Flea beetles—commonly found on beet, cabbage, and nightshade family crops—also spread this disease. Alternaria leaf spot affects the older leaves of cucurbit family crops first. When they drop their leaves as a result, immature fruits often develop sunscald (see page 54 in chapter 1) because they have lost the shade that the leaves provided. Please note that Alternaria leaf spot is referred to as early blight on eggplants, potatoes, and tomatoes; refer to that profile on page 124 to learn more about how it affects those crops.

CROPS MOST COMMONLY IMPACTED:

Cabbage family crops (arugula, broccoli, Brussels sprouts, cabbage, cauliflower, collards, kale, kohlrabi, mustard, radishes, rutabagas, turnips), cucurbit family crops (cucumbers, melons, pumpkins, and summer and winter squash)

WHAT TO LOOK FOR

Round, brown leaf spots containing concentric rings, which are primarily on older leaves near the crown of the plant; spots may be surrounded by yellow halos; centers of spots sometimes drop out of the leaves, giving them a "shothole" appearance.

Broccoli and cauliflower

Black, sooty spores on leaves and curds; leaves turn brown and die.

Cucurbit crops

Fruit spots.

The spots on this broccoli leaf are caused by Alternaria leaf spot.

Notice the concentric rings within the spots on this leaf.

Alternaria leaf spot on a head of cabbage.

ORGANIC STRATEGIES

> Look for resistant varieties. Refer to the Vegetable Disease Resistance Abbreviations chart on page 166.

> Keep plants healthy so they are less likely to suffer severe fungal infections.

> Space plants appropriately so there is good air circulation around them.

> Cover the soil surface with mulch to reduce the chance of spores splashing up onto the plants.

> Practice crop rotation to limit potential spread of this disease.

> Avoid overhead watering to keep the leaves as dry as possible.

> Don't work with your plants when they are wet.

> Remove damaged leaves from the plants and dispose of them.

> Keep up with the weeding in and around your garden to remove alternate host plants for this disease and also to improve air circulation around the plants.

> Avoid overuse of high-nitrogen fertilizers as this promotes lush, green growth that attracts the fungus.

> Control damaging insects such as flea beetles that can spread this disease, using organic products or methods.

> Remove plant debris at the end of the season and dispose of it.

> Apply biofungicide, copper fungicide, horticultural oil, or sulfur fungicide as a preventive measure. Refer to the Organic Disease Control and Prevention Products section beginning on page 168 for more information.

ANTHRACNOSE

Type: Fungal   **Caused by:** *Colletotrichum* species

DESCRIPTION

Anthracnose can cause significant damage to many types of vegetables and their fruits. This fungus overwinters in seeds, soil, and plant debris for up to four years and also on weed host plants belonging to the same plant family. It is particularly prevalent in areas with high humidity and prolonged periods of wet weather. Spores spread by splashing water, rain, and contaminated tools. Anthracnose can infect fruits if they touch the soil and spreads more easily when vegetables are planted too closely together.

CROPS MOST COMMONLY IMPACTED:

Corn, cucurbit family crops (cucumbers, melons, pumpkins, summer and winter squash), legume family crops (beans, peas), lettuce, nightshade family crops (eggplants, peppers, potatoes, tomatoes), spinach

The spots on this cucumber leaf are caused by anthracnose.

WHAT TO LOOK FOR

Round, sunken spots on fruit, often with black concentric rings; elongated brown or round yellow spots on leaves or stems. Here are the signs on specific crops:

Beans, peas

Sunken, brown marks on stems; red leaf veins that turn brown; reddish-brown spots on the pods.

Corn

Leaves have oval, water-soaked spots with pale centers and dark borders; the lesions enlarge, causing the leaves to die.

Cucumbers, melons, pumpkins, squash

Brown leaf spots with center of some spots dropping out; leaves and vines die; young fruits turn black and die; mature fruits develop round, water-soaked lesions. Cucumber leaves have spots with yellow halos, stems have brown, elongated streaks.

Eggplants, peppers, tomatoes

Round, sunken spots on both immature and mature fruits that often develop a secondary mold; pink masses of spores ooze from the lesions; spots may appear on leaves and stems.

Lettuce

Small, rounded, water-soaked spots on the outer leaves, which turn brown; the centers often fall out, leaving holes; romaine and head lettuce are more susceptible than leaf lettuce.

Potatoes

Tubers have brown or gray discoloration; all parts of plant are covered with tiny, black dots (sclerotia).

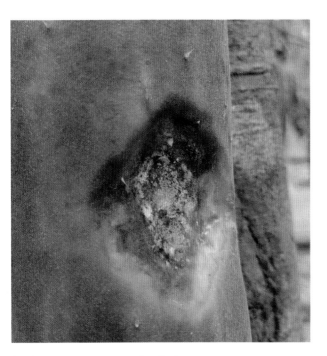

Anthracnose on a cucumber fruit.

The sunken spot on this pepper is a sign of anthracnose.

ORGANIC STRATEGIES

> Practice a three-year crop rotation.

> Choose disease-resistant varieties.

> Make sure your soil drains well; if it doesn't, add compost or shredded leaves; regularly monitor the moisture in the soil to make sure it isn't staying too wet.

> Properly space your plants.

> Grow tomato, eggplant, and pepper plants in cages or on stakes to prevent the leaves from contacting the soil. Grow beans, peas, and cucurbit family crops on trellises or other vertical supports.

> Place mulch on the soil to prevent spores from splashing up onto the plants.

> Avoid overhead watering. If that is your only option, water in the morning so the plants' leaves will dry quickly.

> Avoid working with the plants when they are wet.

> Keep up with the weeds in and around your garden as many are hosts for anthracnose.

> Remove infected fruits right away and dispose of them. Clean up plant debris at the end of the season; do not compost infected material.

> Don't save the seeds of infected plants.

> Apply biofungicide, copper fungicide, plant extracts, or sulfur fungicide as a preventive measure. Refer to the Organic Disease Control and Prevention Products section beginning on page 168 for more information.

BACTERIAL BLIGHT

Type: Bacterial

Caused by: Species of *Pseudomonas*, *Xanthomonas*

DESCRIPTION

Bacterial blight is common in regions that experience prolonged periods of warm temperatures and high humidity. Two main types of bacterial blight will affect the leaves and pods of beans and peas: common blight, which is caused by *Xanthomonas axonopodis*, and halo blight, caused by *Pseudomonas syringae*. Common blight bacteria exist on a variety of plants and weeds but only infect legume family crops. The bacteria of each blight overwinter in seeds and infected plant debris. If you have not had a problem with it before, bacterial blight is usually brought into the garden in contaminated seeds. Once it arrives in your garden, it spreads by water splashing off contaminated plants, from tools that have had contact with diseased plants, and from insect feeding activities. Once on the host plant, the bacteria enter the leaf tissue through wounds or natural pores called stomata. Infected plant tissue still carries viable bacteria, even when the plants are stunted, lose their leaves, and die. Be aware that bean pods that are infected by the bacteria while they are developing will contain infected seeds.

CROPS MOST COMMONLY IMPACTED:

Legume family crops (beans, peas)

WHAT TO LOOK FOR

Common blight
Dry, brown spots or lesions located along the outer margins of the leaves that are surrounded by a yellow border.

Halo blight
Small water spots appear on the undersides of the leaves and turn brown; surrounding leaf tissue becomes pale, creating a halo around each spot, which is how the disease got its name; the spots become sunken and ooze a pale substance. In both forms of bacterial blight, lesions are located between the veins on the leaves; sunken, water-soaked spots on bean and pea pods become dry and develop a brown border; pea stems turn purple or black.

This bean leaf illustrates signs of halo blight; note the yellow halos surrounding the spots.

The sunken spots on these pods were caused by common bacterial blight.

ORGANIC STRATEGIES

> Practice a three-year crop rotation plan.

> Choose varieties that are resistant to bacterial blight. Refer to the Vegetable Disease Resistance Abbreviations chart on page 166.

> Always disinfect pots and seed-starting flats with a 10 percent bleach solution (1 part bleach to 9 parts water); do not reuse potting medium.

> Cover the soil surface with mulch to keep water from splashing up onto the leaves.

> Avoid overhead watering.

> Don't work with the plants when they are wet as this can spread the bacteria.

> Check plants regularly for any signs of infection.

> Avoid injuring plants through pruning cuts or cultivation around the roots; these can provide openings for bacteria to enter.

> Remove and dispose of infected plant material; do not compost it.

> Diagnose the problem correctly before proceeding with possible treatments.

> Do not save seeds from infected plants.

> Apply biofungicide or copper fungicide as a preventive measure. Refer to the Organic Disease Control and Prevention Products section beginning on page 168 for more information.

BACTERIAL LEAF SPOT

Type: Bacterial

Caused by: Multiple species of *Pseudomonas* and *Xanthomonas*

DESCRIPTION

Bacterial leaf spot is caused by bacteria within the genera of *Pseudomonas* and *Xanthomonas*. The bacteria are flagellated, having a whiplike tail that allows them to swim. Each species has an ideal temperature range for reproducing via cell division, but all require wet conditions. When they are splashed onto a leaf, they use their mobility to enter the plant tissue through stomata or in areas damaged by insects. Despite its name of bacterial leaf spot, the bacteria also will infect the stems and fruits of tomatoes and peppers. The bacteria can be brought into a garden by infected seeds and seedlings. They spread easily from plant to plant through rain, splashing water, overhead watering, and contaminated tools. Weeds that belong to the same plant family as the affected vegetable crop are also hosts. The bacteria overwinter on plant debris but will die once it has decomposed. For some species of bacterial leaf spot, turning the crop debris into the soil is sufficient for eradicating the bacteria, but removing and disposing of it as a general practice is a good idea.

CROPS MOST COMMONLY IMPACTED:

Arugula, broccoli, Brussels sprouts, cauliflower, celery, kale, lettuce, peppers, tomatoes

WHAT TO LOOK FOR

Arugula, broccoli, Brussels sprouts, cauliflower, kale

Tiny, black spots with yellow halos on outer leaves that coalesce into larger, papery tissue.

Celery

Water-soaked spots that turn yellow, then change to brown dead spots that have yellow halos.

Lettuce

Small, angular, water-soaked spots that spread between veins; brown areas that turn black and papery-dry.

Peppers and tomatoes

Dead spots on the leaves, stems, and fruits; ¼-inch (0.6 cm) water-soaked spots on leaf undersides; leaves turn yellow and fall off; fruits develop raised scabs, but these do not cause fruit to rot, although secondary decay can occur from other organisms. To test for the presence of bacteria, place a cut stem in water and watch for a milky substance oozing from it within a few minutes.

Bacterial leaf spot on lettuce leaves.

Bacterial leaf spot on tomato leaves.

ORGANIC STRATEGIES

> Use crop rotation methods to avoid planting the same families of susceptible crops in the same location within a three-year period.

> Look for resistant varieties, when available. Refer to the Vegetable Disease Resistance Abbreviations chart on page 166.

> Start your own plants from seed or purchase seedlings from a reliable source that follows good sanitation practices to keep plants healthy. Always inspect seedlings prior to bringing them home.

> Stake or cage tomato and pepper plants to keep foliage off the ground and provide good air circulation around them.

> Mulch planting beds to prevent bacteria from splashing up onto the plants.

> Avoid overhead watering.

> Don't work with susceptible plants when they are wet.

> Wash your hands and sterilize any tools that have been in contact with infected plants. Refer to the Organic Strategies Explained section (page 164) to learn the best practices for this.

> Keep up with your weeding so you won't provide host plants for the bacteria.

> Pull up any volunteer vegetable plants because the bacteria can survive on them.

> Clean up and dispose of infected plant debris.

> Apply biofungicide or copper fungicide as a preventive measure. Refer to the Organic Disease Control and Prevention Products section beginning on page 168 for more information.

BACTERIAL SOFT ROT

Type: Bacterial

Caused by: *Pectobacterium caratovorum* (formerly *Erwinia carotovora*); species of *Bacillus*, *Cytophaga*, and *Xanthomonas*

DESCRIPTION

This bacterial disease affects all parts of a plant but most commonly impacts tubers, fruits, stems, bulbs, or other fleshy tissues. Damage can occur while the plants are growing or after harvest. If potatoes and onions are infected while growing or during harvest, they will decompose in storage. The soil-dwelling bacteria thrive under warm, moist conditions. They infect plants in many ways: from water that splashes up from the ground, leaf contact with the soil, contaminated tools, and insect vectors. Within the soil, bacteria enter roots and tubers through natural openings or feeding wounds caused by insects. Tubers damaged during harvest also provide the bacteria with an entry point. Once inside plant tissue, bacteria multiply rapidly and produce enzymes that break down cell walls. As the infection progresses, the area becomes soft, watery, and slimy. The ooze of infected material further spreads the bacteria. Badly rotted produce frequently is accompanied by a foul odor.

CROPS MOST COMMONLY IMPACTED:

Beet family crops (beets, spinach, Swiss chard), cabbage family crops (arugula, broccoli, cabbage, cauliflower, collards, kale, kohlrabi, radishes, rutabagas, turnips), carrot family crops (carrots, celery, parsnips), corn, cucurbit family crops (cucumbers, melons, pumpkins, squash), lettuce, nightshade family crops (eggplants, peppers, tomatoes, potatoes), onions

WHAT TO LOOK FOR

Water-soaked tissue; rotting tissue usually accompanied by oozing liquids and a foul odor; onion leaves turn yellow and brown; onion necks are soft; rotting scales inside onion bulbs; the flesh of stored squash becomes soft and rots; potato stems have lesions, become soft, and contain a slimy liquid; potato tubers become soft and rot; heads of broccoli, cabbage, and cauliflower develop depressions of decaying plant tissue.

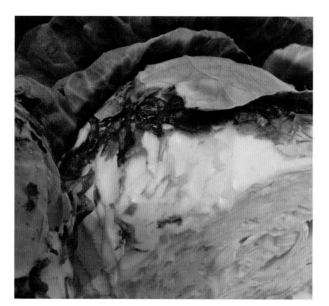

Bacterial soft rot on a head of cabbage.

Bacterial soft rot on a pepper.

Bacterial soft rot on potatoes.

ORGANIC STRATEGIES

> Practice a three-year crop rotation to avoid planting the same crops in the same location.

> The soil should be well-drained. Add compost to improve drainage, as needed.

> When growing potatoes, start with tubers that are certified to be disease-free. Plant them whole, rather than cutting them into chunks, which would be more susceptible to this disease.

> Do not plant in extremely wet soil.

> Space plants appropriately to promote good air circulation between them.

> Do not overwater the plants. Water them early in the day to give them time to dry off before nightfall.

> Avoid injuring plants, bulbs, tubers, or fruits at planting time, while cultivating around them, and at harvest time.

> Harvest susceptible crops during dry weather.

> Cure onions prior to storing them. Place them in a cool, dry area until their skins are papery-dry; afterwards, store them in a cool, dark location.

> Harvest winter squash and pumpkins before frosts occur, and cure them for two weeks in a warm, light area that is protected from the weather, prior to storing them at 50°F to 55°F (10°C to 13°C). Do not store damaged fruits; use them right away.

> There is no cure for this disease. Destroy infected plants; do not compost them.

BACTERIAL WILT

Type: Bacterial

Caused by: *Erwinia tracheiphila* (cucurbits), *Ralstonia solanacearum* (nightshade crops)

DESCRIPTION

Cucurbit family crops are very susceptible to bacterial wilt. The bacteria enter the plants through wounds caused by the feeding activity of cucumber beetles. Adult beetles become carriers of the virus by feeding on infected plants. The beetles spread the disease to other plants through their mouthparts and the bacteria overwinter in the guts of the beetles. The virus is not passed to beetle eggs or larvae. Cucumbers and melons are the hardest hit and die very quickly, but squash and pumpkins also can be impacted by this disease. Because plants will not survive bacterial wilt infections, the only way to stop the disease is by controlling cucumber beetles. The bacteria don't live in seeds or in the soil.

There are two other names for the bacterial wilt that affects nightshade crops. Southern wilt impacts tomatoes, eggplants, and peppers. Brown rot infects potatoes. Both are caused by *Ralstonia solanacearum*. This soilborne bacterium thrives in warm, moist soil and can survive outside of a host plant for several years. Infection takes place when the bacteria contact the roots of a developing host and enter through natural openings or from wounds made by root-knot nematodes (microscopic roundworms that live in the soil). The bacteria disrupt a plant's vascular system, which interferes with the flow of water and nutrients throughout the tissue. Once this occurs, the plant will die. There are no organic controls for either of these types of bacterial wilt.

CROPS MOST COMMONLY IMPACTED:

Cucurbit family crops (cucumbers, melons, pumpkins, summer and winter squash), nightshade family crops (primarily potatoes and tomatoes but also can impact eggplants and peppers)

These tomato plants have bacterial wilt.

Bacterial wilt on a cucumber vine.

This is a simple test for bacterial wilt; note the clear ooze between the cut surfaces of this squash stem.

WHAT TO LOOK FOR

Cucurbits

Sudden wilting of leaves and stems; leaves wilt during the day, recover at night, and then wilt again the next day; spots on fruits; yellow leaves with brown edges, which wilt and die; entire vine dies; brown streaks in the vascular tissue within stems.

Nightshade crops

Sudden wilting; rotting roots; brown stem cankers; plants die.

For both families of crops, there are two tests for detecting the presence of bacteria: (1) Cut a wilted stem in two, pull it apart, and look for a sticky substance oozing from the stem. (2) Place a cut stem in water and watch for a milky substance oozing from it.

ORGANIC STRATEGIES

> Practice crop rotation to avoid planting members of susceptible plant families in the same place each year.

> Plant disease-resistant varieties of cucurbit crops. Refer to the Vegetable Disease Resistance Abbreviations chart on page 166.

> Control cucumber beetles in your garden through the use of cucumber beetle traps or the application of one of the following organic products: kaolin clay, Neem, pyrethrins, or spinosad.

> Mulch heavily around the base of the seedlings to prevent adult beetles from laying their eggs in the soil.

> Place floating row cover (refer to page 38 in the Bug Issues section of chapter 1) over seeds or seedlings as soon as you plant them and remove it when the young plants begin flowering

> Remove and dispose of infected plants and clean up plant debris at the end of the season.

BEET CURLY TOP VIRUS

Type: Viral

Caused by: Beet Curly Top Virus (BCTV)

DESCRIPTION

Viral diseases are always challenging to control and this one is no exception. Beet curly top virus is transmitted by the beet leafhopper (*Circulifer tenellus*). The virus overwinters in host plants. In early spring, the leafhoppers initially feed on weeds such as mustards and Russian thistles and then move to vegetable crops. They ingest the virus on infected plants, incubate it within their bodies, and spread the virus through their feeding activities. Leafhopper eggs do not contain the virus and it is not transmitted by seed. It is more prevalent in arid regions that experience prolonged periods of high heat and low humidity. Symptoms appear one to two weeks after infection.

CROPS MOST COMMONLY IMPACTED:

Beans, beets (both regular and sugar beets), cucurbit family crops (cucumbers, melons, pumpkins, summer and winter squash), nightshade family crops (peppers, potatoes, tomatoes), spinach

WHAT TO LOOK FOR

Stunted growth; distorted leaves; deformed fruits; young, infected seedlings usually die. Here are signs for specific crops:

Beans

Leaves turn yellow, pucker, and curl downwardly; bean pods don't develop normally; plants die. It's easy to confuse the symptoms with those of mosaic virus (refer to page 136), but beet curly top virus impacts younger leaves while mosaic virus affects older foliage.

Beets

Leaves are puckered, twisted, curl up into a roll, and develop blisters; roots are deformed and sometimes hairy; plants die.

Cucurbits

Deformed, stunted growth; leaves turn pale yellow; fruits are undersized and misshapen, or don't develop at all; vine tips bend upward.

Peppers and tomatoes

Leaves roll upward, twist, become thick and turn yellow; veins on the undersides of the leaves usually turn purple; plants produce abnormally, developing fruits appear dull and wrinkled, or don't produce fruit at all; stunted growth; plants eventually die.

Potatoes

Plants are slow to develop; distorted leaves that are upwardly cupped; tubers are undersized or don't develop at all.

Beet leafhoppers are vectors for beet curly top virus.

Notice the distorted leaves on this beet plant.

ORGANIC STRATEGIES

> Choose resistant varieties, if available. Refer to the Vegetable Disease Resistance Abbreviations chart on page 166.

> If your growing season permits, plant tomatoes and peppers one to two weeks later to avoid peak activity by beet leafhoppers.

> Cover plants with floating row cover or a mesh barrier to keep leafhoppers away from plants. The cover can remain in place for the entire season if the crop doesn't require pollination. Otherwise, remove once the plants begin blooming.

> Weed the areas in and around your garden regularly to remove potential host plants.

> Intercrop vegetables that aren't attractive to beet leafhoppers within susceptible crops.

> Research has shown that dense plantings are less attractive to leafhoppers, yet this can increase the risk of other disease problems.

> Remove, destroy, and dispose of infected plant material as soon as you notice and identify the cause.

> Insecticides aren't effective, primarily due to the migrant nature of leafhoppers.

> Plant susceptible crops in a partly shady area or under shade cloth; leafhoppers prefer to feed in sunny locations.

This bean plant is suffering from beet curly top virus.

BLACK ROT

Type: Bacterial   **Caused by:** *Xanthomonas campestris*

DESCRIPTION

Black rot is a major disease that affects all members of the cabbage family (*Brassicaceae*). While it's a nuisance to vegetable gardeners, black rot causes major losses to farmers worldwide. Infected seeds and seedlings are the two primary ways the bacteria are brought into a garden. The bacteria spread during warm, wet weather via splashing water, wind, insects, and contaminated tools. The pathogens can remain on infected plant debris for up to two years. Weeds belonging to the same plant family also can become hosts. Bacteria enter plants through specialized pores (called hyathodes) that are located near the leaf margins or through wounds caused by insect feeding activity. Flea beetles are an insect vector. Black rot affects plants systemically by moving from the leaves to the stems, vascular tissue, and roots. Once a plant is infected, there is no cure.

FUN FACT

Have you ever noticed that xanthan gum frequently appears in lists of ingredients on food packaging? While it also is used to manufacture certain medications, xanthan gum is a food additive that helps thicken and stabilize products. It is a common ingredient in gluten-free and vegan baking products. What most shoppers don't realize is that it's made by fermenting sugar with *Xanthomonas campestris* bacteria—the very same bacteria responsible for black rot on our cabbage family crops. Sorry to ruin your appetite!

CROPS MOST COMMONLY IMPACTED:

Cabbage family crops (arugula, broccoli, Brussels sprouts, cabbage, cauliflower, collards, kale, kohlrabi, radishes, rutabagas, turnips)

WHAT TO LOOK FOR

Plants grown from infected seeds might not show symptoms for several weeks.

Seedlings

Leaves wither, turn yellow, and plants die suddenly.

On older plants

Plant leaf edges turn yellow, then form V-shaped wedges of yellow tissue from the margin to the leaf's midrib; if you hold a leaf up to the light, you might see a network of black veins throughout it; stems turn brown or black; veins become dark; vascular tissue in stems turns black; black veins in roots; heads of broccoli, cabbage, and cauliflower might be stunted; plants wilt and die prematurely.

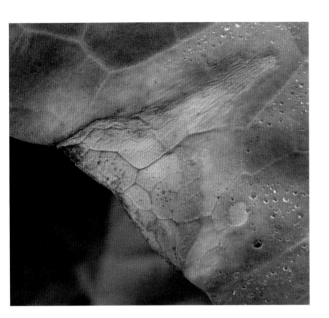

Notice the V-shaped wedge of damaged tissue on this cabbage leaf.

Black rot on a cabbage plant.

ORGANIC STRATEGIES

> Practice a three-year crop rotation plan to avoid growing cabbage family crops in the same location.

> Choose disease-resistant varieties. Refer to the Vegetable Disease Resistance Abbreviations chart on page 166.

> If you plan to start your plants from seed, always disinfect your seed-starting flats first with a 10 percent bleach solution.

> The soil in your planting bed should drain well. If it doesn't, add compost to remedy this.

> Space plants correctly to provide good air circulation between them.

> Avoid the use of overhead watering and don't work with plants while they're wet.

> Keep up with the weeding in and around your garden, especially weeds belonging to the same plant family.

> If you spot signs of black rot on some of your plants, remove the whole plants immediately; do not compost them. Monitor the remaining plants regularly.

> Sanitize any tools that have been in contact with infected plant material. Refer to the Organic Strategies Explained section (page 164) to learn the best practices for this.

> Control flea beetles and other leaf-chewing insects in your garden.

> Apply sulfur fungicide as a preventive measure. Refer to the Organic Disease Control and Prevention Products section beginning on page 168 for more information.

BUCKEYE ROT

Type: Fungal

Caused by: *Phytophthora capsica, P. drechsleri, P. nicotiana* var. *parasitica*

DESCRIPTION

Buckeye rot is a fungal disease that is prevalent in regions that experience high humidity. It primarily occurs on both mature and green tomato fruits, but peppers and eggplants also are susceptible. Potatoes can be alternate hosts. The above species of *Phytophthora* are soilborne. Infection takes place when fruits are in direct contact with the soil, or hang just above it, and occurs during warm, wet weather. The fungi are spread by splashing rain, by overhead watering, and within the soil; the spores do not move through the air. Infection rates increase when soil moisture is especially high. The infections take place right through the skin of the fruits, rather than at the site of a plant injury. The fungi do not infect the leaves on plants. Buckeye rot can be brought into vegetable gardens on contaminated seeds and seedlings, and it can spread via muddy boots and tools. Tomato fruits damaged by buckeye rot have a similar appearance to those afflicted with late blight (refer to page 130). Buckeye rot lesions are smooth and have firm edges while late blight lesions are rough to the touch and have slightly sunken boundaries. Blossom-end rot (page 46), which is a physiological disorder, causes leathery patches near the bottom end of fruits due to a calcium deficiency.

CROPS MOST COMMONLY IMPACTED:

Eggplants, peppers, tomatoes

WHAT TO LOOK FOR

Small brown spots on fruits, usually where they come into contact with the soil; spots enlarge into lesions with tan and brown concentric rings; white fuzzy growth appears on the lesions during wet conditions; fruits rot internally.

This is how buckeye rot affects pepper fruits.

Buckeye rot completely ruins tomato fruits.

ORGANIC STRATEGIES

> Look for *Phytophtera*-resistant varieties. Refer to the Vegetable Disease Resistance Abbreviations chart on page 166.

> Practice crop rotation to avoid planting nightshade family crops in the same bed during a three-year period.

> The soil in your planting beds should be well-drained. If not, add organic material such as compost to improve drainage.

> Space plants appropriately to provide them with good air circulation.

> Stake or cage plants to prevent tomato, eggplant, or pepper fruits from contacting the soil.

> Remove the lowest branches of the plants to reduce the chance of fruits developing near the soil surface.

> Place a thick layer of mulch onto the soil surface to prevent soil from splashing up onto the fruits.

> Avoid overhead watering as well as overwatering. The soil should be lightly moist.

> Remove and dispose of infected fruits.

> Harvest fruits as soon as they are ripe. In the case of tomatoes, pick them at the breaker stage, which is when the green, immature skin begins to lighten in color prior to changing to its mature color. They will finish ripening indoors.

> Clean up and dispose of all plant debris at the end of the season. This includes unripe fruits since pathogens would grow and multiply in them. Do not compost the debris or fruits.

> Apply biofungicide or plant extracts as a preventive measure. Refer to the Organic Disease Control and Prevention Products section beginning on page 168 for more information.

CERCOSPORA LEAF SPOT

Type: Fungal

Caused by: Several species of *Cercospora*

DESCRIPTION

Cercospora leaf spot infects many different families of vegetable crops. The spores of this fungus are brought into the garden on contaminated seeds or seedlings, or they can be blown in by the wind. In asparagus and leafy greens such as spinach and beets, one infected plant can contaminate an entire bed. The fungal infections cause round spots or lesions to develop, from which new spores are later released. Once in your garden, this resilient fungus survives from season to season on plant debris, in the soil, and on weeds. The spores are spread in the garden by wind, splashing water, insects, and contaminated tools. It is especially prevalent during warm, wet weather. The leaves must remain wet for an extended period to become infected. The spores enter plants through their leaf stomata. Because plants often lose their infected leaves, this exposes the developing fruits in the cucurbit and nightshade families to sunscald damage. While Cercospora leaf spot might not kill your plants outright, it weakens them, reduces your harvest, and makes edible leaves unappealing.

CROPS MOST COMMONLY IMPACTED:

Asparagus, beans, beet family crops (beets, spinach, Swiss chard), cabbage family crops (arugula, broccoli, Brussels sprouts, cabbage, cauliflower, collards, kale, kohlrabi, radishes, rutabagas, turnips), carrots, cucurbit family crops (cucumbers, melons, pumpkins, squash), nightshade family crops (eggplants, peppers, tomatoes)

WHAT TO LOOK FOR

Small round spots on leaves and petioles; wilting and dying leaves.

Asparagus

Brown lesions with red borders on the needles and stems that progress upward; their ferns turn yellow and die.

Beet family crops

Small, round, tan to brown spots with red borders.

Cabbage family crops

Round, white spots with dark borders.

Carrots

Small brown, water-soaked spots on leaves and petioles with yellow halos; leaf undersides turn gray and have tiny, black spores.

Cucurbit crops

Round leaf spots with brown centers and yellow halos.

Eggplants

Small, pale leaf spots that turn brown and tiny, dark circles of spores.

Peppers

Round, water-soaked leaf spots up to ½-inch (1.3 cm) in diameter.

Tomatoes

Leaves have lesions in between the leaf veins; leaves curl.

Cercospora leaf spot on a melon leaf.

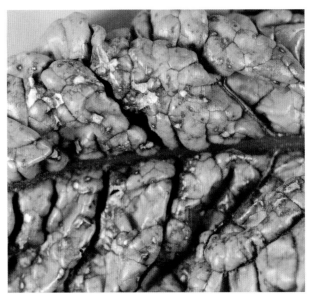

Cercospora leaf spot on a Swiss chard leaf.

ORGANIC STRATEGIES

> Practice a three-year crop rotation to avoid planting susceptible crops in the same location each year.

> Plant resistant varieties when they're available. Refer to the Vegetable Disease Resistance Abbreviations chart on page 166.

> The soil in the planting bed should be well-drained; add compost to improve drainage, as needed.

> Space plants appropriately to allow for good air circulation between them.

> Place mulch on soil surface to reduce the chances of pathogens splashing up onto plants.

> Avoid overhead watering. Water plants during the day so leaves aren't wet at night or for extended periods of time.

> Don't work with plants when they are wet.

> Keep up with the weeds in and around your garden to reduce host plants.

> If you spot this disease early, remove each infected plant entirely and bag it immediately. This will slow the spread. Do not compost infected plant tissue.

> Apply a biofungicide, copper fungicide, horticultural oil, or sulfur fungicide as a preventive measure. Refer to the Organic Disease Control and Prevention Products section beginning on page 168 for more information.

CORN SMUT

Type: Fungal

Caused by: *Ustilago zeae* (*Ustilago maydis*)

DESCRIPTION

This disease is aptly named because I've experienced it in my own garden and it is disgusting! The first time I spotted it, I stopped dead in my tracks and tried to fathom what had caused those swollen, gray areas on my formerly healthy plants. Corn smut is a fungal disease that can be present in corn ears, tassels, or stalks, and gives them a disfigured appearance. This fungus overwinters as teliospores in the soil and crop residue. During warm, moist soil conditions, they germinate and create the new spores that will infect crops. Once conditions become dry, the spores are transported to corn plants by the wind. Spores that land on leaves and stalks require moisture to invade the plant tissue. Spores that land on the silks use hyphae to move down into the kernels. The infected area of the plant develops gray or black powdery galls that are covered by a membrane. Once it dries, the membrane breaks open, and spores either drop down to the soil or blow around on the wind. Heat or drought stress during pollination increases the prevalence of corn smut. The tender foliage and tissue of younger plants are more susceptible. Excessive amounts of nitrogen in the corn patch increase the occurrence of this disease because it accelerates the growth processes of the plants.

Did you know corn smut on young ears is considered a delicacy in parts of the United States and Mexico? It is gathered one week before the actual corn harvest and used in a variety of recipes. I haven't had any personal experience with this, but, if you're feeling adventurous, look for additional information and recipes online by searching for the word "cuitlacoche."

CROPS MOST COMMONLY IMPACTED:

Corn

WHAT TO LOOK FOR

Gray or black powdery galls covered by a membrane on any aboveground portion of a corn plant; distorted kernels within the ears.

Corn smut distorts the kernels on ears of corn.

It's pretty hard to miss corn smut on your cornstalks!

ORGANIC STRATEGIES

> If corn smut has been a problem in past seasons, wait several years before planting corn again.

> Plant varieties that are smut-resistant. Refer to the Vegetable Disease Resistance Abbreviations chart on page 166. Note that varieties with the label "SE"—which stands for "sugar-enhanced"—are more resistant to this disease.

> Plant corn as soon as the danger of frost has passed; the warmer the weather, the higher the risk of this disease. Consider planting short-season varieties so you can harvest the ears earlier.

> Don't overfertilize your corn patch with nitrogen; use a balanced fertilizer instead.

> Avoid overhead watering.

> Place a thick layer of mulch on the surface of the soil to prevent water from splashing up onto the plants.

> Avoid injuring plants while working among them as this provides entry points for the spores.

> If you spot a gall, remove it immediately and dispose of it; do not add it to your compost pile.

> Clean up and dispose of all plant debris at the end of the season.

> If your neighbors are also dealing with corn smut in their gardens, let them know how important it is to completely dispose of infected plants.

DAMPING-OFF DISEASE

Type: Fungal

Caused by: Species of *Pythium*, *Rhizoctonia*, *Fusarium*, *Phytophthora*, and others

DESCRIPTION

Damping-off disease kills the seeds or seedlings of most vegetable crops. If this disease occurs when you are starting seeds indoors or outdoors, it's not important to determine which species of fungus has caused the problem. You just need to know how to prevent this from happening again!

When you experience a poor seed germination rate, it can be easy to think the seed quality wasn't good when, in fact, fungi were responsible for the problem. Damping-off disease impacts seeds and seedlings in three different ways: The fungi kill seeds before they can germinate; they kill seedlings before they emerge through the potting or garden soil; or they stunt or kill seedlings soon after they have sprouted through the soil. In most cases, large swaths of seedlings quickly die. Many factors put seeds and plants at risk, but the most common include planting them in cool, wet soil, or planting seeds in contaminated containers or potting media. The fungi live in garden soil and plant debris for several years.

CROPS MOST COMMONLY IMPACTED:

Nearly all vegetable crops

WHAT TO LOOK FOR

Seeds fail to emerge from the soil and are soft or rotten; seedlings emerge but wilt, collapse, and die; seedlings emerge with lesions at soil surface and either die or fail to thrive; fluffy, white growth on seedlings. Cabbage family seedlings are susceptible to "wire stem," in which the fungi create a canker on their stem; it doesn't kill them but significantly affects their growth.

The fungi that cause damping-off disease create lesions at the base of seedling stems.

ORGANIC STRATEGIES FOR INDOOR SEED-STARTING

> Always start with clean, sterile containers and equipment. Soak them in a 10 percent bleach solution for 30 minutes to accomplish this.

> Use a sterile, soilless potting or seed-starting mix. Do not use garden soil as it likely contains pathogens. Potting mixes also drain well.

> After planting seeds, sprinkle a light layer of milled sphagnum moss over the surface of the potting mix. The moss naturally inhibits fungal growth.

> Do not overwater the potting mix. Also, it's best to water flats from the bottom up, rather than getting the seedlings wet from overhead watering.

> Remove the humidity dome or plastic bag from the planting flats as soon as the majority of seeds have germinated.

> Provide good air circulation around your seed-starting containers; a small fan works well for this.

> Apply biofungicide, milled sphagnum moss, or plant extracts as a preventive. Refer to the Organic Disease Control and Prevention Products section beginning on page 168 for more information.

ORGANIC STRATEGIES FOR OUTDOOR SEED-STARTING

> Plant seeds when the soil temperature is correct for each crop.

> Space plants appropriately to increase air circulation.

> Don't overwater your planting bed. The soil should drain well. Add compost or other organic matter to help aerate heavy soils.

> If you notice damping-off disease beginning, stop watering the bed immediately to slow the fungal growth.

> Clean up plant debris at the end of the season.

> Apply a biofungicide, milled sphagnum moss, or plant extracts as a preventive. Refer to the Organic Disease Control and Prevention Products section beginning on page 168 for more information.

Wilting and dying seedlings are a sure sign of damping-off disease.

MILLED SPHAGNUM MOSS

I've been starting most of my vegetable seeds indoors for many years. Not long after hearing how devastating damping-off disease can be, I read that milled sphagnum moss contains natural chemicals that inhibit those fungi. As soon as I've planted and covered the seeds, I sprinkle a very fine layer of milled sphagnum moss over the top of the planting medium. My seedlings have never been victims of damping-off disease! It's easy to locate this product online and a little goes a long way.

EARLY BLIGHT

Type: Fungal

Caused by: *Alternaria tomatophila* or *solani* (tomato), *A. solani* (potato)

DESCRIPTION

This common fungal disease infects tomatoes, eggplants, potatoes, and weeds belonging to the nightshade family. Peppers are not susceptible to it. It usually doesn't kill plants, but weakened plants will produce smaller and damaged fruits. Early blight can be brought into the garden on contaminated seeds or seedlings of tomatoes and eggplants. *Alternaria solani* fungus can be present in contaminated seed potatoes. Early blight overwinters on infected plant debris, in the soil, and on host weeds. Spores are splashed up from the soil onto the lower leaves of developing plants by rainfall or overhead watering. The spores are also wind-dispersed during dry weather. Wet leaves assist wind-blown spores in attaching to a host plant. Once a plant is infected, the fungus continues to produce spores that generate additional infections and spread. The disease is initially evident on the older, lower leaves of the plants but progresses to developing fruits. Early blight causes dark, sunken spots on the stem end of tomatoes and eggplants, compared to blossom-end rot, which infects the opposite end of the fruits.

In potatoes, it usually only attacks leaves and stems, but, in severe cases, it also will invade tubers. Alternaria leaf spot (page 100) infects many other vegetables, such as cabbage and cucurbit family crops. If you see spots on the leaves of those crops that sound similar in appearance to what is described here, please refer to that disease profile.

CROPS MOST COMMONLY IMPACTED:

Eggplants, potatoes, tomatoes

WHAT TO LOOK FOR

Brown leaf spots with concentric rings and yellow halos, starting on oldest leaves first; spots enlarge and spread; leaves turn yellow and may fall off, causing sunscald (page 54) on newly exposed fruits; sunken spots or dark, leathery lesions on stems; a dark, sunken spot with concentric circles on the stem end of eggplant or tomato fruits; the fruits may fall off the plants. Potato tubers can develop lesions that become sunken. Stem lesions on young tomato or eggplant seedlings will girdle and kill them; this is known as "collar rot."

Early blight causes lesions near the stem end of tomato fruits.

Early blight spots on a tomato leaf.

This stem lesion is a symptom of early blight.

ORGANIC STRATEGIES

> Use a three-year crop rotation, or skip growing eggplants, potatoes, or tomatoes for a couple of years.

> Start with disease-free seed potatoes and resistant tomato or eggplant varieties (look for "EB" on packets).

> Stake or cage eggplant and tomato plants to prevent their foliage from contacting the soil.

> Prune off the lowest branches to prevent foliage from touching soil.

> Cover soil surface with mulch.

> Avoid overhead watering and don't work with the plants while they are wet.

> Do not overfertilize with high-nitrogen fertilizers as lush growth is easily infected.

> Keep up with the weeds in and around your garden, especially those belonging to the nightshade family.

> Clean up and dispose of infected plant debris.

> Remove and dispose of volunteer plants.

> Don't save seed from infected plants.

> Apply biofungicide or copper fungicide as a preventive measure. Refer to the Organic Disease Control and Prevention Products section beginning on page 168 for more information.

FUSARIUM WILT

Type: Fungal

Caused by: *Fusarium oxysporum* and other *Fusarium* species

DESCRIPTION

Fusarium wilt, which is also referred to as yellows or Fusarium yellows, is a disease that you really don't want in your garden. Why? The fungi can live in the soil for a very long time. They survive on infected plant debris, and they are seedborne as well. Infected seedlings from an outside source also will introduce this disease into your garden; always check plants thoroughly before purchasing them. Most commonly identified on tomato crops, this fungus affects many vegetable crops—as well as weed hosts from the same plant families. Pathogens in the soil enter through root wounds caused by cultivation or from nematode damage. They quickly multiply and spread throughout the vascular system, limiting or completely restricting the flow of water through the plant. As you might guess, the primary symptom is wilting, which might give the appearance that plants aren't getting enough water when in actuality the cause is a clogged vascular system. One way to identify the disease is by cutting a plant stem and examining the interior for dark, longitudinal streaks. At this time, no organic fungicides are available to control Fusarium wilt. Three other diseases cause similar symptoms: bacterial wilt (refer to page 110), Southern blight (page 146), and Verticillium wilt (page 152). Be aware two insect pests—squash bugs and squash vine borers—can also cause wilting damage on cucurbit crops.

CROPS MOST COMMONLY IMPACTED:

Asparagus, cabbage family crops (arugula, broccoli, Brussels sprouts, cabbage, cauliflower, collards, kale, kohlrabi, radishes, rutabagas, turnips), cucurbit family crops (cucumbers, melons, pumpkins, summer and winter squash), legumes (beans, peas), lettuce, nightshade family crops (eggplants, peppers, potatoes, tomatoes), spinach

WHAT TO LOOK FOR

Young seedlings die; older leaves of plants turn yellow and wilt, often on one side at first; leaves wilt during the day and recover at night; stunted plants; plants die a few days after the wilting begins; brown vascular tissue in the stem, crown, or roots; white fungus might appear on dead plants.

Peas

Lower leaves on plants turn yellow; plants produce stunted or few pods.

Potatoes

Leaves turn yellow, bronze, or red, and curl up; wilting leaves; tubers are sunken where they attach to the stem.

ORGANIC STRATEGIES

> Look for vegetable varieties that are resistant to Fusarium wilt. Refer to the Vegetable Disease Resistance Abbreviations chart on page 166.

> If you are starting your own plants from seed, use sterile potting mix and clean containers.

> Purchase certified, disease-free seed potatoes.

> Keep up with the weeds in and around your garden as many are alternate hosts within the same plant families you are growing.

> Avoid overfeeding plants with high-nitrogen fertilizers; this promotes tender foliage that will be more susceptible to this disease.

> Sanitize your tools after working with them.

> Remove and dispose of infected plants; do not compost them.

> Consider solarizing your soil to eliminate pathogens from the soil.

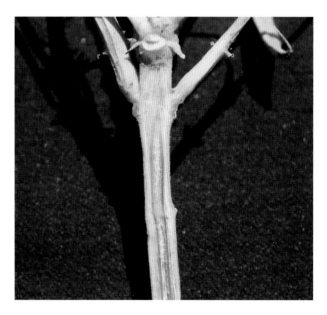

To diagnose Fusarium wilt, clip off a section of affected stem, cut it in half lengthwise, and look for dark streaks within the plant's vascular system.

The presence of yellow leaves on one side of a tomato plant is common with Fusarium wilt.

The leaves of plants infected with Fusarium often wilt during the day and recover at night.

GRAY MOLD

Type: Fungal   **Caused by:** *Botrytis cinerea* and other species

DESCRIPTION

Gray mold is also known as Botrytis blight and affects a wide variety of vegetable crops. Neck rot is a form of gray mold that specifically infects garlic, from either too much moisture or failing to cure the bulbs long enough before storage. In all cases, the spores overwinter in the soil and on rotting plant debris. They also infect plants through wounds caused by insect damage or cultivation activities. Cool, wet conditions are ideal for the spread of infection. Gray mold often occurs after a plant host has been infected with downy mildew (see page 132) or another plant disease. It can infect stored produce and also thrives in poorly ventilated greenhouses.

CROPS MOST COMMONLY IMPACTED:

Artichokes, beans, beets, cabbage, carrot family crops (carrots, celery, parsnips), garlic, lettuce, onions, rutabagas, tomato family crops (eggplants, peppers, tomatoes), turnips

Lettuce plants infected with gray mold exhibit decaying crowns.

WHAT TO LOOK FOR

Fuzzy, gray fungus on any aboveground plant parts; brown, rotting plant tissue; dark lesions on plants; wilting leaves; tiny black sclerotia on leaves and stems.

Garlic

Gray mold between cloves; seedlings fall over and die.

Lettuce

Plants have brown, decaying crowns; rotting outer lettuce leaves and stems.

Tomatoes

White or yellow halos on immature and mature fruits.

Gray mold is growing on this tomato fruit.

Gray mold causes stem lesions on plants.

ORGANIC STRATEGIES

> Keep your plants healthy and unstressed through the cultural practices listed in chapter 1.

> Make sure the soil in your planting beds is well-drained; if not, add compost or other organic matter to improve drainage.

> Space plants appropriately to allow good air circulation between them.

> Place a layer of mulch on the surface of the soil to prevent water from splashing up onto the leaves.

> Stake plants to increase air circulation around them and to prevent the foliage from contacting the soil.

> Avoid overhead watering to keep the leaves dry. Do not overwater.

> Be careful not to injure plants when working with or around them because this exposes them to infection.

> Clean up plant debris to eliminate host material for the spores. Remove infected leaves, fruits, and flowers to decrease the chances of further infection.

> Let garlic tops mature before lifting the bulbs from the garden; it is best to wait until the lowest four or five leaves turn brown. Cure garlic in a dry, sheltered area until the skins and stems are completely dry.

> Apply biofungicide, copper fungicide, or plant extracts as a preventive measure. Refer to the Organic Disease Control and Prevention Products section beginning on page 168 for more information.

LATE BLIGHT

Type: Fungal   **Caused by:** *Phytophthora infestans*

DESCRIPTION

Late blight is the disease responsible for the Irish potato famine that began in 1845. Over one million people starved to death. It is caused by a fungus-like microorganism that primarily infects potatoes and tomatoes as well as weeds in the nightshade family. The microorganism is a water mold that lives in water or soil. The pathogens overwinter in plant debris and on infected potato tubers. They are easily spread through the air or in water during cool, wet conditions. Infected plant seedlings are also a source. While early blight (see page 124) symptoms are similar to those of late blight, look for this difference: Late blight affects new growth near the top of a plant whereas early blight first affects lower leaves before moving up through the plant. Tomato fruits damaged by late blight also have a similar appearance to that of buckeye rot (see page 116).

CROPS MOST COMMONLY IMPACTED:

Primarily potatoes and tomatoes, but can also infect peppers and eggplants.

WHAT TO LOOK FOR

Water-soaked spots on younger leaves; white mold on the undersides of leaf lesions; brown spots coalesce and have yellow or light green halo; dark lesions on stems; tomato fruits are mottled with gold to brown sunken spots, which turn dark and become leathery; potato leaves have brown blotches; tuber skin is brown or purple with sunken areas.

Late blight on a tomato plant.

ORGANIC STRATEGIES

> Look for disease-resistant varieties and plant certified, disease-free seed potatoes. Refer to the Vegetable Disease Resistance Abbreviations chart on page 166.

> If purchasing tomato seedlings, inspect them thoroughly for dark spots on the leaves or stems.

> Use a three-year crop rotation plan to avoid planting nightshade family crops in the same location.

> Space plants appropriately for good air circulation.

> Stake or cage tomato plants to reduce the chances of foliage contacting the soil.

> Apply a thick layer of mulch on the soil surface to prevent foliage from directly contacting soil.

> Avoid overhead watering to keep the leaves as dry as possible. If hand-watering, water the soil, not the leaves.

> Monitor tomato and potato plants regularly, especially during wet weather.

> Pull up and dispose of any volunteer plants because they might be infected.

> Keep up with the weeding in and around your garden, especially weeds in the nightshade family.

> Pull up any infected plants immediately and dispose of them; do not compost them.

> Harvest potato tubers after the vines have been killed by frosts; avoid harvesting them when the soil is very wet; be sure to harvest all the tubers and dispose of infected tubers.

> Check your stored potatoes frequently for any signs of infection.

> If you've had problems with late blight in the past, or it is prevalent in your region, apply a biofungicide as a preventive measure. It will not be effective after infection. Refer to the Organic Disease Control and Prevention Products section beginning on page 168 for more information.

Look for sunken, dark areas on your potato tubers.

This infected tomato plant has dark lesions on its stems.

MILDEW, DOWNY

Type: Fungal

Caused by: Species of *Peronospora*, *Pseudoperonospora*, and *Bremia*

DESCRIPTION

Downy mildew is caused by fungus-like microorganisms. They overwinter on infected plant debris and weeds belonging to the same plant family as the vegetable host crop. While this disease affects aboveground plant parts, it can impact root or bulb development in certain crops. Leaf spots on the older leaves are the most common sign, along with a gray, fuzzy mold on leaf undersides. Downy mildew can be confused with powdery mildew (page 134), which is a true fungus that only affects the upper sides of plant leaves. Cool, damp conditions are ideal for infection of plant tissue. It is spread by rain, by splashing water, through the air, and by cucumber beetles.

The spots on the upper surface of these cucumber leaves are symptoms of downy mildew.

CROPS MOST COMMONLY IMPACTED:

Beet family crops (beets, spinach, Swiss chard), cabbage family crops (arugula, broccoli, Brussels sprouts, cabbage, cauliflower, collards, kale, kohlrabi, mustard, radishes, rutabagas, turnips), cucurbit family crops (cucumbers, melons, pumpkins, summer and winter squash), legume family crops (beans, peas), onions

WHAT TO LOOK FOR

Angular yellow or pale green leaf spots in between leaf veins on the upper surface of leaves; gray or purplish fuzzy growth on the undersides of the leaves that becomes darker; leaves turn yellow, wilt, and die; distorted or stunted plant growth; fruits infected with downy fuzz may be stunted; onion plants have fuzzy brown or purple spots that can girdle the leaves and affect the development of the bulb.

Beans, peas

Pods have brown lesions and mold inside the pods.

ORGANIC STRATEGIES

> If downy mildew has been a problem in your garden, plant susceptible crops later in the spring to avoid cool, damp conditions.

> Consider skipping a year or two of growing crops within a particular plant family if they are annual targets of downy mildew.

> Practice a three-year crop rotation to avoid planting vegetables within the same plant family in the same location.

> Plant varieties that are resistant to downy mildew.

> Well-draining soil is a must; add compost or other organic amendments to improve drainage.

> Space plants properly to permit good air circulation between them.

> Place a thick layer of mulch on the soil of your planting bed.

> Avoid overusing high-nitrogen fertilizers as they promote foliage that is susceptible to infection.

> Keep up with the weeds in and around your garden because many of them are alternate hosts.

> Avoid overhead watering, do not water in the evenings, and refrain from watering during wet conditions. Don't work with your plants when they're wet.

> Monitor your plants regularly and remove infected leaves. Remove infected plant debris at the end of the season.

> If cucumber beetles are present in your garden, control them with traps or apply kaolin clay, Neem, pyrethrins, or spinosad.

> Apply biofungicide, copper fungicide, or plant extracts as a preventive measure. Refer to the Organic Disease Control and Prevention Products section beginning on page 168 for more information.

Mold on the undersides of leaves is a sign of downy mildew.

MILDEW, POWDERY

Type: Fungal

Caused by: Multiple species of *Erisyphe, Leveillula, Pythium, Sphaerotheca,* which are specific to certain hosts

DESCRIPTION

This common disease causes white, powdery spots that slowly spread across the leaves of many different vegetable crops. It often looks like someone has sprinkled baking flour onto the plants. Dispersed by wind, the spores germinate on the leaves and then develop threadlike strands (hyphae) that drill down into the cells so they can feed upon their nutrients. Powdery mildew typically occurs during temperatures that range from 60°F to 80°F (16°C to 27°C), and when the relative humidity is high at night. This disease does not tolerate very high temperatures or direct sunlight.

The spores primarily affect the upper surface of leaves but can spread to the undersides and plant stems as well. Some plants will lose leaves, which exposes fruits to the risk of sunscald. The fungus occasionally infests a crop's fruits, such as on pea pods. The powdery mildew spores that affect certain crops—cucumbers, lettuce, melons, peas, pumpkins, summer and winter squash—will overwinter on plant debris. That means garden cleanup is essential.

Although they have similar names, powdery mildew and downy mildew (refer to page 132) are caused by different types of fungi. If you have a magnifying glass or microscope, you can determine which disease is impacting your plants: Powdery mildew spores develop in chains whereas downy mildew spores form a more branchlike structure.

CROPS MOST COMMONLY IMPACTED:

Artichokes, beets, cabbage family crops (arugula, broccoli, Brussels sprouts, cabbage, cauliflower, collards, kale, kohlrabi, mustard, radishes, rutabagas, turnips), carrot family crops (carrots, parsnips), cucurbit family crops (cucumbers, melons, pumpkins, summer and winter squash), legume family crops (beans, peas), lettuce, nightshade family crops (eggplants, peppers, potatoes, tomatillos, tomatoes), okra

WHAT TO LOOK FOR

White, powdery spots on upper leaf surfaces of most of the vegetables listed above; yellow blotches on the leaves of artichokes, peppers, and tomatoes.

Some plant leaves have markings that appear to be powdery mildew; that is not this case here because the silvery pattern is typical of certain varieties of summer squash.

Powdery mildew on a squash plant.

Powdery mildew on tomato leaves.

ORGANIC STRATEGIES

> Look for crop varieties that are resistant to, or at least tolerant of, powdery mildew. Refer to the Vegetable Disease Resistance Abbreviations chart on page 166.

> Plant susceptible vegetable crops in full sun.

> Space plants appropriately to increase air circulation around them.

> Avoid over fertilization of your vegetable plants since new foliage is more susceptible.

> Water early in the morning.

> Clean up and dispose of infected plant debris, do not compost it.

> Use crop rotation techniques to avoid planting susceptible crops where spores might be present.

> When powdery mildew develops late in the growing season, gardeners usually find it is more of an aesthetic issue rather than one they need to act upon. If powdery mildew is an annual problem in your garden—particularly on squash and pumpkin plants—apply one of the following products as a preventive: biofungicide, copper fungicide, horticultural oil, plant extracts, or sulfur fungicide. Refer to the Organic Disease Control and Prevention Products section beginning on page 135 for more information.

MOSAIC VIRUS

Type: Viral

Caused by: Several strains of mosaic virus

DESCRIPTION

Many strains of mosaic viruses infect vegetable crops; examples include cucumber mosaic virus (CMV), squash mosaic virus (SqMV), tomato mosaic virus (ToMV), and zucchini yellow mosaic virus (ZYMV). The pathogens can live in seeds, soil, weeds, and unrelated host plants. With other diseases, weeds that belong to the same plant family as the vegetable hosts usually become infected with and spread the virus. Not so with mosaic virus. Weeds from different plant families can infect crops as well, which is quite worrisome. The virus also survives on perennial weeds, which helps the disease reappear year after year. This disease is spread by the feeding activities of insects such as aphids, leafhoppers, thrips, and cucumber beetles. Other means of spread include contact with contaminated soil, plant debris, and tools. Cucumber mosaic virus (CMV) affects vegetable and fruit crops, weeds, and both herbaceous and woody plants. Mosaic virus is systemic: It progresses through the plant and gets worse over time. Once vegetable plants are infected, there is no way to control it, so it's best to remove and dispose of the infected plants right away.

CROPS MOST COMMONLY IMPACTED:

Celery, cucurbit family crops (cucumbers, melons, pumpkins, summer and winter squash), garlic, legume family crops (beans, peas), nightshade family crops (primarily peppers and tomatoes), spinach

WHAT TO LOOK FOR

(*Note: Plant symptoms vary based on the crop host and other factors. Consider having a sample analyzed by an educational institution with a horticultural program for a definitive diagnosis.*) Edges of seedling leaves roll inward; true leaves are distorted; yellow-and-green mottled pattern on leaves; stunted plants; little or no flowers and fruits; undersized fruits that are dark green with yellow spots; vines wither; plants die.

Garlic

Plants have mottled and striped leaves, stunted plants, and undersized bulbs.

Tomatoes

Plants develop thin, narrow leaves that are distorted.

The mottled pattern on these cucumber leaves is a sign of mosaic virus.

Cucumber fruits are also mottled from this disease.

This tomato fruit is infected with mosaic virus.

ORGANIC STRATEGIES

> Choose disease-free varieties when available. Refer to the Vegetable Disease Resistance Abbreviations chart on page 166.

> Control cucumber beetles and sap-sucking insects such as aphids, leafhoppers, and thrips through the use of the following:
>   - Floating row cover
>   - Reflective plastic mulch placed on the soil surface; its highly reflective surface makes it difficult for the pests to find the plants.
>   - Sticky traps to catch leafhoppers, thrips, and cucumber beetles
>   - Do not use insecticides because they will not act quickly enough to curtail the insects' feeding activities. The chemicals might even stimulate their appetites before they die, which would increase the spread of the disease.

> Avoid working with healthy plants if you have handled infected plant material. Wash your hands thoroughly and disinfect any tools.

> Keep up with the weeds in and around your garden because they are alternate hosts for this virus; as noted on the opposite page, the weeds don't even have to be in the same plant family, so they are important to control.

> Remove and dispose of infected plants as soon as you see them; also clean up and dispose of plant debris at the end of the season.

POTATO SCAB

Type: Bacterial   **Caused by:** *Streptomyces scabies*

DESCRIPTION

Potato scab is a common disease caused by *Streptomyces* bacteria that live in the soil and on diseased potato plants and tubers. It is also prevalent when hot, dry weather occurs while the tubers are developing. These resilient bacteria can survive going through the digestive system of livestock and later spread in their manure. The bacteria are present in most soils but proliferate in alkaline soils or sandy soils that are low in organic matter. Bacteria overwinter in the soil on unharvested potatoes as well as in weed roots and other organic material. They get into the garden on infected seed potatoes and can be moved from place to place through contaminated soil on tools and boots.

Although *Streptomyces* are bacteria, they are also fungus-like in that they produce spores. When a spore in the soil comes into contact with a developing potato, it enters the skin through natural openings or damaged areas and begins the infection. This induces the potato to grow the corklike cells to isolate the bacteria. As the tuber grows, the infected area enlarges, causing the potato to continue producing extra cells. Potato scab won't impact the size of your potato harvest. Russet potatoes are less susceptible to potato scab than smooth-skinned varieties.

CROPS MOST COMMONLY IMPACTED:

Primarily potatoes, but this also can affect root crops such as beets, carrots, parsnips, radishes, rutabagas, and turnips

WHAT TO LOOK FOR

Raised, corky lesions on the skin of potatoes or fleshy root crops.

ORGANIC STRATEGIES

> Use a three-year crop rotation plan that does not include root crops.

> Always buy seed potatoes that are certified to be disease-free, from a reliable source. Do not save scabby potatoes for planting the next year as they will pass along the problem.

> Choose varieties that are resistant to scab, such as Norland, Russet Burbank, Kennebec, and Superior. Susceptible varieties include Red Pontiac, Russet Norkotah, and Yukon Gold. Refer to the Vegetable Disease Resistance Abbreviations chart on page 166.

> Add compost to the potato bed soil to increase organic matter; do not use animal manures as they will raise the soil pH.

> Growing your potatoes in grow bags or pots is another way to control potato scab. Fill the containers with sterile potting soil and add amendments such as bonemeal and organic fertilizer.

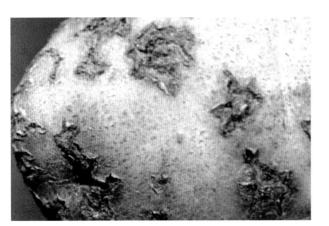

Potatoes with scab have raised, corky lesions on their skin.

> Water plants consistently throughout the season.
> Apply biofungicide, plant extracts, or sulfur fungicide as a preventive measure. Refer to the Organic Disease Control and Prevention Products section beginning on page 168 for more information.
> Harvest all potatoes at the end of the growing season.
> Store scabby potatoes in a dark, cool location to prevent rotting.

Potato hollow heart is often unnoticeable until you cut through a tuber.

POTATO HOLLOW HEART

Have you ever harvested a potato that has an open cavity in the middle? Potato hollow heart is a physiological problem that is caused when a gardener waters their plants inconsistently and then overcompensates by giving them too much water. As a result, this speeds up the development of the tubers to the point where these cavities develop. The simple solution is to provide the plants with regular water throughout the growing season.

RUST

Type: Fungal   **Caused by:** Species of *Albugo, Puccinia, Uromyces*

DESCRIPTION

Rust is a foliar disease that is easily recognized by the appearance of rust-colored spots and blister-like pustules. Plants struggle with it because rust disrupts the leaves' ability to conduct photosynthesis. The life cycle of some rusts involves multiple stages and often more than one type of plant host, including weeds belonging to the same plant family. For example, corn rust spores rely on both corn plants and wood sorrel to complete their life cycle; these types of spores aren't able to overwinter in the soil. Other rust strains overwinter as teliospores in the soil and on crop residue that is left in the garden. When conditions are favorable in the spring, they germinate and release airborne spores that cause new infections. While there are differences in their overwintering behaviors, the way rust infects plants is basically the same: Spores are released into the air and infect a host when they land on a wet leaf. High relative humidity and heavy dew promote the development of rust. This means overhead watering is not a good idea. Once rust has begun an infection, it will produce new spores to spread on its host and nearby plants. Because spores can remain in the soil for a few years, it is crucial that you remove and destroy infected plant material. Rust is particularly problematic on leafy crops—i.e., kale, lettuce, and spinach—since the leaves are what gardeners harvest and consume.

CROPS MOST COMMONLY IMPACTED:

Asparagus, beans, beet family crops (beets, spinach, Swiss chard), cabbage family crops (arugula, broccoli, Brussels sprouts, cabbage, cauliflower, collards, kale, kohlrabi, mustard, radish, rutabagas, turnips), carrots, corn, lettuce, potato

WHAT TO LOOK FOR

Rust-colored spots and blister-like pustules; foliage turns yellow and dies. Here are signs on specific crops:

Asparagus

Spears and new shoots develop sunken, pale green spots that turn yellow.

Beans

Reddish-brown spores appear on plants' leaves, stems, and pods during warm, moist weather.

Corn

Rusty-brown pustules on the upper and lower leaf surfaces; spores can develop on the ears of corn and their tassels.

Spinach and cabbage family crops

Yellow spots on the upper surface of leaves; white, spore-producing pustules on the undersides.

ORGANIC STRATEGIES

> Choose rust-resistant varieties when possible, especially if your region is prone to extended periods of high humidity. Refer to the Vegetable Disease Resistance Abbreviations chart on page 166.

> Follow a three-year crop rotation plan since spores can remain viable in the soil for a few years.

> Avoid overhead watering, which promotes spore development.

> Use balanced fertilizers rather than those high in nitrogen, which promote susceptible new growth.

> Focus on controlling weeds that are in the same plant family as rust-prone crops because the weeds also act as hosts to the spores.

> When harvesting asparagus spears, cut them below the soil surface so you won't leave exposed tissue that can be infected.

> Dispose of all infected plant debris; do not compost it or turn it into the soil.

> Apply biofungicide, copper fungicide, plant extracts, or sulfur fungicide as a preventive or when pustules start appearing on plant leaves. Refer to the Organic Disease Control and Prevention Products section beginning on page 168 for more information.

Rust pustules are visible on both the upper and lower sides of corn leaves.

Rust on a bean leaf.

VEGETABLE PLANT DISEASE GUIDE

141

SEPTORIA LEAF SPOT

Type: Fungal   **Caused by:** Species of *Septoria*

DESCRIPTION

Septoria leaf spot is a disease that affects the leaves and some fruits of plants. It most commonly infects celery, tomatoes, winter squash, and pumpkin plants, although other members of their respective plant families can be infected by the fungus. The pathogens overwinter on infected plant debris and weed hosts. This disease is especially prevalent during prolonged periods of warm, wet weather. The spores are spread by splashing water or rain. Gardeners will first notice spots on the lowest leaves of their plants, which then spread up through the plant. Once the leaves turn yellow, they wither and drop off. If a plant loses significant amounts of leaves, developing fruits will be at risk of sunscald. Early blight (page 124) is another fungal disease that first affects the lower leaves of tomatoes and other nightshade family crops but has accompanying signs that are quite different.

CROPS MOST COMMONLY IMPACTED:

Celery, cucurbit family crops (cucumbers, melons, pumpkins, winter squash), nightshade family crops (eggplants, peppers, potatoes, tomatoes), peas

WHAT TO LOOK FOR

Celery
Small, yellow spots on leaves and petioles that turn brown; leaves die.

Cucurbit family crops
Small, water-soaked leaf spots that are brown or white; older spots have small black fruiting bodies (spores); fruits have small, white, raised spots.

Nightshade family crops
Small, brown spots with yellow halos on leaves and stems; leaves turn yellow and fall off plant; leaf spots start on the lowest leaves of the plant.

Septoria leaf spot on tomato leaves.

Septoria leaf spot on a field pea.

ORGANIC STRATEGIES

> Choose disease-resistant varieties. Refer to the Vegetable Disease Resistance Abbreviations chart on page 166.

> Practice a three-year crop rotation plan to avoid planting cucurbit or nightshade family crops in the same location each year.

> Space plants appropriately for good air circulation between them.

> Apply mulch to the soil surface to make it difficult for the spores to release up to the plant.

> Stake or cage plants to prevent foliage from contacting the soil.

> If this disease has been a problem in past growing seasons, remove the lowest leaves from your plants both at planting time and early in the season.

> Avoid overhead watering because it's important to keep plant leaves dry to decrease chances of infection. Water the soil, not the leaves.

> Don't work with the plants while they're wet.

> Wash your hands and disinfect your tools, especially if the disease is present in your garden.

> Remove and dispose of infected leaves as soon as you see them, but do not remove more than one-third of the leaves on the plant. In addition, pick up any leaves that fall off the plants as quickly as you can, to prevent spores from going into the soil.

> Keep up with the weeds since members of the same plant family can also infect your crops.

> Don't save seeds from infected plants.

> Clean up and dispose of plant debris at the end of the season; do not compost it.

> Apply biofungicide, copper fungicide, or sulfur fungicide as a preventive measure. Refer to the Organic Disease Control and Prevention Products section beginning on page 168 for more information.

SOOTY MOLD

Type: Fungal   **Caused by:** Several genera of fungi

DESCRIPTION

Have you ever noticed dark, sticky leaves on some of the plants in your garden? That is sooty mold, a fungal disease that is spread by spores. While it might look awful on your plants, it is generally not harmful to them. It is actually an indicator of an insect problem on or near the affected plants. This fungus readily grows on honeydew, which is excreted by aphids, leafhoppers, and whiteflies while they suck sap from plant leaves or stems. Those pests, as well as scales and mealybugs, also excrete honeydew on ornamental plants. If ornamental shrubs or trees (maples are particularly bad) are hanging over part of your vegetable garden, the honeydew might be dripping from them rather than initiating on the veggies themselves. Even though the fungi don't infect the plant tissues or otherwise parasitize them, they do reduce the amount of sunlight hitting the leaves, which affects their ability to conduct photosynthesis. In some instances, plants may be stunted, and heavily coated leaves may die. The bottom line is this: If you control the honeydew-secreting insects, sooty mold won't be a problem. Ants are a secondary insect problem that you might encounter. They play an interesting role in the lives of the above insects. Ants protect them from predators because they want to feed on their honeydew. This means you will need to deal with them to get the problem under control. Sooty mold is typically present during warm, dry conditions, and the fungal spores spread by splashing water and in the air.

Sooty mold looks quite startling on vegetable plants.

CROPS MOST COMMONLY IMPACTED:

Artichokes, beets, cabbage family crops (arugula, broccoli, Brussels sprouts, cabbage, cauliflower, collards, kale, kohlrabi, mustard, radishes, rutabagas, turnips), corn, cucurbit family crops (cucumbers, melons, pumpkins, summer and winter squash), legume family crops (beans, peas), lettuce, nightshade family crops (eggplants, peppers, potatoes, tomatoes)

WHAT TO LOOK FOR

Sticky leaves; leaves covered with dark green or black dots or a film; stunted plants

ORGANIC STRATEGIES

> Keep your vegetable plants healthy because they will have fewer insect problems. Attract beneficial insects to your garden.

> Gently wipe off the leaves and/or fruits with a damp cloth. For a thicker buildup of sooty mold, use a mixture of very mild soap and water. The fruits will still be edible.

> If you aren't able to remove the sooty mold from your plants, you can prune off the damaged leaves, provided there will be enough foliage remaining to conduct photosynthesis.

> Control sap-sucking insect pests that produce honeydew (aphids, leafhoppers, whiteflies) by using organic products such as diatomaceous earth, insecticidal soaps, kaolin clay, Neem, plant extracts, or pyrethrins. You also can use physical barriers such as floating row cover to protect plants; remove it when plants begin blooming to allow for pollination. Sticky traps work well on leafhoppers and whiteflies.

> If ants are present in large numbers, control them by using organic methods such as barriers or organic products.

> Prune overhanging shrub and tree branches.

Aphids are one type of insect that excretes honeydew.

Whiteflies also excrete honeydew.

SOUTHERN BLIGHT

Type: Fungal   **Caused by:** *Sclerotinium rolfsii*

DESCRIPTION

Southern blight also goes by the names of Southern wilt and Southern stem rot. While this disease is commonly known for affecting tomato plants, it has a wide range of plant hosts: over 500 species within more than 100 plant families! This makes crop rotation as a control method very difficult, although corn is considered resistant to the disease. Southern blight is prevalent in regions that experience extended periods of hot, humid weather. The fungi also are more active in acidic soils. They overwinter in the top 3 inches (8 cm) of the soil and on plant debris for many years. They survive on decaying organic matter and are spread by infected soil and plant debris. The fungus does not produce spores. Infection occurs where plant tissue contacts contaminated soil. What is especially disturbing is that the sclerotia will grow across the soil surface to infect a plant. Southern blight starts at a plant's roots and crown and then moves up the stem. Similar diseases of tomatoes include Bacterial wilt (page 110), Fusarium wilt (page 126), and Verticillium wilt (page 152).

Southern blight causes lesions at the base of tomato plants. Eventually, the entire plant is affected.

CROPS MOST COMMONLY IMPACTED:

Beans, beets, carrots, cucurbit family crops (primarily melons and pumpkins), nightshade family crops (eggplants, peppers, potatoes, tomatoes), onions

WHAT TO LOOK FOR

(*Note: The presence of sclerotia is the primary way to identify Southern blight.*) Dark lesion on stem at soil surface, which usually girdles it; stems or entire plants suddenly wilt, fall over, and die; thin, white mold (mycelia) on stem and nearby soil that is soon covered with small (1/16 to 1/8 inch [0.2 to 0.3 cm]) brown sclerotia that look like small seeds. Fruits rot on undersides if they are touching the soil.

Beets

Yellow, wilting leaves; rotting lesions on their fleshy root.

Carrots

Taproot is decayed at soil surface; yellow, wilting leaves.

Onions

Bulbs are stunted and soft; leaves turn yellow.

The presence of sclerotia (resting fungal structures) is the most definitive way to identify Southern blight.

This tomato plant is wilting from the damage caused by Southern blight.

ORGANIC STRATEGIES

> Adjust acidic soil pH to 7 by adding lime. This will prevent the sclerotia from germinating.

> Plant susceptible crops earlier to avoid ideal conditions for fungal development.

> If Southern blight has been a problem in the past, apply an organic fungicide prior to planting as a preventive measure.

> Use a plastic sheet mulch, rather than organic mulch, to create a barrier between the soil and the plants. Another option is to wrap the lowest 2 to 3 inches (5 to 8 cm) of the stem with aluminum foil.

> Keep up with the weeds to eliminate alternate hosts.

> Remove and dispose of infected plants right away, along with about 6 inches (15 cm) of soil surrounding the roots. If you see any white mycelia attached to the soil or mulch, remove them as well. Do not compost the debris because the sclerotia are resistant to the average temperature of compost piles. Be careful where you put the soil; it shouldn't be placed anywhere within your vegetable garden.

> Solarize your soil during peak summer temperatures for two to four weeks. Refer to page 163 for more information.

VEGETABLE PLANT DISEASE GUIDE

TOBACCO MOSAIC VIRUS

Type: Viral

Caused by: Tobacco mosaic virus (TMV)

DESCRIPTION

In the mid-1800s, tobacco mosaic virus was a serious problem for European tobacco farmers. At that time, only bacteria and fungi had been identified by scientists. Dutch microbiologist Martinus Beijerinck was able to isolate the virus in the late-1800s. Unfortunately, identifying it hasn't solved the problem: Tobacco mosaic virus remains a significant concern for farmers and gardeners all over the world because there is no cure for the plants infected with it. The disease affects over 350 species, including tobacco and other nightshade family crops, as well as many ornamental plants. While the virus only multiplies within a living cell, it can remain in infected plant debris in a dormant state for up to 50 years. The virus enters a plant through tiny wounds and then systematically infects all parts of the plant. Tobacco mosaic virus is spread by contaminated seeds, plant sap, tools, hands, and infected soil where the disease was present. Tobacco products made from infected plant material can contain both tobacco mosaic virus and tomato mosaic virus (ToMV). The virus transmits through plant sap and persists for a very long time. It even survives on plant supports. The virus is not transmitted by sap-sucking insects such as aphids, leafhoppers, or thrips, although grasshoppers and caterpillars might spread it through their chewing activities. Heirloom tomatoes are more susceptible to tobacco mosaic virus. You might need to consult an educational institution with a horticultural program for a definitive diagnosis since it's hard to identify the virus by the plant's symptoms alone. Tobacco mosaic virus and tomato mosaic virus (refer to Mosaic Virus profile on page 136) are in the same family, but each is caused by a different virus.

CROPS MOST COMMONLY IMPACTED:

Beets, cucurbit family crops (cucumbers, melons, pumpkins, squash), lettuce, nightshade family crops (eggplants, peppers, potatoes, tomatillos, tomatoes)

WHAT TO LOOK FOR

(*Note: Symptoms also can look like herbicide damage; examine the plant carefully and look for the symptoms listed here.*) Leaves with light and dark green mottling; distorted or small leaves; stunted plants; few if any fruits; undersized fruits. Tomato fruits may have sunken lesions.

Tobacco mosaic virus on a squash plant.

Tomato plants infected with tobacco mosaic virus have mottled leaves.

Tomato fruits have sunken lesions.

ORGANIC STRATEGIES

> Look for resistant varieties. Refer to the Vegetable Disease Resistance Abbreviations chart on page 166.

> Inspect new seedlings closely for symptoms before bringing them home.

> If you have dealt with this disease in the past, do not plant susceptible crops in the same location.

> Monitor your plants regularly for any signs of this virus throughout the season.

> Wash your hands well after using tobacco products; avoid using these products in your garden. Be aware that your clothing may carry the virus as well.

> Disinfect tools in between working with plants. Refer to the Organic Strategies Explained section (page 164) to learn the best practices for this.

> Keep up with the weeds in and around your garden as they might be alternate hosts for this virus.

> Remove infected plants immediately and dispose of them and any other infected plant debris; do not compost them.

> Disinfect all plant supports that touched infected plant material.

TOMATO SPOTTED WILT VIRUS

Type: Viral

Caused by: Tomato spotted wilt virus (TSWV)

DESCRIPTION

With a name like tomato spotted wilt virus, you would think it only affects tomatoes, right? You'll be surprised to learn the various strains of this virus affect over 1,000 plant species, including other vegetable crops, fruits, and ornamentals. Even weeds are alternate plant hosts. How does it get in our gardens? The pathogens, which exist in plant sap, arrive on new seedlings or plants. This virus thrives in greenhouse settings, which has the potential to impact greenhouse-grown vegetable starts. It isn't spread by seeds. The pathogens are transmitted by several species of thrips while they are feeding. They become infected as larvae and can transmit the virus throughout their life span. Thrips are the only known insect vector of tomato spotted wilt virus and they can appear from neighboring gardens. Because thrips are so mobile, crop rotation isn't a viable option. There is no cure for tomato spotted wilt virus. This disease is similar in appearance to Early blight (page 124).

CROPS MOST COMMONLY IMPACTED:

Beans, celery, cucumbers, lettuce, nightshade family crops (eggplants, peppers, potatoes, tomatoes), spinach

WHAT TO LOOK FOR

(*Note: Symptoms tend to be unique to each host and vary depending on the age of the plant when it was infected.*)

Beans
Bronzing of leaves, stem lesions, stunted plants.

Celery
Yellow blotches, dead patches, and concentric rings on leaves.

Cucumbers
Yellow leaves; stunted plants.

Eggplants
Bronzing of leaves, tip dieback, leaves cup downward, fruits have pale spots with concentric rings.

Lettuce
Dark brown or dead spots on leaves; distorted leaves; stunted plants.

Peppers
Sudden yellowing of leaves; necrotic long streaks on stems; fruits have dead streaks and spots; dead fruits.

Potatoes
Yellow or brown spots; dead ringspots with pale halos; distorted leaves; tubers have ringspots and discoloration.

Spinach
Yellow leaves with necrotic spots; stunted growth.

Tomatoes
Bronzing of leaves; tip dieback; dark streaks on leaves and petioles; leaves cup downward; stunted growth; immature fruits have light green rings with raised centers; mature fruits have orange and red rings.

Tomato fruits infected with this disease have a bizarre appearance.

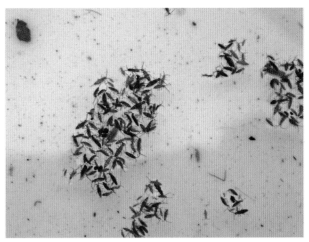

Thrips are the only known insect vector of tomato spotted wilt virus. I trapped some thrips and put them into a bucket of soapy water so you can see what they look like.

ORGANIC STRATEGIES

> Look for resistant varieties, if available.

> Grow your own plants from seed. If you decide to purchase seedlings, inspect them closely for any signs of disease or thrips first.

> Prior to planting, cover the bed with a sheet of reflective plastic mulch. Thrips have difficulty finding the plants because it is so reflective.

> Monitor your garden regularly for thrips and signs of this disease.

> Control thrips in your garden through the use of blue sticky traps, insecticidal soap, Neem, or spinosad.

> Keep up with the weeds in and around your garden as they are alternate hosts for both the disease and thrips.

> As soon as you diagnose the problem, remove and dispose of infected plants immediately.

This tomato plant has tip dieback from tomato spotted wilt virus.

VERTICILLIUM WILT

Type: Fungal

Caused by: *Verticillium dahliae, V. albo-atrum*

DESCRIPTION

This soilborne fungus gains access through a plant's roots and then spreads throughout its vascular system. It infects the seeds as well. The most common signs—yellowing leaves and wilting—typically appear after the plant has set fruit. Verticillium wilt is more prevalent in cool, wet soil and remains in the soil for many years. The fungus also survives on plant debris and on weed hosts. Note that nightshade family crops are most severely impacted by this disease. Asparagus, beans, lettuce, and peas are resistant to Verticillium wilt, and corn is immune to it. Be aware that two insect pests cause damage that is similar in appearance on cucumbers, melons, pumpkins, and squash. Because of this, it's important to do a bit of sleuthing to determine whether you are dealing with damaging pests or a disease. Cucumber beetles are about ¼ inch (0.6 cm) in length and have yellow-and-black stripes or are yellow with black spots. Adult squash vine borers are red-and-black moths. Their inch (2 cm)-long, white larvae tunnel through the stems of the above host plants, causing leaves to turn yellow and vines to wilt and die. Look for puncture holes near the base of the plant's main stem or cut into an affected stem to look for larvae.

CROPS MOST COMMONLY IMPACTED:

Beet family crops (beets, spinach), cabbage family crops (arugula, broccoli, Brussels sprouts, cabbage, cauliflower, collards, kale, kohlrabi, mustard, radishes, rutabagas, turnips), celery, cucurbit family crops (cucumbers, melons, pumpkins, squash), nightshade family crops (eggplants, peppers, potatoes, tomatoes)

WHAT TO LOOK FOR

Stunted plants; V-shaped lesions on leaves that are wider at the leaf margins; yellow leaves that roll inward; stems wilt, causing the leaves to droop; vascular system has dark coloration; leaves wilt and die; plants die prematurely; this disease can initially impact one side of a plant, but it eventually kills the entire plant.

These tomato plants are infected with Verticillium wilt.

The vascular tissue of plants with this disease will exhibit dark discoloration.

V-shaped lesions, such as this one seen on an eggplant leaf, are a typical symptom.

ORGANIC STRATEGIES

> Look for resistant varieties of susceptible crops.
> Plant short-season varieties because you will be more likely to get a crop.
> Plant warm-season crops well after the danger of frost has passed, when the soil and air temperatures are warm.
> Remove the debris of any infected crops and dispose of it; do not compost it.
> Disinfect tools in between use. Refer to the Organic Strategies Explained section (page 164) to learn the best practices for this.
> You can keep infected plants going for a while by fertilizing and watering them, but they will die prematurely.

> Keep up with the weeds in and around your garden to eliminate or reduce potential host plants.
> If this disease has been prevalent in your garden, consider solarizing your soil (see page 163).
> Use a longer crop rotation (four years or more) and avoid following an infected crop with a potentially susceptible crop. Remember that nightshade family crops are particularly problematic.
> Plant cover crops to increase microorganism activity in your soil, thereby decreasing pathogens.

VEGETABLE PLANT DISEASE GUIDE

153

WHITE MOLD

Type: Fungal   **Caused by:** *Sclerotinia sclerotiorum*

DESCRIPTION

White mold is a soil fungus that affects over 400 species in many plant families, including vegetable crops, ornamental plants, and weeds. It is also referred to as Sclerotinia stem rot, Sclerotinia white mold, and watery soft rot. The fungi overwinter as black sclerotia in the soil and on plant debris for up to ten years. Under cool, moist conditions, the sclerotia germinate in the soil and develop special cup-shaped structures, called apothecia, that expel millions of spores. The spores, which live for two weeks, can be spread by plant-to-plant contact, insects, rain, or the wind. Wet conditions caused by heavy dew or the leaves remaining wet for prolonged periods of time will help the spores attack a host plant. The spores primarily germinate on plant wounds and older tissue such as a flower or leaf because they provide nutrients. The fungi grow into healthy plant tissue where they infect the main stem of a plant, which girdles and kills the plant. At that point, white mycelia appear on the stems or soil surface and more sclerotia develop both on and inside the dead plant tissue. If you look closely, sclerotia are usually black or brown, oblong structures that are similar in appearance to mouse droppings. It is important to note that the seeds of a plant can become contaminated by either the sclerotia or mycelia of the fungus.

WHAT TO LOOK FOR

Water-soaked lesions on stems and pods; the leaves on a single stem all die; sudden wilting or premature death of plant; masses of white, threadlike mycelia on stems or soil surface; white to black sclerotia in stem or within mold; plant leaves or flowers rot; fruits rot

White mold on bean pods.

CROPS MOST COMMONLY IMPACTED:

Cabbage family crops (arugula, broccoli, Brussels sprouts, cabbage, cauliflower, collards, kale, kohlrabi, radish, rutabagas, turnips), carrot family crops (carrots, celery, parsnips), cucurbit family crops (cucumbers, melons, pumpkins, squash), legume family crops (beans, peas), nightshade family crops (peppers, potatoes, tomatoes)

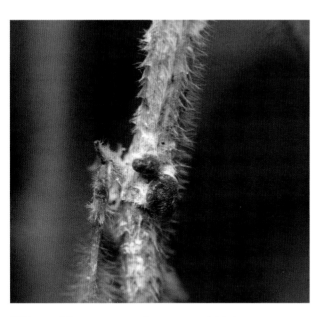

White mold on a tomato plant stem, which is accompanied by black sclerotia.

White mold on a broccoli seedling.

ORGANIC STRATEGIES

> Look for disease-resistant varieties.

> Soil should be well-drained; add compost to improve drainage, if necessary.

> Space plants appropriately to provide good air circulation around them.

> Stake or cage large plants so their foliage or fruits don't contact the soil.

> Don't overfertilize your crops with high-nitrogen fertilizers. Spores will be attracted to the lush growth.

> Avoid overhead watering, and time the watering of susceptible plants so the leaves will dry off quickly.

> Monitor your garden regularly for any signs of white mold infection.

> Remove leaves, flowers, or plants that die naturally to eliminate some of the plant tissue that most commonly gets infected first.

> Keep up with the weeds to eliminate alternate hosts for the fungus.

> Remove and dispose of infected plant material immediately.

> Clean up plant debris at the end of the season to eliminate potential host material for sclerotia.

> Consider solarizing your soil to kill the fungi (see page 163).

> Apply biofungicide or copper fungicide as a preventive measure.

VEGETABLE PLANT DISEASE GUIDE

ROOT-KNOT NEMATODES

While the focus of this chapter is on vegetable diseases, it's important to include a discussion about root-knot nematodes. Why? The damage they cause to the root systems of our crops provides pathogenic bacteria and fungi with entry points into the plants.

Don't confuse root-knot nematodes with beneficial nematodes. The latter are very helpful in controlling damaging insect pests during the soil-dwelling part of their life cycles.

Root-knot nematodes are microscopic roundworms that use their stylets (tubelike mouthparts) to pierce roots. The chemicals they secrete cause root galls, which are rounded swellings. This damage disrupts the root's ability to take up water and nutrients from the soil. Common symptoms of root-knot nematode activity include stunted or wilting plants and yellow foliage.

The life cycle of these damaging nematodes is quite interesting. The eggs overwinter in the soil. After hatching, they go through several different stages. Juvenile nematodes move through the soil, searching for plant roots. After molting a few times, they reach the adult stage. Males move throughout the soil, but females remain within a root. After feeding and enlarging, the females lay eggs in the soil to start the cycle all over again. Root-knot nematodes are spread throughout a garden via contaminated plant roots and infested soil.

The ideal soil temperature range for root-knot nematode activity is 70°F to 85°F (21°C to 29°C). They are not active when the soil temperature drops below 60°F (16°C). Because of this, early-season crops tend not to be bothered by them. Once root-knot nematodes are inside plant roots, there is nothing you can do.

Because nematodes are so tiny, one needs either a microscope or the assistance of a lab to definitively detect their presence. At harvest time, it's important to closely examine the roots for galls so you can devise a strategy for controlling them in future plantings.

Here are some control methods. For better success, use more than one method:

> Practice crop rotation. Don't plant susceptible crops in the same place where you've had problems before.
> Select resistant varieties if they're available. Look for an "N" or "NEM" after the variety's name. It's also possible to alternate plantings of resistant and susceptible crops so the latter will sustain less damage. These crops aren't good hosts for the nematodes: asparagus, corn, garlic, onions, and shallots. Tomatoes, okra, and lima beans are more susceptible.
> Don't overwater the soil as this makes it easier for the nematodes to move about.
> Continue adding organic matter to your soil. This will improve plant health and attract beneficial microorganisms that will parasitize the eggs of root-knot nematodes and feed on other stages of them as well.

Root-knot nematodes are microscopic roundworms.

> Keep up with the weeds in your garden because their roots are also hosts for root-knot nematodes.

> Repeatedly rototill the infested garden soil. This will damage the plant roots remaining in the soil and expose root-knot nematodes to the air. I don't ordinarily recommend disturbing garden soil because this practice damages the important layers created by beneficial microorganisms, but this is a strategy for bad infestations of the nematodes.

> Plant a cover crop of French marigolds (*Tagetes patula*) as a trap crop. The nematodes enter the root system but aren't able to complete their life cycle, so they die without reproducing. Plant the marigolds closely and leave them in place for two months before pulling them, roots and all, and disposing of them.

> Clean up plant debris immediately after harvest and dispose of it.

> Consider soil solarization. Refer to page 163 for details.

Root-knot nematode damage to vegetable plant roots.

ORGANIC STRATEGIES EXPLAINED

CONTAINER GARDENING TO PREVENT PLANT DISEASES

Gardeners grow vegetable crops in containers for many reasons: They might not have a sunny spot for a traditional in-ground garden, they're limited on space because they only have a balcony or a patio, or they want to have their veggies closer to the kitchen. While these are great reasons, there's one more worth noting: If you deal with certain soilborne plant diseases every year, container gardening is a way to protect your vegetables from them.

This works for two reasons: You clean and sterilize the pots first and then fill them with a soilless potting mix, which won't contain any pathogens. If you believe your garden soil contains pathogens, but you don't

have anywhere else to put containers, you still can grow veggies in that spot. Just place a barrier of plastic mulch or landscape fabric over the soil surface and set your pots on it. The barrier will prevent pathogens from moving up from the soil and into the containers.

Even though I haven't had to deal with many soilborne pathogens, I enjoy growing my potato crop in several large pots and cloth grow bags each year. The potatoes do really well and they are so easy to harvest. In the summer, I can easily reach down into the potting soil to pull out a few new potatoes and, at the end of the season, I upend the containers and quickly gather all the tubers. Growing vegetables in containers is a great way to expand your garden without having to dig up a larger area or build more raised beds.

Growing vegetables in containers is a great way to protect them from soilborne pathogens and expand the footprint of your garden.

I have good success with growing potatoes in cloth grow bags and large containers.

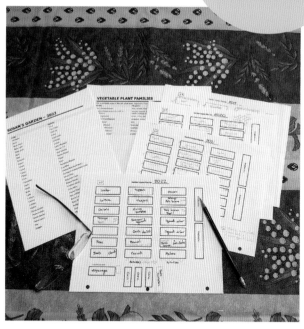

Crop rotation is a useful tool for reducing or eliminating plant diseases in your garden. It requires some record-keeping and a little forethought each year as you decide on the planting layout.

CROP ROTATION

I mentioned crop rotation as a strategy in many of the disease profiles because it is a simple way to give your plants some insurance against having disease issues.

Crop rotation isn't just for farmers. It is important for home gardeners, too. The concept involves keeping track of where you have planted each crop in your vegetable garden during the previous three years or so. When you're ready to lay out your next garden, carefully choose where you are going to grow them to ensure they aren't planted in the same location year after year.

Many years back, I created a template on my computer that represents each of the raised beds in my garden. Every year, I fill in where I've planted each crop and save the record in a binder. Why is this so important? Let's look at an example.

Nightshade family crops (eggplants, peppers, potatoes, tomatillos, and tomatoes) are susceptible to quite a few diseases. If you plant them in the same beds each year, you run the risk of perpetuating disease problems.

When deciding where you want to plant your tomatoes, look carefully at your previous planting layouts and choose a location where none of the nightshade family crops has grown for the past three years. Repeat this method when deciding where to put cucurbit family crops, legume family crops, onion family crops, and so on. This is a simple tool that is well worth the small amount of time it takes to keep good records.

If you have a tiny garden, you can engage in a downsized version of crop rotation. Consider alternating between growing plants in the ground and growing them in containers filled with a soilless potting mix. You can locate the pots in another area of your landscape or, if you don't have room but believe your soil is contaminated with pathogens, put a barrier underneath them as described on page 158. This will help you avoid or, at least, minimize soilborne diseases. If neither of these is an option, look for disease-resistant varieties of the crops you love to grow. (There is a Vegetable Disease Resistance Abbreviations chart on page 166.)

DISEASE IDENTIFICATION TOOLS

If you're feeling overwhelmed by the number of potential vegetable plant diseases, rest assured that you have several options for identifying them.

First, a magnifying glass and your cell phone camera are useful tools. Both enable you to closely examine plant tissue that looks out of the ordinary. For example, you might notice a fuzzy mold or spots on the leaves. By enlarging what you're seeing with the naked eye, you'll be able to list the signs and symptoms, and get closer to a diagnosis. If you really want to get into looking closely at plant parts and bugs, microscopes are very handy tools to have. Oftentimes, you can pick up a used compound microscope for a reasonable price or contact someone who will let you look at your samples on theirs.

There are also phone apps designed specifically for identifying plant diseases. Some are free while others charge a fee. I've listed some in the Resources section on page 217.

You'll find a wealth of resources on the web, but there's a secret to locating reliable, research-based information from educational sites. Let's say you want to know more about powdery mildew. When you type in those words, add a space and then type "site=edu" (like this: powdery mildew site=edu). This phrase will refine your search, so the first results always come from dependable sources.

Educational institutions that have horticultural programs can help you identify a plant disease. To prepare a sample, provide them with fresh plant tissue. Seal the sample inside a plastic bag or jar to avoid spreading disease pathogens. Include information on what the plant is, where it came from, when you planted it, when you started noticing a problem, and any recent changes in your garden that are noteworthy. Photos of the specific problem and of the entire plant are always helpful.

Helpful disease-identification tools include a magnifying glass, microscope, cell phone camera, plant disease apps, reference books, and online resources.

Intercropping involves planting more than one type of crop together to make it more difficult for damaging pests to find their host plants. An example of this technique is seen at the Eden Project in Cornwall, England.

Mulches impede weed growth, help the soil retain moisture, and reduce the spread of pathogens onto plants. Grass clippings from a lawn that hasn't been treated with herbicides make an excellent mulch.

DISPOSAL OF INFECTED PLANT DEBRIS

In the disease profiles, I emphasized the importance of removing diseased plants and fruits from the garden. There's no point in perpetuating pathogens within any parts of the plant. It's not a good idea to add that plant material to your compost pile. Why not? Most compost piles do not generate enough heat evenly throughout them to kill pathogens. Compost piles need to remain between 131°F and 170°F (55°C and 77°C), and also go through a months-long "curing" process in order to kill both pathogens and weed seeds.

To be safe, take a bag to the site of the diseased plants. Carefully pull them up and seal them inside the bag and then dispose of them. Carrying or dragging the plant material throughout your garden on the way to the trash will likely spread infectious spores and cells.

INTERCROPPING

Intercropping is a useful strategy that makes it more challenging for disease-spreading insects to find their target crop. When you plant more than one type of crop together, the pest is less likely to visit the planting. I mentioned this in the beet curly top virus profile (page 112) because beet leafhoppers are vectors for this worrisome disease. Through observation, scientists have learned that these pests are attracted to well-spaced plantings where their target crop contrasts well with its surroundings. Take advantage of that insight by planting more than one type of crop together to disguise the target crop. Throughout this chapter, I have underscored the importance of following proper spacing guidelines to create good air circulation around the plants, making it more difficult for pathogens to spread. But in this instance, your strategy might be to plant two or more diverse crops together in tight spacing, so the targeted plants don't stand out. Because leafhoppers are very challenging to control, I feel it's important to give you as many options as possible.

MULCHING MATERIALS

When plant foliage and fruits come into direct contact with contaminated soil, it's very easy for pathogens to infect the plant. In addition, when water splashes soil up onto the leaves, this spreads disease. If you place a thick layer of mulch on the soil surface, it will dramatically cut down on the chances of either happening.

The most commonly used mulching materials include compost, shredded leaves or newspapers, and grass clippings from a lawn that has not been treated with herbicides. There is one other type of mulch called plastic sheet mulch. While I don't like to recommend the use of extra plastic in our gardens, some plant diseases warrant a more impervious mulch to prevent the spread of pathogens.

Just as its name implies, this type of mulch is made from a plastic material and usually comes in rolls. If you have soaker hoses or a drip irrigation system, place them on the surface of the bed first. Trim the plastic mulch to the dimensions of the top of the bed, put it in place, and use either metal pins or some type of weights to prevent it from blowing away. On planting day, cut a small "X" through which you will plant each seedling. If your irrigation system is underneath the plastic, your plants should get all the water they need. If you have an overhead watering system, be sure to check the soil moisture regularly; you may need to give some supplemental water to your plants so they develop properly.

There is another type of sheet mulch that I mentioned in some of the disease profiles. It is called reflective plastic mulch or metallic plastic mulch. Its purpose is to make it difficult for insects to locate certain types of plants, especially while they are young and susceptible to damage. This is particularly useful since several diseases are spread by insects that are challenging to control. These include aphids, flea beetles, leafhoppers, thrips, and whiteflies. The highly reflective nature of this sheet mulch essentially hides the plants from them, which allows young seedlings to get off to a very healthy start. Later in the season when their foliage covers the majority of the surface of the sheet mulch, insects will be able to find them, but, by that time, the plants are strong and less easy to damage.

The downside to using plastic mulches is that they aren't environmentally friendly, due to the manufacturing process and the difficulty of disposing of them later. I would consider the use of plastic mulches to be more of a last resort. You will need to look at all the options listed in the disease profiles and determine which ones will meet your needs.

PLANT SUPPORTS: WHAT WORKS BEST?

There are two very good reasons for providing vegetable plants with support:

1. They provide growing plants and fruits with good air circulation and increased sunlight.

2. Plant foliage won't be in contact with the soil, which decreases their risk of exposure to soil-dwelling pathogens.

You will find helpful information on choosing plant supports and some fun ways to grow vining crops in chapter 1, starting on page 16.

PURCHASING AND SHARING SEEDLINGS

There is absolutely nothing wrong with purchasing seedlings from a nursery, greenhouse, or plant sale. Smart gardeners know it's their responsibility to examine their purchases closely for signs of disease or insects before taking them home. It's not uncommon for me to hear from gardeners who never had a problem with a certain insect or disease until they brought home some new plants. To save yourself a lot of grief later, take the time to check the leaves, stems, and even the roots of each plant. Do you see any eggs or tiny insects, such as aphids? Are the leaves yellow, puckered, or covered with spots? What about signs of mold? If you see any of these, don't buy the plant!

We gardeners are a generous lot. We enjoying starting plants from seed and sharing them with friends,

If you'd like to grow potatoes, start with seed potatoes that are certified to be disease-free. At planting time, leave the potatoes whole so there is less chance of them rotting or being exposed to soilborne pathogens.

The soil solarization process kills pathogens, insect eggs, root-knot nematodes, and weed seeds.

neighbors, and other gardeners. Before passing those plant babies along to others, make sure you're not sharing an insect or disease problem with them as well. Keep an eye on how the seedlings are developing, and if you suspect a problem, don't pass it along.

SEED POTATOES

If you'd like to grow potatoes, it's very important to start with seed potatoes that are certified to be disease-free. You can find them at garden centers and online sources. When you think about how many diseases potatoes can get, why not get them off to the best possible start?

It's common practice to cut large seed potatoes into chunks, where each one contains at least two "eyes" (these are where the sprouts will emerge). They are allowed to dry for one to two days before being planted to reduce the chance that they'll rot or be

exposed to pathogens. Even with these precautions, pathogens can still attack the exposed raw edges, so I have switched to what I believe is a better method. Instead of purchasing large seed potatoes, I buy small, undamaged ones and plant them whole. This has eliminated the risks, and even though I start with small seed potatoes, the plants always produce full-sized tubers for me.

SOIL SOLARIZATION

In a few of the disease profiles, I suggested solarizing your soil as an organic strategy. But what is soil solarization and why should you be interested in it as an option? Soil solarization involves heating up your soil to kill disease pathogens, insect eggs, root-knot nematodes, and weed seeds. That sounds pretty great, although the downside is that you'll need to take all or part of your garden out of production during the peak of summer to accomplish it.

This process will take about six weeks during peak summertime temperatures. Start by removing plant debris and weeds from the area of your garden that you wish to treat. Water the soil until it is saturated with moisture. Cover the area with a sheet of clear plastic and either bury the perimeter in the soil or securely weigh down the edges to form a good seal. Leave the plastic in place for four to six weeks and then remove it.

Soil solarization is most effective on heavy soils because they retain moisture longer. The combined action of the sun's warmth and moisture will actually produce a steam heat that will kill off your soilborne enemies. Because moisture runs through sandy soils much more quickly, this technique isn't as effective. One solution is to place soaker hoses or drip irrigation lines underneath the plastic so you can remoisten the soil every day without disturbing the sheet.

A negative consequence of soil solarization is that the process will kill beneficial microorganisms. If you decide to use this method, add soil activators that contain beneficial bacteria and fungi once the process is complete.

STERILIZE AND SANITIZE TOOLS AND EQUIPMENT

Disinfecting the tools you use on and around your plants is a very effective way of reducing the spread of disease. Because the majority of garden tools—pruners, trowels, and cultivators, for example—have metal parts, what you use to clean them is very important.

Some gardeners use a bleach solution for this, but I cannot recommend it. Bleach will pit the metal, leaving small pockets that pathogens can attach to. Bleach also causes metal to rust. In addition, if you splash some on your clothing or skin, that's not good either.

Save your bleach for other sterilizing tasks—more on that in a moment—and reach for something that is much safer to handle and better for those tools. Rubbing alcohol, which is officially known as 70 percent isopropyl alcohol, is an antiseptic that is very inexpensive and easy to come by. It isn't corrosive, but it will sterilize your tools. Remember that it is flammable, however. Hand sanitizer is another readily available option that is safe to use on metal surfaces. If there is soil or other debris on your tools, be sure to wash that off with water first, dry off the metal surfaces and then proceed to the sterilization step.

By sterilizing your pruners or other garden tools, you will reduce the spread of disease in your garden.

When making pruning cuts or removing infected tissue from a plant, it's a good idea to sterilize your pruners in between cuts. To do this, keep a small container of rubbing alcohol or hand sanitizer and a dry rag close at hand. Dip the blades into the sanitizing solution and dry them off before the next cut so the solution won't come into direct contact with plant tissue.

When should you use bleach? It is ideal for sterilizing your seed-starting equipment, such as planting flats and inserts, and for cleaning plastic or ceramic pots and other containers—provided they aren't metal, of course. This step is so important for preventing Damping-off disease (page 122), which is caused by several genera of fungi that can quickly kill off your seedlings. Use a stiff brush to remove any remnants of potting media or soil from previous plantings. Fill a large bucket or other container with a 10 percent bleach solution, which is one part bleach and nine parts water. Soak your equipment in it for about thirty minutes, rinse it off, and let it dry. At that point, you can plant in the planting flats and inserts or store the containers for the next season.

VEGETABLE CROP SPACING

It's so important to give your plants plenty of room to grow and not just because they'll be more productive. When there is good airflow around each plant, it will be more difficult for diseases to spread. You will find additional information on this simple strategy as well as a chart of spacing guidelines for vegetable crops in chapter 1 on page 14.

VEGETABLE DISEASE RESISTANCE ABBREVIATIONS

Choosing resistant varieties of vegetables is one way to eliminate or reduce disease issues in your garden. This is a worthwhile strategy if you deal with certain diseases year after year. Seed suppliers have a coding system that indicates which diseases a variety is resistant to. Watch for them when you are shopping for seeds at garden centers, in seed catalogs, or from online sources. See chart of those abbreviations for the applicable diseases in this chapter on page 166.

WATERING METHODS

The method you use for watering your plants can have a big impact on whether they will be susceptible to diseases. Drip irrigation systems and soaker hoses are the two most efficient methods. That's because both are placed on the soil surface, so the water goes right to the root systems. The foliage will stay dry and disease pathogens will not be able to use your irrigation water to move into the plants.

I realize that these two watering methods aren't always an option, so here are a few suggestions:

> If you need to hand-water your plants, consider purchasing a water wand. They aren't expensive and will allow you to water the soil at the base of your plants without having to bend over.

> When overhead watering is your only choice, water at a time of day when the leaves will dry off quickly. Diseases spread easily when foliage remains wet for several hours.

> If you have a sprinkler system, be diligent about placing a layer of mulch on the soil surface to reduce the chance of water splashing up onto the leaves. It will be well worth your time!

DISEASE NAME	VEGETABLE DISEASE RESISTANCE ABBREVIATIONS
Alternaria leaf spot	ALB (Alternaria leaf blight) or AB (Alternaria blight)
Anthracnose	AN
Bacterial blight	BB, HB (Halo blight)
Bacterial leaf spot	BLS
Bacterial wilt	B or BW
Beet curly top virus	CTM (Curly top beet mosaic virus) or CTV (curly top virus)
Black rot	BR
Buckeye rot	PC (Phytophthora blight on peppers)
Cercospora leaf spot	CE (Cercospora leaf spot), C (Cercospora blight), or CLB (Cercospora leaf blight)
Corn smut	S*
Early blight	EB
Fusarium wilt	F or FW

DISEASE NAME	VEGETABLE DISEASE RESISTANCE ABBREVIATIONS
Late blight	LB, TLB (Tuber late blight, potato)
Mildew, downy	DM
Mildew, powdery	PM
Mosaic virus	BMV (Bean mosaic virus) or BCMV (bean common mosaic virus), CMV (cucumber mosaic virus), LMV (lettuce mosaic virus), ToMV (tomato mosaic virus), ZYMV (zucchini yellow mosaic virus), WMV (watermelon mosaic virus)
Potato scab	S* or SCAB
Rust	R or CR (common rust)
Septoria leaf spot	SLS
Tobacco mosaic virus	TMV
Tomato spotted wilt virus	TSWV
Verticillium wilt	V or VW
White mold	WM

* Both corn smut and potato scab have "S" as a disease resistance code. When shopping for sweet corn varieties that are resistant to corn smut, look for the "S" code; for scab resistance in other types of vegetables, look for "S" or "SCAB."

Note: There are also varieties that are resistant to root-knot nematodes. The resistance codes are "N" and "NEM."

WEEDING

It's a safe bet that weeding is at the bottom of all gardeners' lists of fun things to do. Despite that, weeding is really important because your plants will grow more strongly and many weeds are alternate hosts for disease pathogens. Those two reasons should provide some extra motivation for keeping up with them.

I use a couple of strategies to cut down on my weeding duties. The first involves mulching the soil surface. That makes it more difficult for pathogens to get up onto plant foliage and helps the soil retain moisture. Mulch also impedes weed growth by keeping sunlight from hitting weed seeds at the soil surface. If any weeds do sprout, the loose nature of mulch makes it very easy to pull them up.

My other strategy involves the pathways in my raised-bed vegetable garden. Each path is 3 feet (1 m) wide. When I first set up the beds, I used the topsoil from the paths (along with some organic amendments)

to fill them. I then purchased 3-foot (1 m)-wide rolls of heavy-duty landscape fabric, covered each path with it, and placed a few inches of bark mulch on top of it. It's rare when a weed pops up in a path, but when it does, it's really easy to pull up. I can weed my entire garden very quickly because I only have to focus on weeding the tops of the beds.

No matter which strategies you adopt in your own garden, make it your mission to pull a weed whenever you see it and you'll eliminate—or, at least, dramatically reduce—the amount of time you spend on this task.

I should mention that I don't advocate the use of landscape fabric within ornamental landscape beds or vegetable beds. Even though the fabric is permeable, it can interfere with the flow of water and, once the plants' roots infiltrate the fabric, it can be a nightmare to deal with. I feel comfortable using it for the pathways because I know they are permanent features of the vegetable garden.

There are two important reasons to keep wood sorrel out of your garden: They are aggressive spreaders and they are hosts for part of the life cycle of corn rust.

ORGANIC DISEASE CONTROL AND PREVENTION PRODUCTS

Prevention is the most important aspect of dealing with plant diseases. Following good cultural practices in the garden helps our vegetables stay healthy, but sometimes they need extra help from us. It's reassuring to know there are several types of organic products that prevent or control plant diseases. These include biofungicides, copper fungicides, horticultural oil, plant extracts, and sulfur fungicides. All of them are easy to find at garden centers and from online sources.

The following information will help you understand how each product works, the diseases it controls or suppresses, and how to use it. I have to warn you that the use of some products has negative ramifications.

All this information is intended to help you make the best choice when you need some additional help.

When considering a product, remember to read the label directions thoroughly. Double-check that the disease you need to control is included in the list. Read how to mix the product, when to apply and reapply it, precautionary steps you should take when working with it, and any concerns about using it in your garden.

Refer to the Resources section beginning on page 218 for suggested product sources.

Healthy and productive zucchini plants are always a joyful sight in a vegetable garden. It's good to know there are organic products that can help prevent diseases such as powdery mildew.

BIOFUNGICIDES

Biofungicides contain living microorganisms that control certain species of fungal and bacterial plant pathogens. Some of these good guys are soil-dwelling while others exist on plant foliage or within the root system. The root-dwellers create competition for the pathogens, making it difficult for them to become established. Some parasitize the pathogens by directly attacking them. Certain beneficial organisms produce antibiotics that halt the pathogens' development, or they trigger a plant's immune system so it is more resistant to fungal or bacterial attacks.

The bacterial species most commonly used in biofungicides are *Bacillus subtilis*, *B. amyloliquefaciens* strain D747, *B. licheniformis*, and *Streptomyces griseus*.

All biofungicides work best when you use them as a preventive, rather than waiting for a disease to take hold. The products can be applied as a foliar spray or a soil drench. The foliar spray is effective for diseases that infect aboveground plant parts: leaves, stems, flowers, and fruits. Root drenches allow beneficial microorganisms to colonize a plant's root zone so they can eliminate disease-carrying bacteria and fungi; use this method for diseases of roots, fleshy tubers, or parts of a plant that have been in contact with the soil. Biofungicides protect newly planted seeds and seedlings as well.

It's also possible to purchase soil activators that contain beneficial bacteria—including those listed above—as a means to improve your soil, promote healthy plant growth, and fight pathogens.

Biofungicides are not toxic to bees, birds, insects, fish, or animals. You can reapply them every seven to ten days. During humid conditions, which promote the spread of disease, it's possible to increase the potency of the spray and reapply it more frequently. You can use the products right up to the day of harvest.

Wear protective clothing and eye protection, and avoid inhaling the mist. Apply biofungicides in calm, dry weather. Do not use them near storm drains or bodies of water.

USE FOR THESE DISEASES

Alternaria leaf spot, anthracnose, bacterial blight, bacterial leaf spot, buckeye rot, Cercospora leaf spot, damping-off disease, downy mildew, early blight, gray mold, late blight, potato scab, powdery mildew, rust, Septoria leaf spot, and white mold.

Biofungicide.

COPPER FUNGICIDES

The active ingredient in copper fungicides is either copper sulfate or copper octanoate. The former is a powdered form of copper and the latter is a thick liquid that adheres well to plant foliage. These products control fungal and bacterial diseases. For copper fungicides to be most effective, they need to be applied as a preventive or as soon as you notice a fungus starting to develop.

Apply it to both surfaces of a plant's leaves. Use less product for young seedlings and more for older plants with severe disease issues or when extended rainy periods are in the forecast. Be sure to wear protective clothing, protect your eyes, and don't inhale the spray. Copper fungicides are toxic to fish and other aquatic creatures. Do not apply near storm drains or bodies of water.

When considering the use of copper fungicides, it's important to be aware of the potential for a buildup of copper toxicity within your soil. While copper is an important nutrient for vegetable crops, too much of it will stunt plants and the leaves will turn pale or blue in color. Copper toxicity also affects seed germination and adversely impacts microorganisms within the soil. To prevent this, avoid excessive use of copper fungicides, particularly by reapplying them sooner than is recommended on the label.

USE FOR THESE DISEASES

(This varies by the active ingredients in product): Alternaria leaf spot, anthracnose, bacterial blight, bacterial leaf spot, bacterial soft rot, Cercospora leaf spot, downy mildew, early blight, gray mold, powdery mildew, rust, Septoria leaf spot, and white mold.

Copper fungicide.

HORTICULTURAL OIL

Most gardeners know that horticultural oil is primarily used to control insects, such as aphids, spider mites, and scale. It works by smothering their insect eggs as well as their larval and nymphal stages. It also is used to control certain fungal diseases because it interferes with a pathogen's ability to attach to its host plant. Mineral oil is the active ingredient contained in this product.

Avoid spraying oil on young seedlings. Before applying horticultural oil to an older plant, test-spray a small area of it first to make certain it won't burn or damage the foliage. Don't spray horticultural oil in conjunction with sulfur sprays, or within two weeks of the application of sulfur, because it will burn the foliage and make the leaves drop. In addition, avoid spraying horticultural oil when temperatures are above 85°F (29°C). Choose a calm day to apply the oil, so it won't drift to other plantings.

USE FOR THESE DISEASES

Alternaria leaf spot, Cercospora leaf spot, and powdery mildew.

Horticultural oil.

PLANT EXTRACTS

Some plants produce natural chemicals that are effective at controlling both insects and diseases. Here are three noteworthy examples of extracts that will help with disease prevention and control:

GARLIC EXTRACT

While this product is primarily marketed as an insect repellent, it is also used as a preventive for powdery mildew. Commercially processed garlic extract is often mixed with cottonseed oil and corn oil. The recommendations are to start spraying susceptible seedlings as soon as they emerge from the soil and then spray every two weeks throughout the growing season. Do not spray garlic extract on flowers because this might repel bees. It's important to note that the plants you spray with this extract will not taste of garlic.

Garlic extract.

NEEM OIL

Many gardeners use Neem oil as an insecticide, but it will also control anthracnose, powdery mildew, rust, and scab. This oil is extracted from the Neem tree, which grows in Southeast Asia and India. The active ingredient is azadirachtin. Use it as a preventive by applying it to susceptible crops every seven to fourteen days until you are certain the disease isn't going to develop. You can also use the same spray schedule to control a disease that's already present. To prevent powdery mildew, apply it in midsummer and continue spraying; if you have detected powdery mildew, continue spraying to keep it from spreading. Note that Neem oil is toxic to pollinators. Do not spray it near flowers and only spray when pollinators aren't active, such as very early or late in the day. It is also harmful to fish and other aquatic organisms; avoid spraying it near bodies of water.

THYME OIL

This extract is used as a pesticide, fungicide, bactericide, and virucide. It controls pathogens by disrupting their cell membranes. You can use it as often as needed, including up to the day of harvest. Thyme oil is safe for pollinators, but it's best not to spray when they are active. It controls buckeye rot, damping-off disease, downy mildew, gray mold, late blight, and powdery mildew.

SULFUR FUNGICIDES

As you might guess, sulfur is the main ingredient in these products, although some formulations include natural compounds, such as pyrethrins. They are used as insecticides, miticides, and fungicides. In the context of disease control, use sulfur fungicides proactively before a disease is present. The products suppress and control fungi by preventing their spores from germinating.

To use one of these products, apply the spray to all areas of the plant, including new growth and the undersides of leaves. Reapply the spray every seven to ten days. You can use it up to one day before harvest.

Gardeners should be aware of several precautions and concerns about the use of sulfur fungicides. Some plant foliage is sensitive to sulfur and may be damaged by it so be sure to test-spray a few leaves two days before spraying, just to be safe. Never spray sulfur within two weeks of a horticultural oil application as it will burn the plant's leaves.

Avoid spraying during rainstorms or in temperatures that are above 90°F (32°C). Wear protective clothing, avoid inhaling the spray, and don't spray near other humans or around pets. Don't use this spray near bodies of water or when it's windy. Sulfur fungicides are toxic to amphibians, fish, mollusks, and insects.

USE FOR THESE DISEASES

Alternaria leaf spot, black rot, Cercospora leaf spot, potato scab, powdery mildew, rust, and Septoria leaf spot.

Sulfur fungicide.

It's bad enough when you have to deal with deer in your garden, but moose are even more challenging! Tall, sturdy barriers are the most effective solution for keeping them out.

3

CRITTERS IN THE GARDEN

I know I keep telling you that gardening is a joyful experience, but there is one more challenge we need to discuss: unwelcome creatures in our gardens. Some don't cause much damage so we might be willing to overlook their mischief and share a bit of our bounty with them. Others enjoy our produce just as much as we do and apparently think we planted those crops solely for them. That will not do at all.

I mentioned in the last chapter that it's important to follow the principles of Integrated Pest Management (IPM) when dealing with plant diseases. This also applies to dealing with uninvited creatures in your garden. The first step is to identify them and decide if they really are pests that warrant action. If they are, the emphasis will be on preventing them from being a problem by implementing ways to keep them away from the plants they prefer. Always use the most environmentally friendly methods and be sure to document your results just in case you have to deal with that type of pest in the future.

In this chapter, I will cover the birds and mammals that gardeners most commonly encounter. Each of the profiles includes a description of the creature and the type of environment in which you're likely to find it. I'll alert you to signs to watch for to help you identify what you're dealing with. You'll learn which plants are their favorites and find a host of organic controls and strategies that are geared toward helping you outsmart them.

This coyote decoy's original purpose was to scare the quail in my garden. It only worked for about two weeks but quickly became our neighborhood's mascot and has provided many laughs!

Scaring your problem visitor is an example of a strategy. You might accomplish this by using pinwheels, a scarecrow, animal decoys, Mylar balloons, toy snakes, and so on. If you decide to go this route, you should keep three important points in mind:

1. Plan ahead. Start scaring potential troublemakers before they discover a new food source in your garden. If you suspect a pest will eat your vegetable crops, set up your scare tactics before the growing season even begins.

2. Move your scary objects to different locations in your garden on a regular basis. Most creatures will become acclimated to them if they're always in the same spot. You don't want that to happen.

3. Above all, be creative. Find out which methods other gardeners in your area are using successfully. Think about ways to unnerve the birds and animals that visit your garden—even if they might seem silly. If nothing else, you might provide your neighbors with some amusement!

It's so important to identify the culprit you're dealing with because it will help you choose the right methods to keep them away. Start by looking for clues. These include footprints, fecal droppings, the size of bite marks, and how the plants were damaged. For example, pocket gophers typically chew on roots beneath plants and pull them down into their burrows. If your cornstalks have been damaged and knocked over, it's very unlikely a gopher is the guilty party.

Many animal visitors appear under the cover of darkness. Other than staying up late and sitting in your garden with a flashlight, how else can you identify the creature? Game cameras provide us with opportunities to see what's happening in our gardens while we are fast asleep. My husband and I purchased a game camera a few years ago and have been astounded by the number of different animals that come into our yard at night.

Basic game cameras aren't expensive. Ours is motion-activated and records still images to a memory card

This coyote visited our front yard during a nighttime snowstorm.

This white-tailed deer appears to be mugging for the game camera!

whenever the camera is triggered. The camera sits on a small tripod, which makes it easy to move to different locations. Every few days, we view the images to see who has paid us a visit. It turns out our rural landscape is very popular with deer, moose, porcupines, raccoons, rabbits, and coyotes. Even when they're up to a bit of mischief, we have so much fun watching them go about their business while they think no one is the wiser—although I've been wondering if the doe in the above right photo was aware of what was going on.

Game cameras are an effective tool to help you see what is visiting your garden and, if you're lucky, you'll catch the perpetrator in the act. You'll be even more fortunate if you also get to learn about the other animals that are not causing problems but just passing through.

ANIMAL REPELLENTS

There are many organic animal repellents, but not all of them are safe to use in the vegetable garden—so it's always important to check the label before purchasing one. These products are available at garden centers and from online sources. The active ingredients in the organic repellents that are safe to use around edible crops include one or more the following items: black pepper, capsaicin, garlic, cinnamon, aromatic herbs, plant extracts, or dried animal blood. The types of animals these products can repel include chipmunks, deer, gophers, groundhogs, mice, rabbits, raccoons, skunks, squirrels, and voles.

Repellents are most effective if they are applied before a pest has discovered that your garden is a source of food. All are applied around plantings rather than directly on plants, or around the perimeter of a vegetable plot. Be sure to read the label regarding how to apply them and to determine if there is a waiting period before harvesting your crops.

Protect birds by making a cattery for your feline friends. The structure will allow cats to be outside in a pleasant and safe environment.

WHAT ABOUT CATS?

Several of the profiles focus on rodents that can cause a lot of damage to vegetable gardens. While I realize many folks think getting a cat is the perfect solution for controlling them, it's really not a good idea. Here's why: According to the American Bird Conservancy, cats are the number one predator of birds. They estimate domestic and feral cats kill about 2.4 billion birds per year in the United States and have been directly responsible for the extinction of many bird and animal species worldwide.

While I know cats make delightful pets, having them loose outdoors puts cats at risk of injury or death from predators and vehicles driving through the neighborhood. There are two solutions for keeping cats safe and happy: Keep them indoors at all times or, even better, construct a "cattery" for them. Catteries are enclosed structures that provide cats with shelter, perches, maybe a small garden with greenery to eat, and a safe environment so they can enjoy the outside world without coming to harm. Many cat owners attach a cattery to their home and install a pet door so the cat can come indoors and go back out into its outdoor building as it pleases. Cats love these arrangements and this solution keeps birds safe.

TRAPPING, RELOCATING, OR POISONING GARDEN PESTS

As I was researching information on control methods for the smaller mammals that cause problems in gardens, one suggestion frequently surfaced: trapping pests and releasing them elsewhere. Even if this sounds appealing to you, it's important to know there are restrictions and regulations regarding this activity for very good reasons.

Introducing an animal to a different locale will likely upset the balance of that environment. If the animal is diseased, it could spread that disease to healthy animals. The relocated pest won't be familiar with the area so it may have difficulty finding food and shelter. Animals of the same species at the new location will look upon them as a territorial threat and fight with them, or even kill them. Another possibility is that the trapped animal left behind a den of babies somewhere that will starve.

In areas where trapping and relocating animals is permitted, it's always recommended as a last resort. Gardeners should do their best to eliminate the things that are attracting a pest in the first place and set up barriers to keep it away from the garden or structures. Most of the time, that's all that is needed.

When dealing with destructive rodents, sometimes it's necessary to use commercially available kill traps to control the problem. Always contact your regional wildlife or animal control agency to find out what your options are. They will let you know what is legally allowed and can put you in contact with licensed wildlife removal specialists who can resolve the problem for you with the proper equipment.

Poisoning might seem like a quick fix, but the use of poisons should be avoided. Let's say you're having a problem with rats. You head to the store and find poison bait that is supposed to kill them.

You put out the bait and, sure enough, it eventually kills a rat that nibbled on it. A rat slowly dying from poison is an easy meal for a predator, which also will die slowly. That could be a hawk, owl, coyote, or your neighbor's pet.

Poisons have more negative repercussions than many realize. That is why I have focused on the many humane methods for keeping pests away from your garden.

One last thing: Many gardeners ask me if it is safe to eat vegetables and fruits that have been damaged by animals. I always have the same answer: absolutely not. These animals potentially carry a number of transmissible diseases, so you don't want to take any chances.

Keep hawks and other predators safe by avoiding the use of poisons. This female Cooper's hawk perched on my bean arbor while hunting for prey.

BIRDS

DESCRIPTION

I am an avid birdwatcher and have gone to great lengths to create an appealing landscape that will attract them. This includes trees and shrubs of varying heights to provide them with shelter and safety from predators, ponds and birdbaths for drinking and bathing, and birdhouses for raising a family. All these things have successfully attracted many species of birds and I am delighted—except for one thing. Some of the birds are under the impression that the crops I grow in my vegetable garden were planted specifically for them!

There are many insectivorous birds that help us by eating a wide variety of insects in our gardens. Examples include bluebirds, chickadees, grosbeaks, and nuthatches. On the flipside, California quail, starlings, finches, and sparrows have caused a lot of damage within my vegetable garden. Over the years, I've spoken with many gardeners who also have issues with pigeons, pheasants, blackbirds, grackles, cowbirds, crows, jays, and turkeys.

It's hard to be angry with birds as beautiful as California quail, but they cause the most damage in my vegetable garden.

SIGNS OF THEIR ACTIVITY

Multiple small bites that strip the foliage off plants; the more fibrous stems are usually left behind.

FAVORITE PLANTS

Young seedlings, lettuce, and other leafy greens. Birds also will peck holes in ripe melons, berries, and tomatoes.

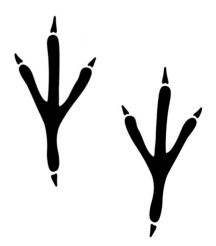

CONTROLS AND STRATEGIES

Birds are very intelligent so we need to give some thought to how we can prevent or, at least, lessen the damage they cause. Scaring them is an effective way to accomplish this and the time to start scaring birds is before they discover a new source of food in your garden. It's important to continually move deterrents around because they will get used to seeing them and no longer be frightened. The other, more reliable approach involves excluding them from our most susceptible plantings. Let's look at viable options for each:

1. Scare them.

> Insert pinwheels into planting beds. Every time a breeze blows, the movement (and sometimes the sound) will startle the birds.

> Hang CDs from strings in areas of the garden. As they move, their highly reflective surfaces shine lights in continually changing patterns.

> Attach Mylar tape or ribbon to stakes. This is also effective because they reflect shining lights in different patterns. Some manufacturers offer humming or buzzing types of Mylar lines. Mylar balloons work well, too.

> Set up a scarecrow or two. I've had mixed results with this, but the key to success is moving them to different areas of your garden on a regular basis as well as changing their wardrobes every few days. As you design your scarecrow, make it easy to move around. This also can be a source of great amusement for your neighbors!

> Anchor a hawk kite above your garden. Whenever it is breezy, the kite will unnerve birds with its continual flapping and diving.

These bush bean plants didn't stand a chance against a covey of hungry quail.

Not all birds are bad! There are many insect-eating birds, such as this European robin, that will help you out in the garden.

> Hang wind chimes here and there. The movement and sounds they make is another deterrent worth trying.

> Experiment with a bird-scaring decoy, such as an owl. Again, they are only successful if you move them around repeatedly. Once the birds get used to them, you'll have to switch to another method.

2. Create a barrier.

> Put floating row cover on hoops to protect seedlings. If the crop doesn't need to be pollinated, the cover can be left in place all season. Agricultural mesh also works well.

> Cover your seedlings by inverting an egg crate over them. The crates have plenty of holes that allow sunlight to hit the plants.

> Create a brick or concrete block perimeter around your seedlings and place a sheet of chicken wire (poultry netting) on the top until the plants are large enough to fend for themselves.

> Use trellises to make it difficult for birds to gain access to vining plants such as cucumbers, melons, small pumpkins, and summer and winter squash.

> Place pruned branches in the ground around seedlings; remove them once the seedlings are less appealing to the birds. In addition, if they frequently take dust baths in a specific planting bed—which can damage seedlings—put branches in their way.

The chicken wire cloches in the foreground have kept birds away from my prized pineapple strawberry fruits. Install plant protectors, which you can find at garden centers and online.

Toy snakes startle birds, provided you move them around regularly. Place toy snakes around plantings or up on trellises. I use them in my garden and try to realistically pose them for maximum effect, which, unfortunately, has startled human visitors from time to time.

Bird netting is very effective at keeping birds away from tender seedlings and leafy crops. Place hoops over the seedlings you want to protect and lay UV-resistant bird or butterfly netting onto the hoops. The goal is to keep seedlings safe and allow them to grow enough so birds can't pull them up or significantly damage them. The netting should have holes that are large enough to permit bees and other pollinators to come and go. Be sure to anchor the perimeter of the netting to keep birds out. It's preferable to have a gap between the netting and the tops of the plants or some birds will land on top of the netting and eat any leaves they can reach.

CHIPMUNKS

DESCRIPTION

Chipmunks belong to the squirrel family, *Sciuridae*, and are in the *Tamias* genus. Depending on the species, they range from 6 to 12 inches (15 to 30 cm) in length, including their tail. They have reddish-brown bodies with a distinctive pattern of black and cream-colored stripes on each side, and large cheek pouches.

Chipmunks are omnivores, eating seeds, berries, grains, insects, fungi, nuts, worms, and even birds and their eggs. They also damage young plants as a result of their digging activities. Their burrows can be up to 30 feet (9 m) long and contain chambers for storing food and raising young. It's not uncommon for them to burrow underneath structures. Chipmunks are active during the day and prefer to move about within the cover of shrubs, rock walls, or brush piles.

Chipmunks have very distinct markings.

SIGNS OF THEIR ACTIVITY

Disturbed or damaged seedlings; chewed corn, tomatoes, and other vegetable fruits; uprooted bulbs; small holes in lawn.

FAVORITE PLANTS

Corn, tomatoes and other succulent vegetable fruits, or young seedlings.

CONTROLS AND STRATEGIES

1. Repel them.

Apply an organic animal repellent to keep chipmunks away from their favorite plants. Read the label for instructions on how to apply it.

2. Create a barrier.

> Use ¼-inch (0.6 cm) hardware cloth to exclude chipmunks from plantings. Line bulb-planting holes with this type of wire as well.

> Surround your garden with a wire fence that has small openings and netting over the top to keep chipmunks out. An alternative is to place heavy-duty netting over your plants and anchor it down well.

3. Use other strategies.

> Provide a water source for chipmunks as a strategy to keep them away from your tomatoes and other succulent fruits. They are after the moisture contained in them.

> Clean up brush piles because they will burrow underneath them or hide within them.

> Mow your lawn at a short height to reduce cover.

> Don't locate birdfeeders near your garden. Clean up spilled seeds regularly.

> Don't feed pets outside.

> If the above measures don't work, trapping may be necessary.

Chipmunks are attracted to the moisture found in tomatoes and other fruits. Provide them with a water source away from your garden.

DEER

You might think deer are only a problem in rural areas, but they are big challenges for gardeners in many settings. Deer are adaptable opportunists and will readily move between wild areas and residential neighborhoods. Much of their foraging activities occur at night when they won't be disturbed by humans. Deer are ungulates, which are four-legged, hoofed mammals. These herbivores are always looking for food and are attracted to well-watered landscapes, particularly during hot, dry conditions.

It's never a good sign when the whole deer family comes for a visit!

SIGNS OF THEIR ACTIVITY

Plants eaten down to the ground, leaves completely chewed off with only their stems remaining, or ragged leaf edges. Oval, brown fecal pellets that are sometimes clumped together near the damage.

FAVORITE VEGETABLE PLANTS

Beans, beets, cabbage family crops, carrots, lettuce and other leafy greens, and peas. They don't care for crops with prickly leaves, such as cucumbers, melons, pumpkins, and squash. Deer also avoid strongly flavored crops such as onions, garlic, and aromatic herbs, but if they are hungry and stressed, they won't be picky!

CONTROL AND STRATEGIES

You can use three main tactics to keep deer away from your plants: Repel them, scare them, or create a barrier to keep them out. To be honest, barriers are the most successful approach. I also want to warn you that what works for one gardener might not work for another. While deer are creatures of habit, they also are adaptable. This means you have to be observant and creative!

1. Repel them.

Because deer have keen senses of smell and taste, commercial repellents can be quite effective. Apply an organic animal repellent to keep them away from their favorite plants. Read the label for instructions on how to use it.

Bars of highly perfumed deodorant soap also work as repellents. Hang the bars at deer nose level in areas you don't want them to go. Long before we built a fence around our small orchard, deer walked through the area nightly, often damaging the trees or eating the fruits and leaves. As soon as I learned about this method and began hanging bars of soap at different spots in the orchard, the deer gave the area a wide berth.

Some gardeners have had success using an ultrasonic animal repellent. These devices emit high-pitched sounds that most humans can't hear but irritate animals enough to make your garden less appealing. The best units are motion-activated and usually battery-powered, but some manufacturers offer solar-powered models. Some even have flashing lights.

A deer nibbled on this pepper plant.

I created this wire barrier to keep deer from jumping through the opening above our two arbor gates during the fall and winter months. To construct each one, I attached short lengths of EMT (electrical metal tubing) to the top and bottom of a long, rectangular piece of heavy-duty deer netting. Each barrier fits perfectly into the gate opening, providing both a visual and physical barrier. I reuse them year after year, and the deer have never breached them.

2. Scare them.

While scaring deer might sound mean, we vegetable gardeners want to protect our crops, right? There are some simple methods for accomplishing this:

Since deer tend to be more active at night, consider stringing some monofilament (fishing line) across paths they frequent or areas they traverse in order to get to your garden. Because it's difficult for deer to see the monofilament in the dark, they are startled when they brush against it and—if all goes according to plan—they will run away from the area.

Motion-activated sprinklers are another scare tactic. They are easy to locate at garden centers and from online sources. Here's how they work: Connect the sprinkler to a hose, adjust the motion sensor to the desired height and distance, and turn on the water to essentially "charge" the hose. When something triggers the sensor, the sprinkler shoots a blast of water in that direction. Of course, one hopes that "something" was a deer and not a forgetful gardener who just got a big surprise!

We have two arbor gates that lead into areas of our backyard. I have hung wind chimes in the openings above the gates to make deer think twice about leaping over the gates. The chimes hang at head level and their nearly constant movements and sounds deter deer from trying to get through. During the fall and winter months, however, I've found that deer are more desperate and willing to take chances to get to food sources. To stymie them, I place a barrier in the openings (see photo on previous page).

3. Create a barrier.

There are many ways to accomplish this. Let's look at the options, from the simplest to the most complex:

Floating row cover (refer to page 30 in chapter 1):
When you suspend row cover on hoops over some of their favorite crops, deer are unaware of what's growing underneath. Even if they do know, they can't access the plants, especially if you weigh down the edges with rocks, bricks, or boards. This is effective for protecting young seedlings and any crops that don't require pollination. Examples include beet family crops (beets, spinach, Swiss chard), cabbage family

Wire barriers work great. It's possible to build or purchase cloches or plant cages made from chicken wire (poultry netting). This commercially made structure keeps deer and other creatures away from their favorite plants. Deer will be able to see the plants underneath, but if the barrier is sturdy enough, they can't get to them. If you use wire cloches, pin them down to the soil with U-shaped metal pins or stakes.

My husband and I combined a 4-foot (1.2 m)-tall field fence with a 3½-foot (1.1 m)-wide strip of deer netting above it to keep deer and moose out of our small orchard and backyard. It has been very successful.

crops (arugula, broccoli, Brussels sprouts, cabbage, cauliflower, collards, kale, kohlrabi, radishes, rutabagas, turnips), and lettuce. A fine mesh screen would also work, but the crop would be more visible through it

Short fences: I have seen raised-bed gardens surrounded by 4-foot (1.2 m)-tall fences, yet they still keep out the deer. How is this possible when these creatures can jump up to 7 feet (2.1 m) high? If the distance between the fence and the edge of the beds is 3 feet (1 m) or less, deer are unlikely to jump over it because they don't think they can land safely. This is a great strategy.

Double fences: You also can construct two relatively short fences that are spaced a few feet apart. Deer can jump vertically but aren't able to jump high and wide at the same time. A similar option is to plant a hedge on one or both sides of a single 4-foot (1.2 m)-tall fence; this works for the same reason and because they can't see where they would land.

Regular fencing: If you wish to build a regular fence as a barrier around your garden, remember that deer can jump about 7 feet (2.1 m) high. This means your fence needs to be that high as well to effectively deter them from the area. One exception to this rule is solid fences that are at least 6 feet (1.8 m) tall. The theory is that if they can't see what's on the other side, they won't jump over it. Just remember to keep the gates closed so they can't wander in or discover there's nothing to be afraid of on the other side. If you don't want a solid fence to disrupt your view of the surrounding area, consider using tall stakes and heavy-duty plastic deer fencing. The beauty of this setup is that it doesn't obstruct one's view like a solid fence would.

I realize that some gardeners encounter larger ungulates, such as elk and moose. Just as with deer, the best defense is a tall, strong barrier.

This double electric fence arrangement keeps deer out of a flower farmer's garden.

Electric fences: Consider erecting two short fences spaced a few feet apart and electrifying them, as seen in the photo above. A flower farmer spaced the fences 30 inches (76 cm) apart. The outer fence has electrified poly tape (a metal ribbon that conducts electricity) set at a height of 20 inches (51 cm), and the inner fence is electrified with two wires at heights of 16 and 36 inches (41 and 91 cm). The only time this method doesn't work is if she forgets to turn on the electricity after tending the flowers!

GOPHERS, POCKET

DESCRIPTION

Gophers are very destructive rodents that belong to the *Thomomys* genus. They are referred to as pocket gophers because they have large cheek pouches, which they use for holding food or nesting materials. Gophers have short, brown fur; small eyes; a short tail; and large front claws that are very effective for digging burrows. They also have four long front teeth, which they put to good use while gnawing on our plants. Their bodies range between 6 and 10 inches (15 and 25 cm) in length.

For the most part, gophers stay in their burrows and use their long whiskers to find their way in the dark. They prefer slightly moist soil as it's easier to tunnel in and, in the winter, they are able to remain active beneath a blanket of snow, undetected by predators. Their burrows are 2½ to 3½ inches (6 to 9 cm) in diameter and consist of many chambers for nesting or food storage. Gophers are generally solitary except while mating or raising their young. They are herbivorous and, for such small creatures, can cause an incredible amount of damage. They generally tunnel beneath herbaceous plants, trees, or vegetable crops, and chew on their roots and stems.

Pocket gopher at the entrance to its burrow.

SIGNS OF THEIR ACTIVITY

Mounds of soil, usually arranged in a semi-circle with a plugged opening; a vegetable or landscape plant leaning to one side of its hole: if you pull on it, the plant comes right up because there aren't any roots to hold it in place; the lower end of root crops has been chewed; the plastic coating of water or buried electrical lines has been gnawed on. *Note: Pocket gophers and meadow voles are easily confused; be sure to read the description of voles and their damage in their profile (page 213).*

FAVORITE PLANTS

All vegetable crops, but gophers prefer root crops such as carrots, parsnips, and turnips.

CONTROLS AND STRATEGIES

1. Repel them.

Apply an organic animal repellent to keep gophers away from their favorite plants. Read the label for instructions on how to apply it.

2. Create a barrier.

If gophers are a frequent problem in your vegetable garden, consider building raised beds and covering the bottoms with wire to exclude them, before filling them with soil. The wire should have a ½-inch to ¾-inch (1 to 2 cm) mesh.

3. Use other strategies

Regional regulations vary regarding the trapping and killing of gophers, so be sure to check them first. If traps are allowed, find a mound of soil and locate one or more of the burrows. Use a pointed stake and push it into the soil near the mound until the stake moves easily into a burrow. Excavate enough of the burrow so you can set a trap. Gopher traps are available at garden centers and online. Check your traps frequently and carefully remove captured gophers. Monitor the area for more gophers as they sometimes take over a vacated burrow.

There are many natural predators of gophers, including owls, hawks, and snakes. Make them welcome on your property so they can hunt for the gophers.

Don't try to flood gophers out of their burrows with a hose because their tunneling system is too extensive and this method is rarely successful. It also wastes water.

Please do not use poison.

This is what a typical gopher mound looks like.

GROUNDHOGS (A.K.A. WOODCHUCKS, MARMOTS)

DESCRIPTION

Groundhogs (*Marmota monax*) are the same as woodchucks and marmots. They are also referred to by the humorous name of whistle pigs because of their high-pitched warning calls. These rodents are members of the squirrel family (*Sciuridae*). Despite their name, they can climb trees. Native to North America, groundhogs are usually found near wooded areas and dig extensive burrows, which can reach up to 50 feet (15 m) in length. If they tunnel under structures, their burrows can undermine the foundation. They are active during the day, although they hibernate from about October to February.

Groundhogs eat about 1½ half pounds (0.6 kg) of food each day, with vegetables and plant roots being their favorites items. This means they can destroy a vegetable garden very quickly.

Yellow-bellied marmot.

SIGNS OF THEIR ACTIVITY

Widely spaced bite marks on plants and fruits; carrot foliage chewed off; wilting and/or dying plants; 12-inch (30 cm)-diameter hole with the excavated soil surrounding it; gnawed tree bark.

FAVORITE PLANTS

Beans, cabbage, cantaloupes, carrots, corn, cucumbers, lettuce, tomatoes, zucchini

CONTROLS AND STRATEGIES

1. Repel them.

Garlic repels groundhogs. Consider interplanting it with their favorite crops.

Repellents made with plant extracts such as peppermint oil, cinnamon oil, and/or garlic oil are safe to use around edible crops. Always read the label prior to purchasing and applying repellents.

2. Scare them.

Frighten them with a motion-activated sprinkler.

3. Create a barrier.

Build a fence around your garden area. You will need wire that is about 5 feet (1.5 m) tall. Prior to installing it, dig a trench around the perimeter of the area and bury the bottom 12 inches (30 cm) of the fencing. Attach the fence to posts, but bend the top 12 inches (30 cm) of the wire outwards. Electric fencing is another option.

4. Use other strategies.

Remove tall weeds to eliminate vegetative cover.

Trim shrubs to eliminate cover.

Harvest vegetable crops as soon as they're ripe.

If you compost kitchen scraps, use a closed system to keep groundhogs away from the compost.

A groundhog chewed on the leaves of these bean plants.

MICE

There are many species of mice, but house mice (*Mus musculus*) and deer mice (*Peromyscus maniculatus*) are two species gardeners might encounter. Mice are smaller than rats—ranging from 5 to 7 inches (13 to 18 cm) in length—have beady black eyes, scaly tails, and brown or gray fur. Deer mice are unusual in that they have white undersides and large hind feet, which they use for jumping. Deer mice are typically encountered in rural settings and nest in hollow tree trunks, under rocks or brush piles, in abandoned bird or squirrel nests, or in structures. Deer mice spread hantavirus, a serious respiratory disease that can be fatal. They shed the virus in their droppings and urine. Since these rodents often take up residence in outbuildings, humans usually contract hantavirus by inhaling contaminated dust while cleaning up and removing mouse nests and feces. Instead of sweeping the area, it's important to wet down the materials with a disinfectant first, do the cleaning, and wash your hands thoroughly afterwards.

All mice primarily eat grains but will also eat fruits and vegetation. They gather and store grain in their dens and will even dig up and carry off seeds that have been newly planted in the garden. In my garden, they have chewed through the stems of young pepper and pea plants and carried off the entire plants! Mice are nocturnal.

House mouse.

SIGNS OF THEIR ACTIVITY

Small (¼-inch (0.6 cm) or less) brown droppings the shape of grains of rice; small bites out of plants; burrowing activity in loose soil; small 1-inch (3 cm)-diameter holes in the ground that haven't been plugged with soil.

FAVORITE PLANTS

Beans, corn, peas, peppers, squash, and vegetable seeds

CONTROLS AND STRATEGIES

1. Repel them.

Apply an organic animal repellent to keep mice away from their favorite plants. Read the label for instructions on how to apply it.

2. Scare them.

Set up motion-activated lights to startle mice. Don't keep a light on all night or they will become used to it.

3. Create a barrier.

Exclude mice from outbuildings and other structures by covering openings and creating barriers with fine-meshed wire.

4. Use other strategies.

Remove brush piles, garden debris, or dense vegetation to eliminate hiding places.

Clean up dropped bird seeds.

Don't leave pet food outside at night.

Snap traps baited with peanut butter are effective; take precautions when handling mice.

Do not use mothballs because they are toxic.

Please do not use poison.

Deer mouse.

A mouse chewed out the interior of this carrot.

MOLES

You might think moles are a type of rodent, just from looking at their appearance. Actually, they are insectivores because they solely eat worms and insects. There are several species of moles, including Eastern moles (*Scalopus aquaticus*), Townsend's moles (*Scapanus townsendii*), star-nosed moles (*Condylura cristata*), and European moles (*Talpa europaea*). No matter which species you encounter, the most important thing you need to know is that moles will not try to eat your vegetable crops. They specifically hunt for grubs, earthworms, and other invertebrates within the soil. Unfortunately, their tunneling habit can dislodge soil and damage plant roots if they venture into your garden.

Moles range from 5 to 7 inches (13 to 18 cm) in length, have pointed or star-shaped snouts, silvery-black fur, and short limbs equipped with impressive claws for digging and pushing soil. They have very poor eyesight but excellent senses of smell and hearing. Moles are active year-round and are primarily found in areas where the soil is loose and moist; this is why they usually are attracted to lawns. Just like gophers and voles, they create a network of tunnels that are about 2 inches (5 cm) in diameter. They push up soil into conical mounds while excavating their tunnels, some of which are about a foot (30 cm) below the surface. They tunnel right below the surface when hunting for their prey.

A mole.

SIGNS OF THEIR ACTIVITY

Conical molehills on a lawn or soil surface; raised tunnels near the soil surface; disturbed plant roots.

FAVORITE PLANTS

None, they are carnivorous, but they might damage plant roots while tunneling.

CONTROLS AND STRATEGIES

1. Repel them.

Mole repellents containing castor oil as the active ingredient are available. They cannot be used around edible crops, but they do work well in lawns and ornamental beds. Always read the label for instructions on how to use a product as well as any restrictions.

2. Create a barrier.

Place a wire barrier around the area you wish to protect. Use wire with ¾-inch (2 cm) or smaller openings. It needs to be buried 2 feet (61 cm) deep and rise 6 inches (15 cm) above the soil surface.

3. Use other strategies.

Consider setting mole traps, which are available in different styles at garden centers and from online sources. To be effective, they must be set in active tunnels. Push your foot down on a surface tunnel; if the mole pushes the soil back up later, it's an active tunnel. If it doesn't, test other areas before setting a trap.

Don't try to flood moles out of their burrows with a hose because their tunneling system is too extensive for this to be successful.

Please do not use poison.

These are molehills in a lawn.

OPOSSUMS

DESCRIPTION

To be honest, opossums (*Didelphis virginiana*) aren't the most attractive animals that might visit your garden. They are similar in appearance to rats—with gray hair, a pointed face, dark ears, and a scaly tail—but aren't related to them. Virginia opossums—so named because that's where Europeans first encountered them—are the only marsupial that is native to North America, with a range from southern Canada to Costa Rica. Marsupials are mammals that give birth to undeveloped young, which they carry and nurture in a pouch. When not rearing young, opossums lead solitary lives. Adults are about the size of a house cat, reaching as much as 36 inches (91 cm) in length (including their tail) and weighing between 4 and 15 pounds (2 and 7 kg). The young can hang from branches by coiling their tail around them.

Opossums, which are commonly referred to as possums, aren't aggressive, even though they will hiss and bare their teeth when feeling threatened. The popular phrase "playing 'possum" arose out of their instinctive reaction to danger, where they fall over, appear to be dead, and can lie motionless for up to four hours. These nocturnal creatures are attracted to wooded areas or open terrain located near bodies of water. Opossums live in dens or burrows that were created and abandoned by other animals. They also will shelter in brush piles or under structures. They can have fleas, lice, and ticks, but they are known to kill and eat large quantities of ticks every year.

As omnivores, they will eat slugs, snails, grubs, insects, small rodents, amphibians, birdseed, fruits, and some vegetables. Opossums prefer rotting vegetation and will often look for food in compost bins or garbage cans.

Adult opossum.

SIGNS OF THEIR ACTIVITY

Because opossums are nocturnal, it can be difficult to detect their presence. In addition, the appearance of their feces varies widely due to their omnivorous diet. You might notice that outdoor pet food or fallen fruits have been eaten, your compost pile has been disturbed, or discover empty snail shells.

FAVORITE PLANTS

They are primarily attracted to rotting fruits and vegetables, but also will eat beans, broccoli, carrots, peas, Swiss chard, and tomatoes.

Female opossum with young on her back.

CONTROLS AND STRATEGIES

1. Repel them.

Garlic and onions repel opossums. Consider planting them near or surrounding their favorite crops.

Use commercial opossum repellents. Follow the label directions, especially regarding their use around edible crops.

Do not use mothballs because they are toxic.

2. Scare them.

Set up a motion-activated sprinkler in an area they frequent to frighten them.

3. Create a barrier.

Physical barriers such as netting or wire are the most effective. Erect fencing with small openings around the areas of your garden that you are trying to protect. The top of the barrier should angle away from your garden. This makes it more difficult for opossums to get over the top.

Clean up brush piles and block the entrance to burrows.

Cover any potential entrances that go under your home, porch, or outbuildings to prevent opossums from establishing a den there.

Since opossums are attracted to compost piles, make them inaccessible by covering or containing them. Otherwise, don't compost kitchen scraps.

Secure your trash can lids.

4. Use other strategies.

Do not leave pet food outside at night and bring pets indoors to eliminate the chances of encounters with opossums.

Pick up any fruits that fall to the ground.

Don't let birdseed accumulate on the ground. Consider putting your feeders away while you're trying to discourage opossums from visiting your property.

PORCUPINES

DESCRIPTION

Porcupines are slow-moving rodents that are found worldwide. Members of the North American species *Erethizon dorsatum*, porcupines like to visit my garden a few times each year. Their bodies are up to 2½-feet (0.7 m) long and they can weigh up to 30 pounds (14 g). They are good at climbing because they have curved claws. Porcupines have brown and black fur, and their backs are covered with quills. When they flare the quills as a defensive maneuver, the quills make a rattling sound, which also frightens off potential predators. It is a myth that porcupines "throw" their quills when feeling threatened. The quills actually have to be in contact with something before they will detach from their body. Because the quills are barbed, it's a very painful experience for the recipient to have them removed. Porcupines have an astounding 30,000 quills on their body and grow new ones whenever they lose some.

These herbivores are found near forested areas. They generally lead solitary lives except during breeding season and while raising their young. The females usually give birth to a single baby, which is called a porcupette. I'll bet you didn't know that! They sure are cute, but I don't appreciate it when their mom brings them along to see our all-you-can-eat buffet.

Porcupines do not hibernate. They have poor eyesight but make up for it with their good senses of smell and hearing. They have two large front teeth, which they use to gnaw on tree bark, often seriously damaging or killing the trees, and they are very attracted to salt. Porcupines nest in hollow logs, in abandoned animal dens, within rock piles, or under structures. They are primarily nocturnal.

This porcupine visited my garden a few years ago.

No matter which type of plant a porcupine goes after, the damage looks the same: trampled, broken stems and branches. These were my raspberry canes.

SIGNS OF THEIR ACTIVITY

Bites taken out of melons and squash; plant stalks broken; plants trampled; chewed leaves; gnawed tree bark; bites taken out of tree fruits and berries.

FAVORITE PLANTS

Cabbage, carrots, grass, leafy greens, melons, potatoes, squash; tree fruits and berries.

CONTROLS AND STRATEGIES

1. Repel them.

If you spot a porcupine in the garden, get a hose! They hate to be sprayed with water and you can chase them as far as your hose will reach.

There are organic animal repellents that are safe to use around vegetable crops and other edible plants. Be sure to follow the label directions regarding their use and to learn when it is safe to harvest your crops.

2. Create a barrier.

Erect a fence around your garden where the upper section is angled outward to make it more difficult for a porcupine to go over it. It's a good idea to bury part of the fence belowground to thwart digging.

To protect trees, place a 30-inch (76 cm) aluminum cylinder around tree trunks; this will discourage gnawing and climbing. You can also use 18- to 24-inch (46 to 61 cm)-tall chicken wire as a barrier.

If a porcupine has taken up residence under a structure on your property, block the entrance to it and to any other potential access points below your porch and other outbuildings. You'll want to do this in the evening while the porcupine is out and about.

3. Use other strategies.

Don't leave pet food outside at night as it might attract porcupines.

Keep pets indoors at night to eliminate the chance of their being injured during porcupine encounters. Dogs instinctively want to bite and jump on top of a porcupine, which unfortunately provides the contact needed for the quills to be released.

RABBITS

DESCRIPTION

Rabbits have a reputation for being fluffy and cute, but gardeners draw the line when they feast upon their vegetable plants. These creatures vary in size depending on the species, but they are easily recognizable from their large ears, brown- and cream-colored fur, and their hopping gait. They nest on the ground in dense, tall grasses, or in burrows. Rabbits hide from their natural predators (hawks, owls, and foxes) underneath hedges, shrubs, and brush piles.

They prefer to eat tender foliage, particularly that of young seedlings. Rabbits avoid some edible plants but will eat just about anything if they are stressed enough. It's important to monitor your garden for signs of them. Start your control tactics early in the season if you've had problems with rabbits in the past. Otherwise, they'll already be aware of the banquet in your garden and how to get to it!

This cottontail rabbit was snacking on the clover growing in turfgrass, which seems harmless enough.

SIGNS OF THEIR ACTIVITY

Plants disappear overnight. Foliage has been cleanly clipped off of plants, rather than torn. Brown, pea-sized droppings. Clumps of their hair in areas where they've been active.

FAVORITE PLANTS

Beans, beets, broccoli, carrots, lettuce, okra, peas, sweet peppers

PLANTS THEY DISLIKE

Basil, garlic, hot peppers, mint, onions, rhubarb, squash, tarragon, tomatoes

CONTROLS AND STRATEGIES

Rabbits are challenging, but there are many tactics worth trying to repel them from the plants they love, scare them from the area, or physically block them from your garden:

1. Repel them.

Commercial rabbit repellents are available at garden centers and online. Choose an organic product that is safe to use around edible crops. An alternative is to apply a regular repellent to the perimeter of your vegetable garden or other areas where rabbits have been active; follow the label recommendations regarding the minimum required distance from edible crops.

Place bars of strongly perfumed deodorant soap near, but not touching, the plants you want to protect.

Interplant vegetable and herb plants they dislike (see list on previous page) among their favorite crops to disguise the scents.

2. Scare them.

Place pinwheels near plants you want to protect. Move them around frequently so the rabbits won't get accustomed to seeing them.

Set up a motion-activated sprinkler in an area they commonly visit. Connect the sprinkler to a hose, adjust the motion sensor to a rabbit's height and the desired distance, and turn on the water to "charge" the hose. When the sensor is triggered, the sprinkler will shoot a blast of water in that direction.

3. Create a barrier.

Cover plantings with well-anchored bird netting, chicken wire (poultry netting), or floating row cover that is supported by hoops.

Keep plants safe underneath commercially made chicken wire cloches or plant cages (refer to pages 182 and 188).

Rabbits and vegetable gardens are not a good combination!

Protect the perimeter of your garden beds with chicken wire; it should be a minimum of 2 feet (61 cm) tall and also have 6 inches (15 cm) buried in the soil in case the rabbits try to dig underneath the barrier.

Grow vegetables in extra-tall raised beds.

Consider using electric fence netting around specific crops or surrounding your garden if you're not having much success keeping the rabbits away.

4. Eliminate hiding areas.

Block potential entrances underneath sheds, decks, or porches.

Remove debris piles.

RACCOONS

DESCRIPTION

Raccoons (*Procyon lotor*) are easily identifiable by their dark bandit masks; thick, gray-brown fur; lighter fur on their muzzles and above their eyes; and tails that have alternating light and dark rings. Adults range from 2 to 3 feet (61 to 91 cm) in length and weigh anywhere from 8 to 30 pounds (4 to 14 kg). Raccoons are extremely intelligent and easily remember the location of food sources they have visited. They can use their hand-like paws to gain access into containers that stymie other types of animals, and they are very adaptable.

Raccoons live throughout North America in many types of habitats. They prefer wooded areas but have adapted well to both urban and suburban settings. The adults prefer dens in brush piles, hollow tree trunks, and rock piles; they also will try to nest within or underneath structures.

These mammals are primarily nocturnal and are omnivores. As such, they will eat insects, amphibians, small rodents, bird eggs, fruits, nuts, vegetables, birdseed, and pet food. Raccoons also dig in lawns for earthworms and grubs, and they are attracted to fishponds. They are solitary most of the year, except during mating season and while caring for their young.

It's important to be aware that they are carriers of rabies, distemper, and roundworms.

Adult raccoon and baby.

Raccoons damaged these cornstalks.

FAVORITE PLANTS

Beans, corn, melons, peas, potatoes, squash

SIGNS OF THEIR ACTIVITY

Distinctive, five-toed pawprints in the soil; cornstalks knocked over with ears partially eaten; torn-up areas of your lawn; disturbed compost pile; empty birdfeeders

CONTROLS AND STRATEGIES

1. Repel them.

Apply an organic animal repellent to keep raccoons away from their favorite plants. Read the label for instructions on how to apply it.

Some gardeners have had success using an ultrasonic animal repellent. These devices emit high-pitched sounds that most humans aren't able to hear but irritate animals enough so they find your garden less appealing. The best units are motion-activated and usually battery-powered, but some manufacturers offer solar-powered models. Some even have flashing lights.

2. Scare them.

Raccoons are sensitive to noise. Consider placing a radio in your garden that is either motion-activated or turn it on at dusk to repel them. Remember to be considerate of your neighbors!

Scare them with a motion-activated sprinkler.

Install a motion-activated light in the area they frequently visit.

Pinwheels will startle raccoons, but they will become accustomed to them; remember to move them around to different areas of your garden, especially where a breeze will make them move.

3. Create a barrier.

Find out what is attracting raccoons and either remove or secure it to eliminate a potential source for food or shelter.

Install a sturdy wire fence around your garden or an electric fence.

Block any access to potential dens, such as underneath buildings or within an attic, after determining raccoons aren't inside the structure.

Secure your trash can lids and put out your cans on trash-collection day, rather than the night before.

Use a closed composting system, if possible, or avoid composting kitchen scraps outdoors.

4. Use other strategies.

Do not intentionally attract raccoons to your garden, especially by putting food out for them.

Since raccoons are active at night, use a game camera to verify they are responsible for the garden damage.

Do not leave pet food outside at night.

Clean up any fallen fruits or nuts that will attract them.

If raccoons are eating birdseed, either remove the feeders until the problem is resolved, or use a single type of seed rather than mixes that easily spill onto the ground from feeders.

RATS

Black rats or roof rats (*Rattus rattus*) and Norway rats (*Rattus norvegicus*) are the two most common species of rats a gardener might encounter. Rats are larger than mice, have long, scaly tails, and brown, gray, or black fur. They are found all over the world but tend to be present wherever humans provide them with easy access to food and shelter. They dig burrows and a network of tunnels, often under structures. Sometimes they will build nests inside the walls of outbuildings and houses. Rats are omnivorous, eating a wide variety of foods, including fish, birds, grains, nuts, fruits, and vegetables. They also require water and shelter. Rats are primarily nocturnal and have poor eyesight. They carry fleas, ticks, and several diseases.

Black rat/roof rat.

SIGNS OF THEIR ACTIVITY

Half-inch (1 cm)-long, brown, cylindrical droppings, especially near pet food dishes or other food sources; 2½-inch to 3½-inch (6 to 9 cm)-diameter burrows in the garden; damaged plants; burrows under compost piles

FAVORITE PLANTS

Carrots, corn, parsnips, pumpkins, squash, turnips

CONTROLS AND STRATEGIES

1. Create a barrier.

Keep trash cans secured with lids.

Do not compost meats, fats, or grains in your compost pile. Only compost vegetable scraps and use an enclosed compost bin.

2. Use other strategies.

Keep your garden neat by pruning back thick vegetation to provide fewer hiding places.

Clean up brush piles, stacks of lumber, rocks, or piles of mulch.

Trim plants away from walls that rats travel along to expose them to predators.

If rats are active in your compost pile, do not use the compost on your edible crops. Similarly, if they nibble on any vegetables, throw them away.

Fix dripping faucets or leaky hoses to eliminate water sources for rats.

Don't leave pet food out at night.

Clean up fallen fruits and nuts, and clean up garden debris frequently.

Snap traps work well, but place them where children or pets won't be harmed by them.

Please do not use poison.

Norway rat.

Typical rat damage to a tomato fruit.

SKUNKS

There are three species of skunks that gardeners might encounter, depending upon where they live: striped (*Mephitis mephitis*), Western spotted (*Spilogale gracilis*), or Eastern spotted (*S. putorius*). Striped skunks are easily recognized by their black bodies and two white, lengthwise stripes. Spotted skunks are also black and white, but, as their name implies, they have white spots rather than stripes. All have clawed feet, which make them efficient diggers. While striped skunks are native to North America, spotted skunks have a larger range that extends from North America down through South America. Striped skunks are larger, with a length ranging from 25 to 30 inches (64 to 76 cm), including their tail, and spotted skunks are 14 to 20 inches (36 to 51 cm) long.

In addition to their appearance, skunks are notorious for their ability to spray an offensive, oily substance from their scent glands when they are startled or cornered. Contrary to what you might think, they spray as a last resort because it takes up to ten days for their bodies to replenish the musk, which leaves them defenseless during that time. Striped skunks stomp their feet as a warning while spotted skunks stand on their front feet with their hind feet and tail up in the air. They are carriers of rabies and many diseases that can adversely impact pets and other animals.

Skunks are primarily active at night. Their vision is poor, but they make up for it with excellent senses of smell and hearing. They use abandoned burrows or brush piles for their dens and also make dens under structures. Skunks are omnivores, feeding on mice, rats, voles, ground-nesting birds and their eggs, amphibians, dead animals, grubs, bees and other insects, fruits, nuts, birdseed, pet food, and vegetables. They dig for grubs and earthworms in lawns and garden beds. The good news is that they eat cutworms and Japanese beetle grubs. If you have a large infestation of the latter, that may attract skunks to your yard.

Striped skunks.

SIGNS OF THEIR ACTIVITY

Three-inch to 4-inch (8 to 10 cm)-deep holes in lawns and garden beds; skunk odor; damaged or disturbed vegetable plants; birdseed on ground eaten; pet food eaten; disturbed compost piles

FAVORITE PLANTS

Corn is their favorite, but they will sample berries, melons, and other vegetable fruits.

Spotted skunk.

A skunk has upturned this section of sod in search of grubs and earthworms to eat.

CONTROLS AND STRATEGIES

1. Repel them.

Apply an organic animal repellent to keep skunks away from their favorite plants. Read the label for instructions on how to apply it.

Some gardeners have had success using an ultrasonic animal repellent. These devices emit high-pitched sounds that most humans can't hear but irritate animals enough to make your garden less appealing. The best units are motion-activated and usually battery-powered, but some manufacturers offer solar-powered models. Some even have flashing lights.

2. Scare them.

Install a motion-activated floodlight to take advantage of the skunk's sensitivity to light.

3. Create a barrier.

Block entrances beneath buildings. Wire works best, especially if you bury 6 inches (15 cm) of the wire to stymie their attempts to dig under the wire.

Place fencing around your garden.

Don't compost kitchen waste outdoors unless you are using a closed, secure system.

Cover and secure trash cans.

4. Use other strategies.

Never intentionally feed skunks.

Harvest ripe vegetables promptly.

Clean up fallen fruits and seeds below birdfeeders.

Don't feed pets outside or leave their food out at night.

Clean up brush and rock piles.

Control mice and rats to eliminate some of their food sources.

If you have a lot of Japanese grubs in your lawn every year, consider applying beneficial nematodes, milky spore (*Paenibacillus popilliae*) after the beetles have laid their eggs, or *Bacillus thuringiensis* variety *galleriae* to control the adult beetles and grubs.

SQUIRRELS, TREE

DESCRIPTION

Tree squirrels are one of the most challenging creatures a gardener can encounter. There are many species of them, but here are some of the most common ones: Eastern fox squirrels (*Sciurus niger*) have a gray-brown body with reddish undersides and are about 22 inches (56 cm) long, including their tail. Eastern gray squirrels (*Sciurus carolinensis*) have brown bodies with white undersides and range from 9 to 12 inches (23 to 30 cm) long. Western gray squirrels (*Sciurus griseus*) have brown bodies with white undersides and are 18 to 24 inches (46 to 61 cm) long. American red squirrels (*Tamiasciurus hudsonicus*) have red bodies with white undersides and range between 10 and 14 inches (25 and 36 cm) in length. All of them have bushy tails.

Tree squirrels are active during the day and are quite intelligent. Their diet includes seeds, nuts, acorns, fungi, insects, birds and their eggs, fruits, and vegetables. They will nest within hollow tree cavities, or build nests high within the tree canopy next to the trunk, in nest boxes, or in structures.

They cause damage by digging within our lawns and gardens while storing nuts and acorns. They chew on utility wires and also damage buildings while trying to gain access to them. Tree squirrels carry rabies, fleas, mites, and parasites.

American red squirrel.

SIGNS OF THEIR ACTIVITY

Shallow holes in the lawn and garden; vegetables partially eaten; young seedlings that have been chewed on; bulbs dug up

FAVORITE PLANTS

Corn, tomatoes, and other vegetables

CONTROLS AND STRATEGIES

1. Repel them.

Interplant strongly scented plants, such as marigolds, nasturtiums, and aromatic herbs, within your vegetable beds. Garlic and onions also repel squirrels.

Apply an organic animal repellent to keep squirrels away from their favorite plants. Read the label for instructions on how to use it.

Some gardeners have had success using an ultrasonic animal repellent. These devices emit high-pitched sounds that most can't hear but irritate animals enough to make your garden less appealing. The best units are motion-activated and usually battery-powered, but some manufacturers offer solar-powered models. Some even have flashing lights.

2. Scare them.

Set up a motion-activated sprinkler to startle them.

Consider hanging Mylar balloons near the plants you want to protect.

Remember that dogs live for chasing squirrels! They will frighten squirrels away from your yard—but only while the dogs are outside.

3. Create a barrier.

Trim shrub branches and tree limbs that are near structures. Your utility company might help you with this if the branches are located near their lines. Consider adding wide metal baffles on tree trunks to keep squirrels from climbing them.

Exclude squirrels from your home by securing any areas where they could gain access, no matter how small, because they will gnaw on openings until they can get inside. Seal attics, roof vents, and dryer vents with a sturdy screen to prevent access.

Build or purchase wire cages to place around the vegetables you want to protect. Chicken wire cloches and crop protectors work well for this.

Cover crops with floating row cover that is suspended on hoops over susceptible crops. Be sure to weigh down all edges.

If you enjoy putting out birdfeeders, try hanging a squirrel-proof model. These are available from many sources although are not always successful. Hang the feeders on poles, away from any trees or structures.

4. Use other strategies.

Do not intentionally feed squirrels or provide them with nest boxes.

Don't feed your pets outdoors because the food residue will attract squirrels.

Harvest vegetables promptly and keep all garden debris picked up, especially tomatoes that have fallen from the plants. Clean up fallen fruits and nuts that will attract squirrels.

Please do not use poison.

Squirrels enjoy eating tomatoes and other garden vegetables.

VOLES, MEADOW

DESCRIPTION

There are many species of meadow voles within the *Microtus* genus; they are also commonly called meadow mice. They are similar in appearance to mice, but they don't try to get into houses or other structures. Voles are easily confused with gophers because of their appearance and the damage they cause. These smaller rodents have short bodies and longer tails than gophers, although their tails are not as long as those of mice. Voles have small ears and eyes, dark brown fur, and slightly hairy tails. They are between 5 and 8 inches (13 and 20 cm) long. Their droppings are about ³⁄₁₆ inch (0.5 cm) long and green or brown in color.

Another reason voles are confused with gophers is because they also create networks of burrows, although vole burrows are smaller in diameter (1½ inches to 2 inches [4 to 5 cm]). Voles do not generate mounds of soil. Their surface "runways" are unique and usually seen in lawns, with an occasional small hole around which the grass has been shortly clipped.

Voles are typically found in rural or agricultural areas and are active year-round. They are extremely prolific, with females producing up to ten litters of three to six young in a year's time. They are herbivores, eating plants, bulbs, and tree bark just above the soil level. The damage they cause to plants is usually at the soil surface or just below, which often girdles them; this is another difference from gophers.

Meadow vole.

SIGNS OF THEIR ACTIVITY

Runways throughout the lawn or within block plantings of lettuce and other salad greens; small holes with the surrounding grass clipped short; gnaw marks on plants near the soil level; girdled plants; plants that have fallen over

FAVORITE PLANTS

Artichokes, beets, Brussels sprouts, cabbage, carrots, cauliflower, celery, lettuce, onions, potatoes, spinach, sweet potatoes, tomatoes, turnips

---

CONTROLS AND STRATEGIES

1. Repel them.

There are mole and gopher repellents that contain castor oil as the active ingredient. They cannot be used around edible crops, but they do work well in lawns and ornamental beds. Always read the label for use and restrictions.

There are also organic animal repellents that will keep voles away from their favorite plants. Check the label for instructions on how to apply them near vegetable crops.

2. Create a barrier.

Create low barriers around the plants you need to protect. To do this, use wire that has ¼-inch (0.6 cm) or smaller holes. It should be 12 inches (30 cm) aboveground and 10 inches (25 cm) belowground. Don't let weeds grow around the barriers as they might encourage voles to be active in the area.

Voles created these surface runways and holes in my lawn during the winter.

3. Use other strategies.

If your garden or raised beds are surrounded by lawn, keep the grass shortly mowed to reduce vole habitat.

Keep up with the weeds in and near your vegetable garden so voles are less likely to inhabit the area. Also reduce thick mulch that could encourage voles.

Snap traps work well. Place them within the runways. Wear gloves and handle dead voles carefully because they can have parasites and also carry diseases.

Voles have many natural predators, such as owls, hawks, and snakes. Make them feel welcome.

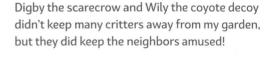

Digby the scarecrow and Wily the coyote decoy didn't keep many critters away from my garden, but they did keep the neighbors amused!

RESOURCES

If you are interested in delving even deeper into organic vegetable gardening, plant diseases, animal pests, and insects, I have compiled a list of reliable resources below. While it is by no means comprehensive, these suggestions will help you achieve your goal of being a well-informed gardener! You'll find wonderful books that are brimming with great ideas, enjoyable and informative podcasts, and useful websites. There's even a table of suppliers for many of the products I mentioned throughout the book so you can check out your options.

BOOKS

- *American Horticultural Society Pests and Diseases*. Pippa Greenwood, Andrew Halstead, A. R. Chase, Daniel Gilrein, 2000.
- *Deerproofing Your Yard & Garden*. Rhonda Massingham Hart, 2005.
- *Deer-Resistant Design*. Karen Chapman, 2019.
- *Growing Under Cover*. Niki Jabbour, 2020.
- *The New Organic Grower*, 3rd Edition. Eliot Coleman, 2018.
- *No Dig Organic Home & Garden*. Charles Dowding and Stephanie Hafferty, 2017.
- *The Organic Gardener's Handbook of Natural Pest and Disease Control*. Fern Marshall Bradley, Barbara W. Ellis, and Deborah L. Martin, 2009.
- *Solving Deer Problems*. Peter Loewer, 2003.
- *The Vegetable Garden Pest Handbook*. Susan Mulvihill, 2021.
- *The Vegetable Gardening Book*. Joe Lamp'l, 2022.
- *What's Wrong With My Plant? (And How Do I Fix It?)*. David Deardorff and Kathryn Wadsworth, 2009.
- *The Winter Harvest Handbook*. Eliot Coleman, 2009.
- *The Year-Round Vegetable Gardener*. Niki Jabbour, 2011.

ORGANIC GARDENING PODCASTS

- Gardenerd Tip of the Week with Christy Wilhelmi. gardenerd.com
- Green Organic Garden with Jackie Marie Beyer. organicgardenerpodcast.com
- The Grow Guide with Maggie Wysocki and Dave Hanson. thegrowguidepodcast.com
- The joe gardener™ Show with Joe Lamp'l. joegardener.com/podcasts
- The Organic Gardening Podcast with Chris Collins and Fiona Taylor. gardenorganic.org.uk/podcast

ONLINE HELP WITH INSECT, DISEASE, AND ANIMAL PEST IDENTIFICATION

APPS

Insects

> Picture Insect – Bug Identifier
> Insect Identification*
> Leps by Fieldguide
> Seek by iNaturalist

Plant disease

> Identify Tomato Plant Diseases
> Online Plant Doctor
> Plant Disease Identifier*

* (Available for Apple only)

WEBSITES

> Disease-resistant tomato varieties from Cornell University: vegetables.cornell.edu/pest-management/disease-factsheets/disease-resistant-vegetable-varieties/disease-resistant-tomato-varieties/

> National Plant Diagnostic Network Website: npdn.org/home. If you're having difficulty identifying a plant disease and you don't have an educational institution with a horticultural program near you, use this website to locate a plant diagnostic laboratory within the United States. There is contact information for each location so you can find out what their hours are, ask how to prepare your plant sample, and find out the cost of this diagnostic service.

> Vegetable Disease Identification Key for Cucurbits and Tomatoes from Cornell University: vegetablemdonline.ppath.cornell.edu/DiagnosticKeys/KeyPage.html

> Facebook Groups. Look for ones that will help you identify insects and plant diseases. These include the Pacific Northwest Bugs, Bug Identification, and What's Wrong With My Plant. To locate a list of groups, log on to Facebook and conduct a search using the words "insect identification" or "plant disease."

EDUCATIONAL RESOURCES

> How to Locate Master Gardener Programs in the United States and Canada: mastergardener.extension.org/contact us/find a program/

> IPM (Integrated Pest Management) Institute of North America: ipminstitute.org/what-is-integrated-pest-management/

> Regional Insect, Plant Disease, and Gardening Information from United States Extension Programs: Because educational institutions occasionally change servers, Susan is maintaining an updated list of suggested Extension programs on her website: SusansintheGarden.com/guides/links.

> United States Department of Agriculture Hardiness Zone Map: planthardiness.ars.usda.gov/

AUTHOR RESOURCES

> SusansintheGarden.com: blog; guides for growing vegetables organically, composting, organic pest control, seed-starting viability and scheduler, and planting vegetables; Susan's weekly garden columns; index to her videos; photo galleries

> Susan's gardening videos: youtube.com/susansinthegarden

Note: We've made every effort to provide current web addresses for these sources, but businesses and educational institutions occasionally change servers or close. If a link doesn't work, please conduct a web search for the name given here. With a little luck, the results should steer you in the right direction.

PRODUCT SUPPLIERS

	Adaptive Tools	Animal Repellents	Barriers (fencing, netting)	Composters	Disease Control	Fertilizers	Grow Bags	Irrigation	Season extension
Arbico Organics 10831 N. Mavinee Dr., Suite 185 Oro Valley, AZ 85737-9531 (800) 827-2847 arbico-organics.com		✔			✔	✔			✔
The Benner Deer Fence Co. (610) 603-6484 bennerdeerfence.com			✔						
Corona Tools USA **22440 Temescal Canyon Rd.** Corona, CA 92883 (800) 847-7863 shop.coronatoolsusa.com	✔								
Deer Busters 144 Cleveland Ave. Waynesboro, PA 17268 (888) 422-3337			✔						
Dramm Corporation rainwand.com/all-products	✔							✔	
Dripworks 190 Sanhedrin Circle Willits, CA 95490 (800) 522-3747 dripworks.com								✔	
FarmTek 1440 Field of Dreams Way Dyersville, IA 52040 (800) 245-9881 farmtek.com		✔	✔						
Fedco Seeds and Supplies P.O. Box 520 Clinton, ME 04927 (207) 426-9900 fedcoseeds.com			✔		✔	✔		✔	✔
Fiskars (866) 348-5661 fiskars.com/en-us/gardening-and-yard-care/products	✔								
Gardener's Edge 241 Fox Dr. Piqua, OH 45356 (888) 556-5676 gardenersedge.com	✔						✔		

PRODUCT SUPPLIERS

	Adaptive Tools	Animal Repellents	Barriers (fencing, netting)	Composters	Disease Control	Fertilizers	Grow Bags	Irrigation	Season extension
Gardener's Supply 128 Intervale Rd. Burlington, VT 05401 (888) 833-1412 gardeners.com	✓	✓	✓	✓		✓	✓	✓	✓
Gardens Alive P.O. Box 4028 Lawrenceburg, IN 47025 (513) 354-1482 gardensalive.com		✓	✓	✓	✓	✓			✓
Greenhouse Megastore (888) 281-9337 greenhousemegastore.com							✓		
Gurney's Seed & Nursery Co. P.O. Box 4178 Greendale, IN 47025 (513) 354-1941 gurneys.com		✓	✓	✓					✓
Harris Seeds P.O. Box 24966 Rochester, NY 14624 (800) 544-7938 harrisseeds.com		✓	✓		✓	✓		✓	✓
Johnny's Selected Seeds P.O. Box 299 Waterville, ME 04903 (877) 564-6697 johnnyseeds.com		✓			✓	✓		✓	✓
Peaceful Valley Farm Supply 125 Clydesdale Ct. Grass Valley, CA 95945 (888) 784-1722 groworganic.com		✓	✓	✓	✓	✓		✓	✓
Planet Natural (888) 349-0605 planetnatural.com		✓	✓		✓	✓	✓	✓	
Safer Brand 24 L. King St. Lancaster, PA 17602 (855) 767-4264 saferbrand.com		✓			✓	✓			
Territorial Seed Company P.O. Box 158 Cottage Grove, OR 97424 (800) 626-0866 territorialseed.com			✓			✓			✓

ABOUT THE AUTHOR

Susan Mulvihill comes from a family of enthusiastic gardeners. Her grandmother introduced her to the world of gardening while she was growing up in Southern California. It wasn't long before Susan was growing vegetables on her own. Her mother loved to garden, and all her sisters enjoy growing beautiful, productive gardens.

Susan and her husband, Bill, live in Spokane, Washington. They enjoy gardening together on five acres, which occasionally involves challenging weather conditions and visits from a wide variety of wildlife. In 2017, their garden was featured on the popular PBS program *Growing a Greener World* (episode 809).

Susan has been a Spokane County Master Gardener for over twenty years and has relished the opportunity to help gardeners sort out numerous horticultural mysteries. She has been affiliated with *The Spokesman-Review* newspaper for over thirty years, as both a newsroom employee and correspondent. Her weekly garden columns run each year from February to October.

She is the author of *The Vegetable Garden Pest Handbook*, an easy-to-use guide to identifying bugs and using organic practices to control the damaging ones. In 2014, she teamed up with her friend and fellow Master Gardener Pat Munts to write *The Northwest Gardener's Handbook*. Both titles are published by Cool Springs Press.

Susan is a longtime member of the professional organization Garden Communicators International. As such, she has received awards for her writing and for the design of her popular blog, SusansintheGarden.com.

She strongly believes in the importance of sharing her gardening knowledge. Several years ago, she embraced the concept of video storytelling as a way to do just that. Susan has created over 400 videos on a wide variety of topics for her YouTube channel, youtube.com/susansinthegarden. She also posts daily to her Facebook page (facebook.com/susansinthegarden) and Instagram feed (instagram.com/susansinthegarden).

Throughout her career, Susan has encouraged everyone to grow a garden and respect the environment by using organic methods. You can reach Susan via email at Susan@SusansintheGarden.com.

ACKNOWLEDGMENTS

Even though an author writes the words, it takes many more people to create a book. *The Vegetable Garden Problem Solver Handbook* is no exception.

Following the success of my previous book, *The Vegetable Garden Pest Handbook*, Jessica Walliser (editorial director for gardening titles at Cool Springs Press) asked me if I would be interested in writing about vegetable plant diseases. As I contemplated it, I started thinking about the many other potential challenges gardeners face as well. I sent an outline to Jessica that incorporated all those things. She loved the idea, and the real work began.

Thank you, Jessica, for having the confidence in my ability to pull together a lot of information and turn it into a useful guide. You are a joy to work with and such a font of horticultural wisdom.

In all reality, this book would not have happened without Bill's unwavering support. We continually bounced ideas off each other and he always had excellent suggestions. I'm so lucky to have a partner who enjoys gardening as much as I do. Thank you so much.

Once the text was written, the behind-the-scenes transformation began. Project Manager Elizabeth Weeks, Art Director Anne Re, and their able teams worked together to create the eye-catching book you are holding in your hands. Thank you to all of you.

My sister, Anne Knapp, shared her tales of dealing with crafty squirrels that love her tree fruits just as much as she does. Anne provided me with a lot of useful information about what worked and what didn't.

I would also like to thank Tom Munson, Lucy Potts, and Marcia Sands for sharing their wonderful photographs so readers can easily identify some of the creatures and bugs that visit their gardens.

I am so pleased that everything came together and I could not have done it without all of you!

PHOTO CREDITS

JLY Gardens: pages 103 (right), 109 (left), 111 (left), 121 (left, right), 125 (left), 130 (left), 131 (bottom), 133 (top), 136, 138, 141 (bottom), 142, 148

Susan Mulvihill: pages 6 (top, bottom left and bottom right), 7, 8, 10, 12, 13, 14, 16, 17, 18, 19, 20, 23 (left, right), 27, 28, 29 (left, right, center), 30 (top, bottom), 31, 32, 33 (left, right), 34, 35 (left, right), 39, 40 (all), 41 (bottom), 42 (all), 43, 45, 47 (top, bottom), 48, 50, 51, 52, 53, 54, 55, 56, 67 (left, right), 69 (left, right), 96, 97, 112, 113 (top left), 116, 120, 128 (right), 130 (right), 133 (bottom), 134, 135 (left), 145 (top, bottom),

151 (top right), 158, 159 (left, right), 160, 161 (left, right), 163 (left), 164, 167, 168, 171, 172, 174, 175, 176, 177 (top left, top right, bottom), 179, 180 (top, bottom), 181 (top, bottom), 182 (top, bottom), 183, 184 (bottom), 186 (top, bottom), 187 (bottom), 188 (top, bottom), 189, 190 (top, bottom), 191, 192 (bottom), 193 (bottom), 194 (bottom), 196 (bottom), 197 (bottom), 198 (bottom), 200 (top, bottom), 201, 202 (top, bottom), 203, 204 (bottom left), 206 (bottom), 209 (bottom left), 211 (bottom), 213 (bottom), 214, 215, 220

Tom Munson: pages 184 (top), 192 (top), 204 (top right), 208, 211 (top)

Lucy Potts: page 41 (center)

Marcia Sands: page 41 (top)

Shutterstock: pages 49, 103 (left), 113 (bottom), 123, 127 (bottom right), 129 (left), 137 (right), 149 (right), 163 (right), 169, 170, 173, 178, 185, 187 (top), 194 (top), 195 (top, bottom), 196 (top), 197 (top), 198 (top), 199, 204 (bottom right), 206 (top), 207 (top, bottom), 209 (top, bottom right), 212, 213 (top)

George Weigel: page 124, 193 (top)

BUGWOOD.ORG

Scott Bauer, USDA Agricultural Research Service: page 131 (top)

William M. Brown Jr.: page 137 (left)

Clemson University, USDA Cooperative Extension Slide Series: pages 129 (right), 139

Whitney Cranshaw, Colorado State University: page 151 (top left)

Jonathan D. Eisenback, Virginia Polytechnic Institute and State University: page 156

Don Ferrin, Louisiana State University Agricultural Center: pages 110, 117 (left, right)

Nancy Gregory, University of Delaware: page 119 (right)

Metin GULESCI, Leaf Tobacco: page 129 (top left)

Mary Ann Hansen, Virginia Polytechnic Institute and State University: page 37

Gerald Holmes, Strawberry Center, Cal Poly San Luis Obispo: pages 102, 108, 109 (right), 111 (right), 115 (left, right), 119 (left), 122, 128 (left), 132, 151 (bottom right), 152, 153 (left, right), 154

Brenda Kennedy, University of Kentucky: page 155 (top right)

Ed Kurtz: pages 98, 99

Rebecca A. Melanson, Mississippi State University Extension: pages 125 (right), 135 (right), 147 (left), 157

Daren Mueller, Iowa State University: pages 144, 155 (top left)

Oliver T. Neher, The Amalgamated Sugar Company: page 113 (top right)

Larry Osborne: page 141 (top)

Alison Robertson: page 143

Howard F. Schwartz, Colorado State University: pages 100, 101 (left, right), 105 (left, right), 107 (right), 127 (top right)

Edward Sikora, Auburn University: pages 127 (bottom left), 146, 147 (right), 149 (left)

Yuan-Min Shen, Taichung District Agricultural Research and Extension Station: page 107 (left)

INDEX

Note: *Italicized page references indicate photos.*

Note: *Italicized page references indicate photos.*